DATE DUE

MAY 29 2012	
WITHDRAWN	

Scapegoats of **SEPTEMBER 11TH**

Scapegoats of

SEPTEMBER 11TH
Hate Crimes & State Crimes in the War on Terror

Michael Welch

RUTGERS UNIVERSITY PRESS
NEW BRUNSWICK, NEW JERSEY, AND LONDON

Critical Issues in Crime and Society
Raymond J. Michalowski, Series Editor

Critical Issues in Crime and Society is oriented toward critical analysis of contemporary problems in crime and justice. The series is open to a broad range of topics including specific types of crime, wrongful behavior by economically or politically powerful actors, controversies over justice system practices, and issues related to the intersection of identity, crime, and justice. It is committed to offering thoughtful works that will be accessible to scholars and professional criminologists, general readers, and students.

Library of Congress Cataloging-in-Publication Data
Welch, Michael, Ph. D.
  Scapegoats of September 11th : hate crimes & state crimes in the war on terror / Michael Welch.
     p. cm. — (Critical issues in crime and society)
  Includes bibliographical references and index.
  ISBN-13: 978-0-8135-3895-2 (hardcover : alk. paper)
  ISBN-13: 978-0-8135-3896-9 (pbk. : alk. paper)
  1. War on Terrorism, 2001—Moral and ethical aspects. 2. September 11 Terrorist Attacks, 2001—Influence. 3. Hate crimes—United States. 4. Arab Americans—Crimes against—United States. 5. Islamophobia—United States. 6. Prejudices—United States. 7. Civil rights—United States. 8. United States—Race relations. I. Title. II. Series
  HV6431.W444 2006
  973.931—dc22

                                                            2006010512

A British Cataloging-in-Publication record for this book is available from the British Library

Manufactured in the United States of America

To all the victims of 9/11 and its aftermath

CONTENTS

PREFACE

Septemeber 11, 2001, is a date that will continue to resonate sharply into the foreseeable future. Still, that day in history is not a static reminder of past atrocities. On the contrary, 9/11 is a dynamic emotional signifier of the present and beyond, capable of evoking not only intense grief but also anxiety, fear, and anger. Regrettably, in post-9/11 America, much of that outrage has been targeted at innocent persons not involved in the terrorist attacks on the Pentagon or the Twin Towers. In a word, those people have become the scapegoats of September 11. This book takes on the uneasy task of sorting out the various manifestations of displaced aggression, most notably hate crimes along with state crimes that have become embarrassing hallmarks of the war on terror at home and abroad.

In so many ways, this project represents a continuation of my research on crime, punishment, and human rights, particularly as informed by race and ethnicity. On September 11, 2001, I had already completed the writing for my book *Detained: Immigration Laws and the Expanding I.N.S. Jail Complex* (2002, Temple University Press). Appropriately, I added an epilogue to that volume describing the challenges facing human rights in the aftermath of 9/11; nevertheless, the thrust of my conclusions has remained largely unchanged. In the days, weeks, months, and even years following the attacks, shameful actions by some Americans and the government merely confirmed my observation that another round of social control was put into motion, aimed largely at so-called racial, ethnic, and religious "outsiders." Rather than simply offering a recent chronology of those developments since September 11, this book delves into the meaning of scapegoating in ways that reveal society's ancient punitive tendencies. In doing so, however, it also sheds an optimistic light on the potential for an emerging awareness of human rights.

Due to the nature of writing, authors often work in isolation while simultaneously remaining deeply connected to the world around them. This work is no exception. Over the past few years, I have benefited from the help and support of a long list of assistants and colleagues. At Rutgers University, I acknowledge my research assistants, Daanish Faruqi, Helay Salam, Hosay Salam, Frank Carle, Nicolle DeLuca, and Igor Draskovic, as well as the dedicated staff at the University's libraries. I also thank my colleagues Professors Lennox Hinds and Albert Roberts, and all members of the Criminal Justice Program Committee, along with Deans Arnold Hyndman, Holly Smith, and Ed Rhodes.

Portions of this book were written while in residency as a visiting fellow at the Centre for the Study of Human Rights, London School of Economics. Many colleagues there helped me navigate uncharted waters, most notably Conor Gearty and Stan Cohen, along with Joy Whyte, Harriet Gallagher, Andrew Puddephatt, Helen Wildbore, Margot Salomon, and Tim Newburn, director of the Mannheim Centre for Criminology at the LSE. In Paris, where I was fortunate to have a flat conducive to reading and writing, I would like to thank Elisabeth Ban and Nick Stevens, as well as all the nice people in the 18th arrondissement.

In terms of converting a manuscript into a book, I have benefited tremendously from the talented staff at Rutgers University Press: Director Marlie Wasserman, Associate Editor Adi Hovav, Production Editor Nicole L. Manganaro, and Prepress Director Marilyn Campbell. Of course, this work became much more readable due to the copyediting of Anne Schneider. Finally, I wish to thank Ray Michalowski, series editor of Critical Issues in Crime and Society at RUP along with Hal Pepinsky who also reviewed the entire manuscript, offering key insights and comments.

Michael Welch
HOBOKEN, NEW JERSEY

Scapegoats of **SEPTEMBER 11TH**

CHAPTER ONE

Talking About Terror

By repeatedly insisting that only he has the tools and the determination to fend off terrorism in the post-September 11 era, Bush has cultivated feelings of crisis, pessimism, anxiety, and a loss of control throughout the nation. He has instilled a sense of dependency in Americans.

—Renana Brooks, "The character myth: To counter Bush, the Democrats must present a different vision of a safe world," *Nation,* 2003

It makes no more sense to attack civil liberties to get at terrorists, than to invade Iraq to get at Osama Bin Laden.

—Al Gore, "This administration is using fear as a political tool," *New York Times,* 2003

I n so many ways, September 11, 2001, bisects history, altering the way people speak, think, and feel about the world around them. Whereas the United States has pockets of political violence scattered throughout its past, until recently it has yet to withstand the full force of a devastating terrorist attack. To say that America changed on September 11 is

3

more than a cliché; the nation's identity as a target—and victim—resonates both symbolically and substantively. As this volume sets out to examine, America is experiencing major shifts in its social, political, and
cultural landscape as it searches for a safer society. The war on terror has
become the most visible manifestation of that desperate need for security. However, as a social invention, the war on terror serves more than
the manifest function of protecting the nation against terrorist strikes.
There are other—deeper—latent functions as well, most notably the desire to exact revenge for the mass killings of innocent civilians on 9/11.
Still, settling that score reaches beyond the mundane task of appre-
hending and punishing certain terrorists. The war on terror, as fiercely
echoed in the speeches by President Bush and other political leaders,
represents a continuation of a more ancient campaign against evil.

Whereas grounding the war on terror within a mystical framework
generates considerable popular support from people who view the world
as a dangerous place with evil lurking in our midst, that way of talking
and thinking about political violence undermines the formulation of
sound counterterrorism policies. Such mysticism in understanding terrorism produces a good versus evil dichotomy rather than a right versus
wrong morality. Consequently, the war on terror—lacking the moral
bearings required to distinguish between right and wrong—recklessly
produces two significant forms of collateral damage. First, current counterterrorism tactics victimize scapegoats, that is, people not associated
with political violence but nonetheless targeted merely because of their
ethnicity and religion, namely Middle Easterners, Arabs, and Muslims, as
well as South Asians. For angry citizens in post-9/11 America, such scapegoats are easy to identify and easy to dislike. Second, the war on terror
has weakened key democratic principles developed to protect all people
against the abuses of government power. The USA Patriot Act along with
a host of illegal and unethical actions in the war on terror continues to
rip away long-standing values of justice.

Scapegoating involves displacing aggression onto innocent people selected as suitable enemies due to their perceived differences in race, ethnicity, religion, and so on. As a social psychological defense mechanism
against confronting the real source of frustration, scapegoating provides
emotional relief for people racked with fear and anxiety. That solace is inevitably short term, prompting scapegoaters to step on a treadmill of endless bigotry and victimization. This book explores in-depth the scapegoats
of September 11 by attending to hate crimes and state crimes in the war
on terror; by doing so, it chronicles the mistakes and missteps in current

counterterrorism tactics. In the face of popular and political cheerleading in the war on terror, this work presents a careful and sober assessment. With few exceptions, any comfort that the war on terror delivers is merely illusory, given the array of self-defeating strategies that fail to contribute to public safety and national security. As this work demonstrates, support for the war on terror involves a good amount of wishful—and in some instances magical—thinking, reducing the battle against terrorism to symbolic ritual in lieu of pragmatic policy. Setting the stage for a critical analysis, this chapter scans discourse in the war on terror, interpreting the way people and politicians talk about threats of terrorism. The discussion begins with a close look at the role of fear in stoking political responses to terrorism and concludes with an overview of the book's scope.

Fear Factor

For decades, criminologists and sociologists have understood the significance of public fear in the formation of criminal justice policies and practices. Indeed, elected officials not only respond to those anxieties over crime and disorder but also have a hand in stoking and exploiting those fears for political gain (Best 1999; Glassner 1999; Welch, Fenwick, and Roberts 1998, 1997). In the wake of September 11th, those emotional and political dynamics have been further galvanized, forcing a tighter bond between genuine public fear and its calculated manipulation by government. Aided by an expanding media, popular and political concerns over terrorism have both widened and sharpened the discourse of fear; consequently, the "dangerous world" mindset has gained considerable currency in the way people and politicians speak about terror (see Altheide 2002).

With these developments in full view, it is important to recognize that public fear of terrorism may be disproportionate to the actual risks, leading to choices and behaviors that are not entirely rational. Jeffrey Rosen, author of *The Naked Crowd: Reclaiming Security and Freedom in an Anxious Age* (2003), discovered this phenomenon first-hand in his investigation into new screening technologies introduced at airports since 9/11. At Orlando International Airport, security officials began testing a device he refers to as the Naked Machine that conducts a kind of electronic strip search by bouncing a low-energy X-ray beam onto the bodies of passengers. The machine exposes all objects concealed by clothing but in doing so it produces an anatomically correct naked image of those being screened; while promising a high level of security, the device sacrifices personal privacy. To remedy that downside of the machine, scientists have adjusted the program in a way that projects images of concealed objects onto a sexless and nondescript figure, what Rosen calls a Blob Machine. That particular modification ensures that same degree of security while also protecting the passenger's privacy. Willing to test the rational choices of prospective passengers, Rosen offered to a group a hypothetical option of being screened by either the Naked Machine or the Blob Machine. His findings seem to confirm a certain level of anxiety that overrides rational choice. "There were some who say they are so anxious about the possibility of terrorism that they would do anything possible to make themselves feel better. They don't care, in other words, whether or not the Naked Machine makes them safer than the Blob Machine, because they are more concerned about feeling safe than being safe" (Rosen 2004a, 10).

Rosen concludes that many people seem willing to accept new laws and technologies that sacrifice personal privacy, even though they do not produce a greater form of protection against terrorism. Indeed, horrific imagery documenting terrorist strikes flowing across television screens 24 hours a day tends to crowd out the rational assessment of risks in the public mind. The irrationality of fear over terrorism coexists with—and in certain circumstances, encourages—government policies that are equally irrational in their formation and implementation. While the war on terror has given President Bush a much-needed lift amid so many unpopular policies (e.g., the war in Iraq, tax cuts for the wealthy), it is irrational for the nation since terrorism is not an enemy in the conventional understanding of war. Rather terrorism is a violent tactic used by politically weaker groups to gain political objectives (see Jenkins 2003).[1] It is at this juncture that the linkages between public fear of terrorism and political actions in the war on terror are becoming increasingly clear. As William Greider puts forth:

> Like the cold war's, the logic of this new organizing framework can be awesomely compelling to the popular imagination because it runs on fear—the public's expanding fear of potential dangers. The political commodity of fear has no practical limits. The government has the ability to manufacture more. . . . "War on terror" is a political slogan—not a coherent strategy for national defense—and it succeeds brilliantly only as politics. For everything else, it is quite illogical. (2004, 11, 14)

As the election year campaigns reached crescendo, John Kerry, on August 11, 2004, criticized the Bush administration for blocking a bipartisan plan to give senior citizens access to lower-priced prescriptions from Canada. That very day, Acting Commissioner of the Federal Drug Administration Lester Crawford told the Associated Press that terrorist "cues from chatter" led him to believe that Al Qaeda may try to attack Americans by contaminating imported drugs. Crawford refused to furnish any details to substantiate his claims (Legum and Sirota 2004, 13). In 2005, the Department of Homeland Security, in an effort to improve the much-criticized funding formula for high-risk areas of the nation, completed a study titled the National Planning Scenarios. The report presented the most plausible or devastating terrorist strikes, including detonation of a nuclear device in a major city, release of the nerve gas sarin in office buildings, and a truck bombing of a sports arena. The report, reading much like a doomsday film script, was not based on any credible intelligence of such attacks. Alarmingly, however, it included specific estimates, such as the aftermath of a bombed chlorine tank, killing 17,500 people and injuring more than 100,000. The Department denied that their objective was to scare the public. Still, the agency's new director, Michael Chertoff, announced: "There's risk everywhere; risk is a part of life" (Lipton 2005a, A16).

The regrettable effects of the "dangerous world" perspective already have been realized in the few years following 9/11: most notably the round-ups, detentions, and deportations of Middle Eastern men proven not to have any links to terrorism, along with injustices at Guantanamo Bay, and, of course, the invasion of Iraq. Still, scholars are concerned over the long-term impact that the fear is likely to have on American political structures. Corey Robin, a political scientist, suggests that fear has tainted liberalism and that 9/11 guarantees the longevity of fear as a political idea, perpetuating distorted visions of terror (2004; Kimmage 2004). Naturally, only time will tell the extent to which the political landscape has been altered. In the meantime, there is plenty of evidence demonstrating that the war on terror influences language, particularly political rhetoric intended to deal with collective anxiety.

Discourse in the War on Terror

Politicians of all stripes have tuned their speeches to the emotional fallout of September 11th. As the center of attention, Bush and his staff have clearly forged new ground in the realm of political talk about terror.

Here several key categories of language are evident, namely the mystical, tough talk, blaming, fabrication, rumors, and domination. Admittedly those forms of political rhetoric overlap considerably, creating what rock musicians call a "wall of noise" referring to a continuous tonal backdrop from which independent but interrelated melodic expressions emerge. Nevertheless, each of these types of talk—or discourse—contains distinct themes and traits worthy of careful consideration.

Discourse in the war on terror was mystified immediately upon the attacks on the World Trade Center and the Pentagon. Due in large part to their horrific magnitude, those events became easily expressed in terms of evil. Indeed, Bush and other political leaders spoke urgently of the need to locate and punish the evildoers. At a memorial service days following September 11, Bush delivered the memorable words that would continue to shape his war on terror: "Our responsibility to history is already clear: to answer these attacks and rid the world of evil" (Lifton 2003b, 12). A scant look at the mystical words contained in the language of the war on terror might lead one to reject their cultural significance as trivial. But that would be a missed opportunity. Speaking of the war on terror in a mystical idiom invokes deeper quasi-religious interpretation of terrorism, paving the way for an almost literal form of demonization, or scapegoating. In doing so, Bush—even by his own admission—assumes a messianic force committed to ridding the world of evil (Woodward 2004). The mystical character of the war on terror continues to generate a groundswell of support from Bush's religious constituency, and in extreme instances transposes historical references to the Crusades into the present. Lieutenant General William Boykin drew considerable attention when it became known that his speeches to church groups not only mischaracterized Islam as an inferior religion but also advocated conversion to Christianity as a tactic in the war on terror (Jehl 2003; Reuters 2003).

The militant motif in the war on terror is difficult to overlook, especially since it blends both figurative and literal meanings. While the term connotes a struggle against terrorism it also plunges head first into warfare: for instance, to justify the invasion of Iraq when weapons of mass destruction could not be found. The militant thrust of the war on terror is commonly conveyed in tough talk, or simply put, "kicking ass." Bush staunchly warned the Taliban that it must deliver those responsible for the attacks of September 11 or soon "they will share their fate" (White House transcript, President Bush's Address to a Joint Session of Congress and the American People September 20, 2001; National Commission on Terrorist Attacks Upon the United States 2004, 337). Tough talk has served as the linguistic foundation for abuse, torture, and homicide in the war on terror, particularly in light of the often-quoted phrase that after 9/11 "the gloves came off." That rally cry has not only been internalized by many military and criminal justice personnel but also civilians who in the course of exacting hate crimes believe that they are acting in the spirit of patriotism by "bashing ragheads" here at home (Welch 2003a). It should also be noted that the "fighting" language embedded in the war on terror is not only a conservative form of speaking but a liberal—and radical—one as well. Even those who do not support Bush's counterterrorism strategy engage in tough talk, not only in reference to defending the nation against terrorism but also in fighting back on behalf of civil liberties and human rights that have come under assault in the war on terror (Chang 2002).

For anyone who followed the televised proceedings of the 9/11 Commission, they saw the blame game in full swing. The Bush team blamed the Clinton administration and vice versa while the FBI and the CIA unleashed at each other a steady stream of salvos. Simultaneously, blaming places the burden of accountability on another actor or agency while removing such responsibility from those issuing the blame. However, that dynamic is circular, creating an endless spiral of accusations and denials. On January 25, 2001, National Security Advisor Condoleezza Rice received a strategy document prepared by Richard Clarke, top White House counterterrorism advisor, outlining proposals for eliminating the threat from Al Qaeda. The document warned the administration that terrorists had staged cells inside the United States and abroad and were planning strikes. To reduce the threat of attacks, the report, *Strategy for Eliminating the Threat from Jihadist Networks of al Qida: Status and Prospects*, issued several specific recommendations, including the destruction of terrorist training camps while classes are in session. Clarke pressed "urgently" for a meeting of principals, including the president's top foreign policy advisors. But for months there was virtually no action on the request. Eventually, the principals' meeting took place on September 4, 2001, a week before 9/11. When Rice was questioned why she did not act until it was probably too late, she said: "No Al Qaeda plan was turned over to the new administration" (Shane 2005, A10).

But Matthew Levitt, an FBI counterterrorist analyst in 2001, disagrees with Rice, and suggests that she is averting blame that squarely falls into her orbit of responsibility. Levitt called the 13-page strategy memorandum "a pretty disturbing document" and whether the document constituted a "plan" as Clarke averred and Rice denied is "a semantic debate." Levitt added: "I think it makes the threat look pretty urgent. I look at this and I see something that to my mind requires immediate attention" (Shane 2005, A10). From a policy standpoint, cross blaming—even in the face of so-called "smoking-gun" evidence—leaves blank any sense of overall government accountability for errors contributing to terrorist attacks. Still, from a deeper psychological view, blaming provides as a potent defense mechanism against accepting responsibility and serves to project one's insecurity and weakness onto another person. Already it is clear that a combination of organizational and personal blaming has yielded considerable harm to America's national security while continuing to undermine effective counterterrorism policies and practices.

Fundamental to communication is language that can be regarded as truthful, and where there is doubt, suspicion lingers. Much of the discourse in the war on terror includes information that is either fabricated altogether or at least greatly exaggerated, prompting criticism from those striving to determine the truth. Christopher Scheer, Robert Scheer, and Lakshmi Chaudhry, authors of *The Five Biggest Lies Bush Told Us About Iraq* (2003), accuse the Bush administration of brazenly inventing new rationales for its foreign policy and the war on terror, shamelessly twisting facts to support them. The first lie that Scheer and his colleagues confront is, "They Attacked Us: Iraq Supported Al Qaeda," in which Bush dished out "the lie that the war and occupation of Iraq can reasonably be linked to the 'war on terror,'" even as former Bush Treasury Secretary Paul O'Neill said publicly that the Bush team was obsessed with Iraq from the early days of the administration (Scheer, Scheer, and Chaudhry 2004, 13; O'Neill 2004).[2] Predictably, outright lies often are met with blatant denial. After years of insinuating a link between Saddam Hussein and Al Qaeda, Vice President Cheney insisted: "I have not suggested there's a connection between Iraq and 9/11" (Krugman 2004a, A27; Rampton and Stauber 2003).

As another example of the many falsehoods in the war on terror, the State Department released its annual report, *Patterns of Global Terrorism,* in which it claimed that in the year 2003 there were 190 total number of terror attacks worldwide, leading to 307 deaths and 1,593 victims wounded. Those figures were dramatically down from the previous year when the State Department reported 205 total number of terror attacks, along with 725 deaths and 2,013 victims wounded. Consequently, the 2003 report was met with skepticism as the Department stood accused of cooking the books in an effort to portray the U.S.-led war on terror as effective. In response to those charges, the Department revised its annual estimates and released another version of the report, finding 208 total number of terror attacks. Moreover, the Department more than doubled the statistics on fatalities and injuries, showing 625 deaths and 3,646 victims wounded. Wrestling to limit the embarrassment facing the Department, Secretary of State Colin Powell attributed the error to "the way the data was being added up" and that the initial 2003 report was "not designed to make our efforts look better or worse" (Knowlton 2004, 1). Phil Singer, a spokesman for Senator John Kerry, said that the Bush administration had "been caught trying to inflate its success in terrorism" (Knowlton 2004, 8; see Sanger 2004a). Especially in the absence of evidence, skeptics charge political officials with deliberately manipulating collective fear for political gain. In 2004, Tom Ridge, Secretary of Homeland Security, announced that flight cancellations and other government actions over the Christmas holiday season—which greatly inconvenienced travelers and their families—prevented a catastrophic terrorist attack by Al Qaeda. However, Ridge could offer no intelligence to prove it conclusively: "My gut tells me that we probably did. But proving an unknown is a pretty difficult thing to do" (Shenon 2004a, A21).

Discourse in the war on terror also involves key manifestations of informal communication, most notably in the realm of rumors. Traveling word of mouth, rumors not only disseminate falsehoods but also contribute to an atmosphere of suspicion and bigotry that marginalizes certain racial, ethnic, and religious groups. For instance, rumors spread that: "Jews stayed home from work at the World Trade Center on 9/11 because they were warned of the attacks in advance" (Krassner 2003, 28). Similarly, urban legends circulating in Jersey City, New Jersey—located directly across the Hudson River from Ground Zero—incorporated the heightened fear of terror in the months following 9/11. In one particular urban legend, a woman waiting her turn at a check-out register in the Newport Mall volunteers to give some small change to a Middle Eastern man so that he could complete his purchase. Moments later, the man approaches her in the parking lot and thanks her again for her generosity; in doing so, he also tips her off not to shop at the mall the next day because there might be a terrorist strike. While not emanating from political leaders or their institutions, rumors and urban legends perpetuate fear in ways that encourage people to accept harsh tactics in the war on terror, including ethnic profiling, detention, and worse—abuse and torture.

Political messages intended to dominate people also have become part of the larger discourse in the war on terror (see Chomsky 2003; McLuhan 1964). While often viewed as a mangler of the English language, Bush is credited with mastering negative emotional language as a political device. Renana Brooks, a clinical psychologist who heads the Sommet Institute for the Study of Power and Persuasion, observes that through his speeches and public statements, Bush exhibits a style of speaking designed to dominate others. "President Bush, like many dominant personality types, uses dependency-creating language of contempt and intimidation to shame others into submission and desperate admiration. While we tend to think of the dominator as using physical force, in fact most dominators use verbal abuse to control others (Brooks 2003b, 20; see Goldstein 2003).

Among those items in his linguistic toolbox, Bush employs empty language to induce others to surrender to his will. Empty language refers to statements that carry little meaning. In fact, they are tremendously broad and vague, making it virtually impossible to oppose. Empty language is not benign; rather it is manipulative precisely because it intends to distract listeners from examining the content of the message. According to Brooks, empty language allows dominators to conceal faulty generalizations; to ridicule viable alternatives; to attribute negative motivations to others. By doing so, critics and skeptics are portrayed as contemptible. In his 2003 State of the Union address, Bush relied heavily on empty language. For example, in his remark justifying the invasion of Iraq, Bush proclaimed: "We will answer every danger and every enemy that threatens the American people" (Brooks 2003b, 21). Similarly, Bush uses pessimistic language that produces fear and disables people from feeling they can solve their problems. On September 20, 2001, and again on October 7, 2002, Bush addressed the public in ways that seem to heighten a sense of national vulnerability:

Americans should not expect one battle, but a lengthy campaign, unlike any other we have ever seen. . . . I ask you to live your lives, and hug your children. I know many citizens have fears tonight. . . . Be calm and resolute, even in the face of a continuing threat. (Brooks 2003b, 21)

Some ask how urgent this danger is to America and the world. The danger is already significant, and it only grows worse with time. Iraq could decide on any given day to provide a biological or a chemical weapon to a terrorist group or individual terrorists. (Brooks 2003b, 21–22)

Periodic elevations on the color-coded warning board would serve to remind Americans that they live within a permanent crisis, producing a dominating dynamic in which people feeling powerless against the threat of terrorism become dependent on the only person who claims to have the strength to defend the nation, that is President Bush. When people are worried and fearful, they are more likely to respond to emotional rather than rational language (see Brooks 2003b; Didion 2003). Of course, most forms of language in the discourse in the war on terror (i.e., the mystical, tough talk, blaming, fabrication, and domination) are facilitated by the media, which either lend cooperation to political elites or become manipulated by them (see Weitzer and Kubrin 2004; Welch, Fenwick, and Roberts 1998, 1997).[3]

A Critical Approach to the War on Terror

Adopting a critical approach, this book examines in great detail America's war on terror and, in its path, the many problems it produces. In doing so, the analysis blends several conceptual viewpoints from the societal reaction perspective of sociology, most noticeably moral panic theory (Cohen, 2002), with recent contributions to the risk society literature (Beck 1992; Heir 2003; Ungar 2001). A few introductory comments about such a framework are instructive. Moral panic, simply put, marks a turbulent and exaggerated response to a perceived social problem whereby there is considerable concern and consensus that such a problem actually exists. Blame is then shifted to suitable villains who absorb societal hostility. Along the way, the perceived threat exceeds proportionate risks, forming a disaster mentality from which it is widely believed that something must be done urgently or else society faces a greater doom.

A classic example is moral panic over crack cocaine, a potent social issue in the 1980s that led to tough mandatory minimum sentences targeting inner city minorities (Reinarman and Levine 1997). The controversy over crack cocaine embodied all of the defining elements of moral panic: concern, consensus, hostility, and disproportionality. Moreover, such panic proved volatile, waning in following years as the media, the political establishment, and the public turned their attention to other social ills and anxieties. Still, left in its wake are institutional changes in law, which continue to place huge volumes of racial minorities behind prison walls (Welch 2004a, 2005a). There lies an unfair and unjust legacy of moral panic and why it is important to confront such panics early in their making (McRobbie and Thornton 1995). To be clear, however, moral panic theory does not necessarily claim that a particular social problem doesn't exist; rather, it suggests that the state response to such a threat is inappropriate. Jailing vast numbers of nonviolent drug violators, for instance, is considered an inappropriate response to drug abuse given the financial and social costs of mass incarceration. Implementing a sound approach to drug control policy that takes into account an array of factors and forces contributing to addiction and trafficking (e.g., social, racial, and economic disparities) seems to be a wiser choice of social action than simply resorting to punitive measures as a means of social control (Welch, Bryan, and Wolff 1999).

Given the breathtaking impact of the 9/11 attacks and a host of institutional changes since then, notably the USA Patriot Act, it is tempting to apply moral panic theory to explain political responses to key events in post-September 11 America (see Hamm 2005; Rothe and Muzzatti 2004). Still, as this book contends, traditional moral panic theory places some limits on such interpretations, most significantly in the realm of volatility—the tendency for panic to fade from the collective psyche. Moral panic theory is by its very nature retrospective insofar as it examines past responses in order to draw conclusions that a pseudo-disaster was manufactured. There is no doubt that many initial responses by the government were driven by panic, such as the brazen round-up of Middle Easterners in the days, weeks, and months following 9/11. This work nevertheless embarks on an extension of moral panic theory that incorporates research on risks in society and the anxieties they produce (Beck 1992; Heir 2003; Ungar 2001). Rather than concentrating solely on the problem of terrorism, the focus also turns to a distinct societal condition exacerbated by 9/11 in which risk—and danger—plays a vital role in influencing how politicians and the public construe the world around them.

Throughout much of the discussion, crucial attention is turned to discourse, a regulated system of producing knowledge. Edward Said (1978) reminds us that all knowledge is codified through a political and cultural filter representing certain interests as well as collective fears and anxieties. This work likewise highlights the significance of knowledge along with language and emotion in a post-9/11 world, particularly how people and politicians think, talk, and feel about threats of terror (see Altheide 2004; Campbell 2004; Chermak, Bailey, and Brown 2004). While taking into consideration the importance of collective anxiety, the thrust of the book concentrates on displaced aggression. As the title suggests, adverse consequences of the war on terror are explored in-depth, especially the creation of scapegoats—innocent people—who become targets of hate crimes and state crimes.

Scapegoats of September 11th covers tremendous chronological and substantive territory, beginning with the tragic day of September 11 and journeying into the present. Arguably an entire book could be devoted to each of the major topics in these chapters (e.g., ethnic profiling, detention, hate crimes, state crimes, torture, Abu Ghraib, Guantanamo Bay). However, this project condenses these subjects into a workable set of interlocking observations. As Chapter 2, *Seeking a Safer Society,* acknowledges, public safety and national security have become dominant themes in political and popular discourse since 9/11. Moreover, much of the talk about threats of terrorism not only expresses collective anxiety but serves to reinforce it as well. With those developments in full view, it is tempting to apply moral panic theory in a straightforward manner (see Rothe and Muzzatti 2004). *Scapegoats of September 11th,* however, takes a slightly different approach by emphasizing a key extension of moral panic research, namely risk. As Cohen (2002) explains, some of the social space once occupied by moral panic has been filled by more undifferentiated fears, anxieties, and insecurities. *Scapegoats* asserts that America's war on terror is better understood in the context of "a risk society" rather than in the traditional realm of moral panic (see Beck, Giddens, and Lash 1994). Correspondingly, the particular fear of street crime is being replaced by a more universal fear over terror, marking a key shift in the sites of social anxiety (see Hollway and Jefferson 1997).

Chapter 3, *Scapegoating and Social Insecurity,* explores the forces and dynamics of blaming, especially as they pertain to scapegoat theory. As discussed, displaced aggression rarely is ventilated randomly. On the contrary, such hostility and violence commonly conform to predictable patterns of prejudice and bigotry. Still, there also remain deeper cultural reasons for that trajectory, most notably the view that modern scapegoating exists as a continuation of ancient rituals of punishment serving to reduce psychic discomfort while symbolically purifying the community. So as to draw linkages to previously examined concepts, the notion of scapegoating is deeply integrated into contemporary cultural theory (Douglas 1966) as well as the risk society paradigm, producing new insights into the culture of control and the criminology of the other (Garland 2001; Young 1999). In a similar vein, *Crusading Against Terror* (Chapter 4) takes a closer look into religious and cultural underpinnings of counterterrorist policies in post-9/11 America. Regrettably, some facets of the war on terror take the term crusade literally in ways that glorify fundamental Christianity while marginalizing Islam, setting the stage for harassment, abuse, and other forms of scapegoating.

Central to the book is its survey of hostility aimed at Middle Eastern (and South Asian) people in the United States since September 11. Chapter 5, *Hate Crimes as Backlash Violence*, offers considerable evidence to the extent that displaced aggression has marred communities across the nation. Ethnoviolence represents a key form of scapegoating and is interpreted as a potent site of social anxiety, becoming one of the chief "faces of oppression" in American society (Young 1990). Moreover, a cultural, ethnic, and religious backdrop serves to make Middle Easterners not only vulnerable targets in post-9/11 America, but so-called "legitimate" targets by those dispensing their own brand of wrath. Those manifestations of hostility are not confined to the angry citizens on the street motivated to avenge the attacks of 9/11. Similarly, the government—at all levels—institutes policies and practices driven by prejudice and bigotry. In Chapter 6, *Profiling and Detention in Post-9/11 America*, the criminal justice apparatus and its commitment to hard-line tactics remains the focus of discussion. In addition to the toxic policy of ethnic and religious profiling, the chapter investigates more formalized campaigns of social control embodied in the Special Registration Program, a dragnet entangling more than 82,000 foreign nationals, many of whom were unjustly detained and deported. The misuse of detention and the abuse of detainees are the legacy of Attorney General John Ashcroft who remained unapologetic, even after the Inspector General at the Department of Justice documented wholesale violations of detainees' rights.

Such abuses emanating from the criminal justice system since 9/11 are also evident in the domain of the military, drawing worldwide condemnation. As Chapter 7 *State Crimes in the War on Terror* reveals, that criticism is well deserved. Retrospectively, the Bush administration justifies the invasion and occupation of Iraq on the grounds that it serves the war on terror. Under international law, that action is illegal, along with the unlawful enemy combatant designation that has led to the indefinite detention of hundreds of detainees at Guantanamo Bay. The despicable scandal at Abu Ghraib, where detainees were denied fundamental protections from the Geneva Conventions designed to safeguard prisoners of war, represents only one of the more visible examples of human rights violations. Other illegal activities such as torture and extraordinary rendition—in which abuse is outsourced to a third party—remain concealed behind a thick wall of secrecy. The chapter takes an exhaustive look into the short- and long-term problems produced by systemic state crimes in the war on terror. Linking those developments with ethnoviolence occurring stateside, there is good reason to believe that hate

crimes and state crimes are twin phenomena, existing as mutually reinforcing entities of displaced aggression.

Of course, moral problems stemming from the war on terror persist
because the government goes to great lengths to claim its effectiveness.
That is one of the most staunchly guarded myths in post-9/11 America.
Chapter 8, *Claiming Effectiveness,* dispels such fiction, carefully documenting the false and exaggerated claims that the war on terror is on the
right track. Presented in detail are numerous bungled cases that leave
even the casual observer wondering why the government is spending
valuable time and resources trying to nail insignificant and inconsequential suspects, especially since they pose little or no threat to public
safety or national security. The chapter also takes a critical glance at secrecy, not only because it undermines the democratic value of a transparency government but also, with particular relevance to false claims
of effectiveness, hides incompetence. The discussion concludes by acknowledging parallels to the failed war on drugs since the war on terror also is driven by ethnic cues, producing an array of ethical predicaments along with harsh and unnecessary confinement. Correspondingly,
Assaulting Civil Liberties, the subject of chapter 9, investigates the breadth
and depth of government intrusions since September 11, all of which occur in an atmosphere of fear and suspicion. At the center of attention is
the Patriot Act, one of the most controversial statutes in recent American
history. Given its sweeping nature, the Act shifts enormous power to the
government with little—and in some cases no—judicial or legislative
oversight. The Patriot Act not only creates havoc within the criminal justice system but also is used to criminalize legitimate protests and stifle
dissent. Despite the near comical implementation of the No Fly Lists—
that snagged both pop singer Cat Stevens and Senator Ted Kennedy—
many Americans do not realize that the war on terror is fraught with mis-
judgment and mismanagement, problems that can be easily corrected by
better checks and balances.

In his highly acclaimed book, *States of Denial: Knowing About Atrocities
and Suffering,* Stanley Cohen examines the social psychological processes
influencing public indifference to human rights violations. Applying that
paradigm to the fallout in the war on terror, my final chapter, "Culture of
Denial," takes another glimpse at the political reaction to hate crimes and
state crimes. Specific focus concentrates on the multiple forms of reinterpretation and spin-doctoring that reinforce cultural denial and perpetuate scapegoating. By discussing the significance of an emergent sociology of denial, readers are reminded of the universal duty to recognize

suffering and challenge institutions that reproduce states of denial (see Barak 2005; Michalowski 1996,1985; Pepinsky 1991).

Scapegoats of September 11th concludes by shedding an optimistic light onto efforts to reduce political violence, most importantly by protecting civil liberties and human rights along with cultivating genuine international relations—a bitter pill indeed for the Bush administration. Improving the study of social phenomena, Antonio Gramsci (1971) encouraged intellectuals and scholars to compile inventories of knowledge in an attempt to make sense of it all. That is precisely the objective of this book: to gather sufficient evidence on the war on terror so as to understand critically its adverse consequences—affecting not only individual scapegoats but society as well.

CHAPTER TWO

Seeking a Safer Society

The measurement is not are we safer, the measurement is are we as safe as we ought to be?"
> —Democratic presidential candidate John Kerry,
> quoted in L. Uchitelle and J. Markoff,
> "Terror, Inc.," *New York Times,* 2004

For the life of me, I cannot understand why the terrorists have not attacked our food supply because it is so easy to do."
> —Secretary of Health and Human Services Tommy G. Thompson,
> quoted in R. Pear, "U.S. health chief, stepping down, issues
> warning: Flu and terror worries," *New York Times,* 2004

Safety has emerged as a dominant social theme in a post-9/11 America. Indeed, protection against terrorist attacks echoes in the chorus of campaign politics. While trying vigorously to extract votes from an already nervous electorate, Vice President Dick Cheney warned: "It is absolutely essential that eight weeks from today on November 2, we make the right choice because if we make the wrong choice then the danger is that we'll be hit again and we'll be hit in a way that will be devastating from the standpoint of the United States" (Sanger and Halbfinger 2004, A1). Democratic vice presidential candidate John Edwards snapped back: "What he [Cheney] said to the American people was that if you go to the polls in November and elect anyone other than us, then another terrorist attack occurs, it's your fault" (Sanger and Halbfinger 2004, A1). Whereas politicians and government officials clearly have a hand in manipulating and exploiting fear and anxiety, they are merely tapping into an existing collective emotional condition. Recent studies reveal that Americans have become concerned, anxious, and fearful of another major terrorist strike (Carey and O'Connor 2004; Lerner et al. 2003; Merkin 2004). Key transformations in America's emotional state, evident since the attacks of September 11 lend themselves to critical analysis, most notably from the standpoint of moral panic theory.

Moral panic theory continues to enjoy growing popularity among scholars studying crime, deviance, and collective behavior, encompassing such issues as juvenile delinquency (Springhall 1998; Welch, Price, Yankey 2004, 2002), school violence (Burns and Crawford 1999; Killingbeck 1999), bad drugs (Hill 2002), pornography (Watney 1987), child abuse (Best 1994; Jenkins 1998; Zgoba 2004), and crack mothers (Humphreys 1999; see Cohen 2002; Welch 2005c). With those contributions in clear view, Sheldon Ungar suggests that: "the sociological domain carved out by moral panic is most fruitfully understood as the study of the sites and conventions of social anxiety and fear (2001, 271). Ungar also goes on to emphasize that as societies undergo change so do phenomena linked to public concern or alarm, becoming new sites of social anxiety. Particularly in the United States, new sites of social anxiety have emerged in a post-9/11 world. That collective uneasiness brings to light the importance of interpreting what Beck (1992) calls a risk society.

This chapter focuses on the conceptual dynamics underpinning popular and political responses to threats of terror. As the public remains uneasy over the risk of political violence targeting the nation, government leaders offer assurances of safety while also averting blame for previous attacks. In doing so, they toss the "hot potato" of accountability onto other government officials or agencies. As this chapter illustrates, that dynamic figures prominently in the political manipulation of public fear. Certainly, such exploitation follows the shifting sites of anxiety from fear of crime to fear of terror. The material consequences of that shifting anxiety are found in ways that government spends—and wastes—tax dollars, a phenomenon that has become known as the homeland security industrial-complex. Setting the stage for this investigation, the discussion begins with an overview of a risk society as an extension of moral panic.

Moral Panic and a Risk Society

While establishing the theoretical grid of this analysis, it is important to acknowledge that the moral panic paradigm has undergone considerable development since it entered the literature more than thirty years ago. The term was used initially by Jock Young (1971) in his examination of police and how they negotiate reality and translate fantasy, but soon Cohen elaborated more fully on the concept in his book *Folk Devils and Moral Panics: The Creation of Mods and Rockers*. In its infancy, moral panic theory incorporated an emerging sociology of deviance and cultural studies, reflecting the changing social mood of the late 1960s. Young and Cohen concede that they probably picked up the idea of moral panic from Marshall McLuhan's *Understanding Media* (1964). According to Cohen, moral panic has occurred when: "A condition, episode, person or group of persons emerges to become defined as a threat to societal values and interest; its nature is presented in a stylized and stereotypical fashion by the mass media and politicians" (1972, 9). Cohen explored the roles of the public, media, and politicians in producing heightened concern over British youths in the 1960s when the Mods and Rockers were depicted as threats to public peace as well as to the social order. Together, the media and members of the political establishment publicized putative dangers posed by the Mods and Rockers; in turn, such claims were used to justify enhanced police powers and greater investment in the traditional criminal justice apparatus.

In 2002, the book's third edition was published, allowing Cohen to look back on how moral panic as a concept has been used—and misused—by academics and journalists. Chronicling its applications, Cohen reviews key advances in several areas of inquiry, including welfare issues and asylum seekers. A greater understanding of moral panic goes beyond recognizing its many territories of expansion; it is also crucial to reveal the depth and complexity of the concept. The third edition of *Folk Devils and Moral Panics* stands apart for its ability to delineate further the explanatory power and meaning of moral panic. Three extensions of moral panic theory are considered: social constructionism, media and cultural studies, and risk. Leaping ahead to the third extension, risk, Cohen recognizes the expanding territory of moral panic theory: "Some of the social space once occupied by moral panics has been filled by more inchoate social anxieties, insecurities and fears. These are fed by specific risks: the growth of new 'techno-anxieties' (nuclear, chemical, biological, toxic and ecological risk), disease hazards, food panics, safety scares about traveling on trains or planes, and fears of international terrorism" (2002, xxv).

Those developments offer conceptual bridges between moral panic paradigm and a risk society, again refining a critical understanding of shifting sites of social anxiety. The construction of risk refers not only to basic information about harmful conditions and events but also the manner of evaluating, classifying, and reacting to them (Beck 1992; Cohen 2002). Those activities inevitably involve claims made by experts and authorities, raising questions over whether there is a moral enterprise in the making.

Efforts to interpret society in a post-9/11 era prompt us to look toward a broader picture of collective anxieties. Ungar (2001, 272) suggests that we "open space for the consideration of other social anxieties that do not quite fit the moral panic paradigm." In his research, Ungar reveals new social anxieties in advanced industrial societies, in particular those involving nuclear, chemical, environmental, biological, and medical concerns (1990, 1992, 1998, 1999, 2000). The threat of nuclear winter along with worries over the greenhouse effect, Three Mile Island, breast implants, massive oil spills, and mad-cow disease (Bovine Spongiform Encephalopathy) represent new risks in society. Taken together, those concerns manifest as new sites of social anxiety in what Beck (1992) calls a risk society (see Hollway and Jefferson 1997). Those new worries are side effects of industrialization and modernization and in extreme form they contribute to the perception of a catastrophic society taken hold by a disaster mentality. Adding to deeper uneasiness, those side effects remain unpredictable and incalculable (Beck, Giddens, and Lash 1994). As society becomes technologically advanced, scientific developments vacate the protective environment of the laboratory and enter the real world. Consequently, "accidents not only come as a surprise but also can provide a crash course in institutional failings" (Ungar 2001, 273). Consider recent worries over the safety of breast implants, a reminder that patients (and cosmetic consumers) are really part of a larger work in progress, subject to risks related to the product itself and the limitations of medicine and regulatory agencies.

Threats of terrorism merely add to the existing fear of crime and broader anxieties embodied in a risk society. Reminiscent of the Cold

War, politicians, military advisors, and civilians share a common dread over the prospects of nuclear attack (Ungar 1990, 1992). Recent political pronouncements conveyed with stark visual metaphors feed that anxiety. On the anniversary of the attack on Pearl Harbor, Bush in 2002, in his run-up to the war in Iraq, warned: "Facing clear evidence of peril, we cannot wait for the final proof, the smoking gun that could come in the form of a mushroom cloud" (Herbert 2004, A17). As we shall discuss in forthcoming chapters, Bush's claim that Saddam Hussein had weapons of mass destruction and was linked to Al Qaeda proved false. Nevertheless, White House concerns about the risk of terrorists gaining access to weapons of mass destruction and biological and chemical armaments are widely shared among national security experts as well as the public (Allison 2004; Clarke 2004; National Commission on Terrorist Attacks Upon the United States 2004).

Compounding matters, the vulnerability of nuclear plants continues to gain public concern. A case in point is the controversy over the Indian Point nuclear plant located north of New York City. A public interest group, Riverkeeper, released a report that asserts that a successful terrorist attack on the plant could cause an apocalyptic disaster. Riverkeeper claims that a strike on the nuclear reactors could kill 44,000 people in a few days, at a range of up to 60 miles; over decades, more than 500,000 people could die from cancer. The group estimates that the disaster could cost 2.1 trillion dollars. Alex Matthiessen, the executive director of Riverkeeper, stated: "Evacuating an area with 17 to 20 million people in it seems fairly hopeless to me. It begs the question, why do we still have a nuclear plant 24 miles from New York City, given this new terrorist era?" (Wald 2004a, B5: see Riverkeeper 2004). The Nuclear Regulatory Commission (NRC) raised doubts over the study and accuses the group of sensationalism, especially considering that their report is titled "Chernobyl on the Hudson?" Still, Riverkeeper has generated considerable public concern and its work became the subject of a documentary aired on HBO called "Indian Point: Imagining the Unthinkable," produced by Rory Kennedy whose brother Robert F. Kennedy, Jr. is an environmental lawyer working for Riverkeeper. Dan Dorman, deputy director of NRC, insists that physical safety at the plant has improved; strangely though, he tries to be reassuring by downplaying the risk of another attack, saying that "terrorists were unlikely to be able to hijack another big jet (Wald 2004d, B5; see Foderaro 2004; Gates 2004).

Contributing further to fear and anxiety is the realization that there is so much that we do not know about the threat of terrorism. As the 9/11 Commission began to delve into its investigation over the attacks it discovered a "'knowledge-ignorance paradox,' [a] process by which the growth of specialized knowledge results in a simultaneous increase in ignorance" (Ungar 2000, 297). Simply put, the more we know, the more we don't know. Indeed, chair of the commission, Thomas H. Kean, conceded that adding to the likelihood of terrorist attacks was the lack of imagination (National Commission on Terrorist Attacks Upon the United States 2004). For political leaders who must manage risk, and for the public who want to have confidence in their government to protect them from terrorist strikes, the emergence of a "knowledge-ignorance paradox," coupled with a lack of imagination cannot be comforting. Perhaps that is one reason why the White House opposed forming the commission. Of course, other major reasons why the Bush administration tried to thwart an investigation have to deal with "covering its ass" and passing the "hot potato."

Hot Potato in the War on Terror

A chief development in a risk society is the "hot potato" in which various actors and institutions scramble to avoid blame. As the "hot potato" makes its rounds, probing questions mount, among them: Why did it take so long for the authorities to inform the public of the risk? In the case of the September 11 attacks, the commission charged with investigating government responses issued that query, especially in the face of the following warnings:

> "Bin Laden Preparing to Hijack U.S. Aircraft and Other Attacks." (Presidential Daily Brief December 4, 1998; Ridgeway 2004, 26)

> "Bin Laden Determined to Strike in US." (PDB of August 6, 2001, National Commission on Terrorist Attacks Upon the United States 2004, 261)

> The July 10, 2001 FBI memo from Phoenix sent to headquarters advising "possibility of a coordinated effort by Usama Bin Laden to send students to the United States to attend civil aviation schools." (National Commission on Terrorist Attacks Upon the United States 2004, 272)

White House counterterrrorism expert Richard Clarke warned National Security Advisor, Condoleezza Rice, "Foreign terrorist sleeper cells are present in the US and attacks in the US are likely." (National Commission on Terrorist Attacks Upon the United States 2004, 179)

For the past several years, the 9/11 "hot potato" continues to bounce from the White House, Congress, the FBI, and the CIA, all of which push blame onto other government agencies and even previous presidential administrations (Johnston and Jehl 2004a; National Commission on Terrorist Attacks Upon the United States 2004; Shenon 2004b).

Worries stemming from a risk society and fear of crime represent two coexisting types of anxieties. Fear of crime is more distinguishable, becoming significant discourse in a popular culture imbued with tales of risk, victimization, and the pervasiveness of villains (Best 1999; Glassner 1999). In contrast to late modern risks, fear of crime persists—despite evidence that crime continues to decline—because crime is believed to be "knowable, decisionable (actionable), and potentially controllable" (Holloway and Jefferson 1997, 258; italics in original). In a post-September 11 world, anxieties related to a risk society escalate given that there is so much uncertainty about future terrorist attacks. Consider news coverage on the 9/11 Commission: "The bipartisan commission that investigated the Sept. 11 attacks concluded in its final report on Thursday that the attacks 'were a shock but they should not have come as a surprise.' It warned that without a historic restructuring of the nation's intelligence agencies and a new emphasis on diplomacy the United States would leave itself open to an even more catastrophic attack" (Shenon 2004c, A1). The report was written in blunt and ominous language, "But we are not safe," while calling for urgency: "an attack of even greater magnitude is now possible and even probable—we do not have the luxury of time" (Shenon 2004c, A1: see Clarke 2004; National Commission on Terrorist Attacks Upon the United States, 2004). Those worries are compounded by a general fear of crime, and a host of undifferentiated concerns such as economic insecurity, as well as racial and ethnic tensions.

Understanding fear of terror in a post-September 11 world from the perspective of a risk society allows us to transcend traditional moral panic theory that tends to be retrospective, concentrating on past events. Furthermore, since we are focusing more on a pressing social condition rather than a putative problem we are less concerned with volatility, the tendency for worries to fade from public concern. This does not mean that we will not be dealing with scapegoats who serve as targets of displaced aggression. Much like moral panic, the risk society produces hostility aimed at not only scapegoats but also individuals and government agencies that bear responsibility, such as public officials and agencies asleep at the switch during a terrorist attack. As an extension of moral panic theory that stresses finite problems, this study acknowledges that in a risk society anxieties are more ubiquitous, often spiked by a "stream of emergencies and would-be emergencies" (Beck 1992, 37).

Moral panic models are hierarchical insofar as they involve claims made by authorities (or experts) occupying high social status that instill fear in people at the lower levels of society (McRobbie 1994). Consequently, the public adopts either a fortress mentality (a feeling of hopelessness or paralysis) or a gung-ho spirit, insisting that something must be done and right away. In either event, forms of social control abound insofar as the powerful embark on plans aimed at battling the putative problem, but in doing so place restrictions on certain groups of people, usually the impoverished and racial and ethnic minorities. Panic over crack cocaine produced legislation that funneled increasingly larger numbers of the poor, blacks, and Latinos behind prison bars (Reinarman and Levine 1997; Welch 2004b 1999; Welch, Bryan, and Wolff, 1999; Welch, Wolff, and Bryan 1998). By comparison, a risk society does not conform to that top-down trajectory since it deals with anxieties that are difficult to pinpoint (Ungar 2001). A risk society also has the potential to shift scrutiny onto authorities charged with protecting the public and when there is reason to issue blame, the "hot potato" is put into motion.

Manipulating Fear and Anxiety

The war on terror shares elements of both moral panic and a risk society, especially in light of evidence that the government manipulates fear of terrorism (Scheuer 2004; Robin 2003). Attorney General John Ashcroft, for example, issued several press briefings with ominous threats of terror attacks; however, he often recycled information from previous announcements, some dating back 28 months (Rich 2004, 7). In a May 26, 2004 FBI briefing, Ashcroft stated that intelligence reports indicate that Al Qaeda was close to launching a major attack against the nation. "This disturbing intelligence indicates Al Qaeda's specific intention to hit the United States hard. Beyond this intelligence, Al Qaeda's own public statements indicate that it is almost ready to attack the United States"

(Johnston and Stevenson 2004, A14). Interestingly, the announcement surprised the rest of the government, including the Department of Homeland Security, where officials said they "saw nothing in the threat reporting that warranted increasing the threat level" (Johnston and Stevenson 2004, A14). From the standpoint of a risk society, authorities are becoming increasingly subject to scrutiny; the 9/11 Commission disclosed in detail careless and manipulative government conduct that undermines public safety and national security (see National Commission on Terrorist Attacks Upon the United States 2004).

Moral panic is triggered when political and media opportunists tap into worries that are already in the air. The same holds true for social anxiety in a risk society imbued with uncertainty and unpredictability. Contributing to that anxiety is the realization—consciously or subconsciously—that public safety is subject to roulette dynamics. In light of those risks, government officials in a risk society must be careful not to oversell their ability to protect citizens from terrorist attacks. Indeed, President Bush, Vice President Cheney, and National Security Advisor Rice, Homeland Security Director Ridge, and Attorney General Ashcroft repeatedly told the public that they expect another terrorist strike on the United States sometime before the 2004 national election. The public yearns for safety and is likely to support officials who not only offer assurances on national security but also demonstrate a willingness to "kick ass." We ought to note, however, that a willingness to "kick ass" is actually an admission that the government cannot completely protect the nation against attack. Therefore, "kicking ass" serves symbolic functions related more to retaliation than to national security, especially when it involves the case of the Iraq war.

President Bush and his staff repeatedly issued assurances of national security and their willingness to "kick ass." While on the campaign trail, Bush told a crowd in Iowa: "You need to know something about me. I will never turn over America's national security decisions to leaders of other countries" (Sanger 2005, A16). More aggressively, Bush in his national address on September 20, 2001, overtly blamed Al Qaeda for the 9/11 attacks, the 1998 embassy bombings, and hitting the USS *Cole* and threatened retaliation: "Tonight, we are a country awakened to danger. . . . The Taliban must act, and act immediately. . . . They will hand over the terrorists or they will share their fate" (White House transcript, President Bush's Address to a Joint Session of Congress and the American People September 20, 2001; National Commission on Terrorist Attacks Upon the United States 2004, 337). When the USS *Cole* was bombed 25 days before the 2000 election, vice presidential candidate, Dick Cheney insisted "Any would-be terrorist out there needs to know that if you're going to attack, you'll be hit very hard and very quick. It's not time for diplomacy and debate. It's time for action" (Associated Press, 2000: 1). Similarly, while campaigning as the Democratic presidential candidate, John Kerry also relied on his own brand of tough-talk, announcing: "I can fight a more effective war on terror" (Nagourney 2004a, 16). As we shall explore in-depth in upcoming chapters, tough-talk and "kicking ass," indications of gung-ho spirit, are symptoms of social anxiety, leading to an array of scapegoating activities manifested in blatant human rights violations, such as the abuse and torture scandals at Abu Ghraib prison (Iraq), Camp Mercury (Iraq), Guantanamo Bay (Cuba), and the interrogation center at Bagram air force base (Afghanistan).

Hot Crises and Media Reassurance

Whereas some risks fail to resonate because they are not immediate or concrete enough, such as the ozone hole, other threats are taken very seriously becoming hot crises. As the term suggests: "Hot crises are startling, as presumed invulnerabilities appear challenged. A palpable sense of menace puts the issue 'in the air,' as unfolding events are watched, discussed and fretted over" (Ungar 1998, 37). When government officials announce that a threat is imminent and then take visible measures in response (such as filling city streets with armed National Guardsmen), the public takes notice. One particular hot crisis occurred on August 1, 2004, when the White House declared a high risk of terrorist attacks in New York City, Newark, and Washington, D.C. after receiving "what it described as alarming information that operatives had conducted detailed reconnaissance missions at certain sites" (Lichtblau 2004a, A1). Intelligence information gathered indicated that Al Qaeda had moved forward with plans to detonate car bombs and other modes of attack against prominent financial institutions, including the New York Stock Exchange, the Citigroup building in Manhattan, Prudential Financial in Newark, and the International Monetary Fund and the World Bank in Washington. In response, the Department of Homeland Security raised the threat level to code orange ("high alert") for those localities. Whereas the government had previously issued terrorist warnings, the announcement on August 1 was more dire than in the past because the White House said the information was "highly unusual in its specificity" and "chilling in its scope" (Lichtblau 2004a, A1; see Van Natta and Way 2004).

The media plays a central role in the creation of moral panic, often sensationalizing news events that inflame public fear (Goode and Ben-Yehuda 1994; Welch, Price, and Yankey 2002, 2004). Hot crises, however, create unique opportunities for the media as it attempts to decipher and explain relative risks to the public. Sociologists have discovered that in the midst of a hot crisis, the media, rather than stoking anxiety, tends to issue reassurance. That moderation effect serves to dampen any potential grassroots panic (Sandman 1994; Ungar 1998). In response to the August 1 scare, journalists investigated the claims of the government and found that the intelligence was three or four years old and that the White House had not found concrete evidence that a terrorist plot was underway. That revelation forced government officials to back pedal. In a revised version of events, a senior intelligence official announced: "What we've uncovered is a collection operation as opposed to the launching of an attack" (Jehl and Johnston 2004, A1). In essence, hot crises produce special circumstances in which the media turns off its "rhetoric of endangerment" and switches from fear-inducing to fear-reducing, exhibiting the range of utensils contained in the media tool kit (Carey and O'Connor 2004; Gamson and Modigliani 1989; Ungar 1998).

In confronting government and its claims of imminent terrorist threat, the media not only reassure the public that risk is exaggerated but by doing so also cultivate cynicism over the way politicians handle the war on terror. Indeed, "warning fatigue" has spread, particularly as citizens suspect the government of using terrorist threats to advance partisan interests. While eating a bratwurst in a local diner, Michael Schumacher, a 54-year-old writer confessed: "I don't know who on earth to believe anymore. You feel you're being manipulated all the time" (Kinzer and Purdum 2004, A13). The entire warning process has created a Hobson's choice, especially for well-intentioned public officials. If the government doesn't warn citizens of a potential plot and there is an attack, political leaders will have even more problems gaining public confidence.

Shifting Sites of Social Anxiety

As mentioned previously, fear of street crime is a potent site for social anxiety, serving as an emotional repository in which uneasiness over general risks and concerns are stored. In coping with those anxieties, fear of street crime becomes a social discourse in which people connect, disclosing and sharing their thoughts and feelings about life in a risky society.

Paradoxically, that bond simultaneously assuages and stokes anxiety since the more emotional investment there is toward fear of crime, the greater the uneasiness (Best 1999; Glassner 1999; Hollway and Jefferson 1997). As Ungar (2001) explains, sites of social anxiety are subject to shift. The emotional state of a post-9/11 society is marked by anxiety that migrates from fear of street crime to that of terrorism. That shift echoed in the political season of an election year as discourse over the threat of terrorism replaced previous rhetoric on the war on crime. "Crime, once as much a staple of campaigns as the sight of kissing babies, has become perhaps the biggest non-issue of the 2004 election. But the overriding explanation is that crime has simply fallen under the emotional shadow of the Sept. 11, 2001 attacks. Willie Horton the rapist made notorious by Mr. Bush's father in the 1988 campaign has been replaced by Osama bin Laden as the poster boy for what ails America" (Lichtblau 2004b, 4WK). While citizens still worry about various forms of street crime, including illegal drugs, gang violence, and car theft, the fear of terrorism has emerged as the new hot button topic. As Matt Bennett, a Democratic consultant puts it: "It's hard to argue that anyone is emphasizing terrorism too much because the threat is so great" (Lichtblau 2004b, 4WK).

Even the CIA, for years a clandestine agency operating behind closed doors, has stepped into the public light, sending counterterrorism agents to small towns to instruct local law enforcement officials on how to combat terrorism. "In part, the briefings are a direct response to rising fears of a Qaeda attack sometime this year and reflect the government's willingness to take previously untried steps to detect and possibly deter an attack" (Johnston and Jehl 2004b, 18). The CIA visited Fishers, Indiana, a suburb of 55,000 residents located north of Indianapolis. According to its police chief George G. Kehl: "There's so much concentration on large cities that there is always the possibility of being targeted in a smaller area," even though Kehl concedes that the risk is slight (Johnston, and Jehl 2004b, 18). Shifting sites of anxiety from street crime to terrorism are not only reflected in the way people talk about crime but also in how government officials spend—and waste—money on national security and law enforcement.

Homeland Security–Industrial Complex

In response to growing concern and anxiety over the threat of terrorism, political leaders have strengthened their commitment to the war on terror with considerable financial backing. Both private and public sectors are spending more to beef up security, creating what is becoming known as the homeland security–industrial complex. Whereas investing in national security and public safety makes for prudent social policy, there is a tendency for wasteful spending that benefits certain government agencies and private interests. Making matters worse, such funding extravaganzas are self-defeating since they do not contribute to the protection of society against threats of terrorism.

The homeland security–industrial complex resembles two other entrepreneurial projects, the military–industrial complex and the corrections–industrial complex. In each, government officials form partnerships with private interests that result in raiding the tax base. The Cold War and its ability to consume funding in the arms race has been a subject of intense criticism. In *The Power Elite* (1956), Mills presented evidence of an integrated collective of politicians, business leaders (i.e., defense contractors), and military officials who together determine the course of state policy. President Dwight D. Eisenhower, in his 1961 farewell address, warned that government "must guard against the acquisition of unwarranted influence" by the military–industrial complex (1985, 748; Ungar 1990). Since the 1980s when deregulation gained prominence, the field of corrections has become big business for politicians, business leaders, and criminal justice officials (Adams 1996; Wood 2003). More specifically, the corrections–industrial complex is formed around the iron triangle of criminal justice where subgovernment control is established. Operating well below the radar of public visibility, key players in the corrections subgovernment strongly influence the course of policy and spending. They include (a) private corporations eager to profit from incarceration (e.g., Corrections Corporation of America, Cornell Companies, Global Expertise in Outsourcing), (b) government agencies anxious to secure their continued existence (e.g., Bureau of Justice Assistance, National Institute of Justice), and (c) professional organizations (e.g., the American Bar Association, the American Correctional Association) (Lilly and Deflem 1996; Lilly and Knepper 1993; Welch and Turner 2004). The iron triangle of criminal justice draws on power from each of those sectors in a formidable alliance and, according to critics, is a daunting source of influence over government (see Sheldon and Brown 2000; Welch 2005a, 2003c).

The homeland security–industrial complex borrows from funding tactics developed during the Cold War and more recently the war on crime. Moreover, it rests on a potent form of emotional logic driven by fear.

Gordon Adams, who coordinated national security spending in the Clinton administration, noted the prevailing predicament in a risk society: "The question is: What is enough security? The answer is no one knows, and fear is a powerful driver here. Since we do not know who means us harm, where they are and how long they are going to continue to mean us harm, where do you stop?" (Uchitelle and Markoff 2004, BU8).

Now that the war in Iraq has been reframed from the need to disarm weapons of mass destruction to the war on terror, government officials claim that increased military spending can be justified as a counter-terrorism measure. Among the most significant beneficiaries are the "Big Three" defense contractors, Lockheed Martin, Boeing, and Northrup Grumman. In 2002, the Big Three received more than $42 billion in Pentagon contracts. Those firms were allocated one out of every four dollars spent by the Department of Defense (Hartung 2004). Other private industries also are lining up at the cash trough, including espionage agencies with their eyes on lucrative government contracts. As James Bamford, author of *A Pretext for War: 9/11, Iraq, and the Abuse of America's Intelligence Agencies,* puts it: "The CIA is awash in money as a result of post-9/11 budgetary increases. But because of the general uncertainty over the future, it faces a long delay before it can recruit, train and develop a new generation of spies and analysts. So for now, its building up its staff by turning to the 'intelligence–industrial complex'" (Bamford 2004, WK13). However, as the Abu Ghraib prison scandal illustrates, private intelligence contractors in sensitive positions can lead to disaster. Private intelligence agencies also place larger financial burdens on taxpayers. Eager to fill positions, private agencies offer salaries twice that of salaries for federal employees, then entice CIA agents who already have security clearances. Many of those so-called rent-a-spies resume their old government duties but under the supervision of a private firm. But questions remain over the quality of their work. Bamford interviewed one contractor who had been assigned to analyze e-mail messages: "A lot of it was in Arabic and none of us spoke Arabic—just a little problem. None of us really know what we were doing and we had management who didn't know what they were doing either" (2004, WK13; see Newburn 2005).

Federal tax dollars also are allocated to individual states so that they may guard themselves against terrorist strikes. Demonstrating the futility of the homeland–security complex, such spending has become classic "pork barrel" whereby less populated states receive a greater proportion of funding. That controversy is fueled by an incident in which the state of Alaska proposed to spend a $2 million grant on a jet for the governor, or what critics called an "expensive chariot." The Department of Homeland Security rejected the request but informed the Alaskan legislature that it would be "happy to entertain" another proposal. Alaska is second to Wyoming in the amount of per-resident federal funding it receives in the war on terror, and three times the amount granted to New York (Murphy 2004; Rosenbaum 2004). Funding is based on an age-old Congressional formula that is geared toward distributing wealth among states rather than assessing risk of terrorism. Mayor Michael Bloomberg repeatedly accused Congress of shortchanging New York City, calling the distribution of homeland security money a "slush fund" (Hu 2004, B2). Likewise, municipalities bordering New York City also complain that they are being ripped-off by federal and state governments since they must reach into their own budgets during heightened terror alerts announced by the Department of Homeland Security. Jersey City (NJ) police chief, Ronald Buonocore, said the orange alert is costing his department about $35,000 per day in overtime and expenses: "Our department can barely afford it and the state and federal government has been slow in helping us out" (Holl 2004, B4; Benson 2004).[1]

The financial component of the war on terror is likely to remain out of balance given the influence of special interests and legislators eager to keep them happy. Moreover, wasteful spending, along with an antiquated Congressional funding formula, reveals further hypocrisy among political leaders who campaign on the politics of fear and then engage self-defeating policy decisions that fail to protect the public or improve national security.

Conclusion

Post-9/11 America is in search of a safer society. However, in the years since the attacks, the war on terror has become increasingly politicized and coopted by special interests. Those political and financial forces have produced an array of contradictions for anti-terror policies and practices that undermine even well intentioned efforts to safeguard the nation. Fear of terrorism is now coupled with an emerging public cynicism over government's handling of terrorist threats, thereby stoking rather than assuaging anxiety. The 9/11 Commission brought to light a host of problems and concerns over the government's response to risks of terrorism; despite its recommendations, there is still debate within government over how to institute badly needed remedies, such as intelligence reform. The color-coded warning system also generated greater anxiety and confusion since it alerted the public of heightened risks but then politicians advised citizens to go about their usual business. Hot crises, such as the one on August 1 (2004) that was based on dated intelligence, contribute further to anxiety, adding to warning fatigue since people are growing skeptical of alerts that seem to have a political agenda.

This chapter set out to canvas the conceptual underpinnings of the war on terror by explaining the significance of moral panic theory and its extensions embodied in a risk society. Central to a risk society is social anxiety, a condition that produces numerous and varied consequences (see Kirkpatrick 2005a). Among them is the tendency for tragic events to produce corrosive communities in which government officials deny culpability and feverishly pass the "hot potato" while employing an array of diversion tactics such as blaming scapegoats (Freudenburg 1997). As dust settles from the political fallout of 9/11, it is becoming increasingly clear that official denial and the venting of displaced aggression onto innocent people has become a common reaction to the anxiety over terrorism. As discussed in the following chapters, it is likely that such scapegoating will persist, especially considering that: "the risk society is constituted by a vast number of unfamiliar threats, with new threats always lurking in the background" (Ungar 2001, 276).

CHAPTER THREE

Scapegoating and Social Insecurity

In general terms, throughout history of [hu]mankind, sacrifice, vengeance, and penal justice were not separate notions but different facets of the same process, needed alike to protect the state against the wrath of gods.
    —Nigel Davies, *Human Sacrifice: In History and Today,* 1981

Political leaders in the United States depict the problem of terrorism in richly coded mystical rhetoric, issuing broad proclamations about the threat of evil and evildoers, along with the axis of evil (Frum and Perle 2003; Kirkpatrick 2004a; Nunberg 2004). Framing the issue in that manner reflects and reinforces not only public fear of terrorism, but also an undifferentiated social anxiety over national security, economic woes, crime, racial/ethnic minorities, immigrants, and foreigners. Those tensions compound the need to assign blame even if it means falsely accusing innocent persons for terrorism along with a host of other social problems. That phenomenon, referred to as scapegoating, has a significant cultural, religious, and theoretical history. According to Tom Douglas: "The ancient process of the transfer and of evil, which has come to be known as 'scapegoating,' seems to have existed ever since human beings held the concept that they were under the supervision of divine beings" (1995, ix).

Beyond serving certain mystical purposes, the functions of scapegoating are widely recognized, in particular from the perspective of social constructionism. "When, in times of turmoil, new forms of deviance are needed by a society in order to provide scapegoats for deep social tensions, they will usually be invented" (Jeffrey 1992,1). Modern scapegoating departs from its ancient past insofar as there is less emphasis on mysticism, atonement, and purification. Still, scapegoating nowadays serves other potent social and psychological needs, ranging from the need to assign blame to the need to reduce psychic discomfort. Despite satisfying those needs—however neurotic they may seem—scapegoating in the war on terror is self-defeating since it undermines efforts to identify the real causes and solutions to political violence.

This chapter delves into the phenomenon of scapegoating, tracing its cultural and theoretical progression. The notion has evolved tremendously since it was first introduced as a biblical device to explain the expulsion of evil. Anthropologists, psychologists, and sociologists have all engaged in its conceptual development in attempts to interpret the universal need to blame others for social crises. While reviewing the distinct contributions of those theories, attention is turned toward integrating certain facets of cultural theory with risk society theory, thereby advancing criticism of an emerging culture of control and the *criminology of the other*. Regrettably, some versions of contemporary criminology have embraced questionable methods of assigning blame; such "othering" produces criminal justice policies that are tightly contoured along images of race and ethnicity—as well as social class (Welch 2005b; Young 1999). This chapter applies those dispositions to the war on terror, revealing the counterproductive nature of scapegoating in a post-9/11 society.

Scapegoating Theories

Scapegoating theory has a lengthy and complex history, rooted in religion, anthropology, and social psychology. In the biblical sense, scapegoating refers to a ritual described in a key passage in the Old Testament in which the first of two goats is sacrificed in an act of atonement while the other is chosen to escape, carrying symbolically the sins of the Hebrews into exile. " . . . and Aaron shall lay both his hands upon the head of the live goat and confess over him all the inequities of the people of

Israel and all other transgressions, all their sins, and he shall put them upon the head of the goat and send him away into the wilderness. . . . The goat shall bear all their iniquities upon him to a solitary land" (*Leviticus* 16, 8–10).

In recognizing the significance of rituals, anthropologists in the nineteenth century expanded the concept of scapegoating in an effort to explain a wide range of rites for the expulsion of evil (Stivers 1993). Often scapegoating merges with banishment insofar as certain people are forced from their communities. Occasionally the Athenians would expel from the city people chosen for their distinct attributes—the poor, the deformed, and the ugly—as a campaign to purify it. The view of scapegoats as tainted and polluted, prompting the need for societal purification, is widely recognized by key social theorists (M. Douglas 1966; Durkheim 1912; Girard 1987a, 1986; Levi-Strauss 1968). The Greek word, *pharmakoi*, is rendered into English as "scapegoats" or "offscourings" and the English term "scapegoats" is traced to Tyndale's bible (Bronowski 1972; Mellema 2000). Tom Douglas stresses: "Without some concept of supervision by an all-powerful being with the perceived ability to punish wrong-doing, no development of the rituals of purification and propitiation would ever have taken place" (1995, 15).

Eventually, in the mid-twentieth century, psychologists and sociologists adopted the term in reference to those who are unfairly blamed for a social problem; it is this meaning of scapegoating that prevails in contemporary society. Modern scapegoating is different from its ancient counterpart insofar as it is motivated less by mystical/religious ritual and more by the need to victimize (innocent) targets (Perera 1986). "In modern times the term *scapegoat* has been used to describe a relatively powerless innocent who is made to take the blame for something that is not his fault. Unfortunately he is not allowed to escape into the wilderness but is usually subjected to cruelty or even death" (Aronson 1980, 212).

Social scientists, however, differ in their focus on scapegoating. Psychologists tend to be concerned with the motivation behind scapegoating whereas sociologists explore its consequences. Creating another dichotomy, psychologists distinguish between explanations that suggest conscious intent and those implying unconscious impulse. From the perspective of psychoanalytic psychology, scapegoating represents a form of projection whereby individuals, small groups, and entire societies unconsciously cast onto others qualities they dislike in themselves. In essence, projection is a defense mechanism that relieves psychic discomfort (Freud 1989). Jungian psychologists similarly discuss that dynamic in the context of shadows consisting of the dark side of human nature, including guilt, shame, and regret. Those shortcomings often are too painful to face and easier to identify and condemn in others (Jung 1953–1979; Perera 1986; Szasz 1970).

Through frustration/aggression theory, psychologists have discovered that tension within an ingroup produces aggressive behavior targeted at an outgroup (Allport 1954). Displaced aggression is facilitated by prejudice, especially racism. Erik Erikson (1964) described scapegoats as victims of "pseudo speciation" insofar as they were considered to belong to a different "species" or "inferior race." Moreover, the general prohibition of aggression against members of one's "own species" does not apply to scapegoats (Aronson 1980). "There are two kinds of racism: one that is direct and material, a result of fear of and a desire to subjugate the other race's potential physical, political, or economic power; the other, indirect and symbolic, a consequence of a fear of the other race's standing as a degraded, inferior group. The two racisms are intimately connected" (Brown and Stivers 1998, 710).

Adorno, Frenkel-Brunswik, Levinson, and Sanford (1969) found that there are some persons who are predisposed to prejudice because they possess an authoritarian personality. Those individuals hold rigid belief systems based on conventional values. They also cannot tolerate what they see are "weaknesses" either in themselves or in others, and advocate punishments for transgressions, including those associated with so-called deviance (e.g., illegal drug use, homosexuality). The authoritarian personality is one that is full of suspicion of others while embracing authority with a high degree of respect, obedience, and self-righteousness. All of those characteristics contribute to personal frustration commonly leading to scapegoating.

Attending to the consequences of scapegoating, sociologists point to group solidarity insofar as members of an ingroup experience a sense of belongingness, superiority (often racial), and denial of one's own involvement in evil (Durkheim 1912; Erikson 1966). Scapegoating is particularly evident during moments of social crisis. "These scapegoats are, in turn, 'invented' by moral crusaders to bear the blame for threats to a society's past way of life and basic moral values" (Jeffrey 1992, 1). The power of labeling certain people as different, deviant, and responsible for causing social problems is particularly potent. That dynamic figures prominently in the selection of scapegoats in which outsiders—strangers—serve as symbolic reminders of uncertainty, threat, and ultimately evil. The way in which scapegoats are chosen is not haphazard; on the contrary, it is patterned firmly along observable lines of race, ethnicity, and religion. Contributing to the emergence of what Girard (1986) calls stereotypes of persecution is the process by which scapegoats are accused of having some moral failure that contributes to a social problem. Therefore, it is widely believed that scapegoats deserve blame and punishment.

Social Insecurity and Assigning Blame

Contributing to a deeper understanding of the nature of scapegoating, cultural theory, especially in the work of Mary Douglas (1992, 1986, 1966), offers several key insights. Equipped with a critical and anthropological lens, cultural theory observes thought styles, Douglas's term for how societies think about risk, danger, dread, and insecurity. Thought styles are particularly significant as they pertain to risk-laden issues ranging from nuclear safety to crime and, of course, terrorism. Richard Sparks proposes that criminology can benefit from cultural theory insofar as it reveals that risk discourse is more than just calculative but also moral, emotive, and political. "Thus when we encounter particular political formations of penality in particular times and places—'Prison Works!,' 'Three Strikes,' the 'war on drugs,' 'zero tolerance,' and perhaps anxieties about illegal immigration in Italy or Greece—we can see them for the hybrid formations that they are. They are instrumental *and* rhetorical, archaic sometimes *and* advanced, culturally embedded *and* politically tactical, political speech acts *and* institutional logics" (Sparks 2001, 169).

Government response to the attacks of September 11 has become a notable political formation, creating the war on terror. In light of that monumental development, Douglas's contributions further resonate. While addressing risk and insecurity, she unveils the process of assigning blame for social problems. Disaster and misfortune tend to become moralized and politicized; consequently, someone already unpopular is going to be blamed. At the collective level, blaming is emphatically cultural, having a broad institutional impact on social knowledge. "Blaming is a way of manning the gates through which all information has to pass" (Douglas 1992, 19). Perceptions of risk and insecurity not only facilitate blaming and scapegoating, but in doing so also add to a deepening punitive culture (Simon 2001; Vaughan 2002). In the United States, the punitive culture has produced an array of penalties for criminal infractions (i.e., mandatory minimum drug sentences), leading to unprecedented growth in the prison population along with an expanding roster of criminal penalties.

However, since those measures in and of themselves do not reduce crime, the public passion for punishment serves more expressive than instrumental functions (Garland 2002; Welch 2005a). Likewise, scapegoating, since it involves unfair blaming, also is expressive insofar as it allows for the cathartic ventilation of frustration by displacing aggression onto a suitable target.

Culture of Control

In surveying the consequences of social anxiety, it is important to bear in mind a key observation by Cohen who points to the significance of political morality: "More interesting than 'applying' risk theory to the study of moral panics is to remember that most claims about relative risk, safety or danger depend on political morality" (2002; xxvi). Moreover, the perception and acceptance of risk inevitably lead to efforts to determine who is responsible for causing the hazard. Accordingly, the allocation of blame becomes a central activity (Douglas 1992). In the realm of criminology, there is a popular movement to divert attention from social conditions (e.g., relative deprivation, economic marginalization, racial injustice) and stridently place blame onto certain types of people, thus reproducing the dominant ideology of crime (Barlow, Barlow, and Chiricos 1995a, 1995b; Welch, Fenwick, and Roberts 1998, 1997). That perspective, known as the *criminology of the other*, is notable because it reveals in clear terms the blaming process inherent in scapegoating. To understand the criminology of the other in a broader social context, we turn to the culture of control.

In *The Culture of Control: Crime and Social Order in Contemporary Society*, David Garland (2001) explores conservative social trends in the United States and the UK that have lead to exceedingly punitive responses to crime. While departing from correctionalist criminology and its aim to remedy the causes of criminality, tough on crime initiatives are put forth, creating an array of contradictions. Paradoxically, the United States—a nation committed to individual freedoms and civil liberties—has become the world's leader in incarceration due to its commitment to mass imprisonment. Likewise, American public support for such archaic sanctions as the death penalty and chain gangs are also manifestations of expressive punishments symbolizing collective anger (Kaminer 1995; Welch 2004a).

Expressive punishments embedded in American and British culture draw heavily on the emotional toll of crime. Criminal victimization, as characterized in the British Labour Party's slogan "Everyone's a Victim," has become a collective experience stoked by the media and politicians realizing that they have tapped into a public psyche consumed with undifferentiated anxiety over economic insecurity, racial tension, and an array of other social issues, including immigration and asylum seeking (Bottoms 1995; Chambliss 1999; Stenson and Sullivan 2000). As a consequence, punishments imbued with emotion are commonplace as citizens endorse tough on crime sanctions (e.g., 3-strikes legislation; see Greenberg 2002).

The culture of control marks another significant, albeit regressive, development in criminological thought, namely its emphasis on the consequences of crime rather than its causes. As a result, the focus shifts from the *crime* problem to the *criminal* problem, paving the way for an emergent criminology of the other in which lawbreakers are depicted as menacing strangers who threaten not only personal safety but also that of the entire social order. Capturing the essence of the criminology of the other, Garland elaborates:

> This is a criminology that trades in images, archetypes, and anxieties, rather than in careful analyses and research findings. In its deliberate echoing of public concerns and media biases and its focus on the most worrisome threats, it is, in effect, a politicized discourse of the collective unconscious, though it claims to be altogether realist and "common-sensical" in contrasts to "academic theories." In its standard tropes and rhetorical invocations, this political discourse relies upon an archaic criminology of the criminal type, the alien other. (2001,135)

That way of thinking about crime—and terrorism—draws on popular fears and resentments in ways that perpetuate harsh penal sanctions, including detention, indefinite and otherwise. While the older social democratic criminology has not vanished completely, it tends to be drowned out by the shrill emotionalism that has consumed the crime issue. In sum, the criminology of the other is anti-modern in nature insofar as it rejects modern concepts of crime and progressive methods of dealing with social problems, such as confronting racial and socioeconomic inequality. Conforming to the precepts of moral panic, the criminology of the other re-dramatizes crime, reinforces a disaster mentality, and retreats into intolerance and authoritarianism. In doing so, it clings to criminal stereotypes resonating with racism and classism, and that sense of "otherness" reinforces an "us versus them" worldview (Lea 2002; Young 1999). The criminology of the other is "deeply illiberal in its assumption that certain criminals are 'simply wicked' and in this respect intrinsically different from the rest of us" (Garland 2001,184).

Implications to the War on Terror

Scapegoating theories have tremendous value in their application to the war on terror. Although much of the ancient features of scapegoating have waned, some mystical forces persist in an otherwise secular campaign against terrorism. Much of the political and popular rhetoric pushing the war on terror is mystical, aimed at finding—and eliminating—the evildoers. Not surprisingly then is President Bush's call for sacrifice in requesting billions of more dollars from Congress for the Iraq war—as a means of furthering the war on terror. Consider also the need for purification that goes beyond ridding the world of terrorists deemed not only dangerous but also morally tainted. Purification extends to the threat of pollution. In traditional societies, poisoning was one of the most heinous and immoral crimes, reflecting symbolic and substantive anxiety over pollution. In the fourteenth century, Jewish people (as social and religious outsiders) were accused of poisoning the rivers in Northern France, causing the famous Black Death or Plague. That selection process relied on stereotypes of persecution, which involved the targeting of individuals and groups based on some perceived moral failure (Brown and Stivers 1998). Nowadays, anxiety over pollution and poisoning in the form of chemical and biological weapons and dirty bombs is met with the similar need for protection and purification. Moreover, scapegoating is driven by a familiar selection process patterned on modern racism, or Islamophobia.

As detailed in forthcoming chapters, hate crimes and state crimes are virtually inseparable from scapegoating since they involve the unfair blaming of innocent people—particularly Arabs and Muslims—for the attacks of September 11. Still, identifying precisely the motives and consequences of such scapegoating invites further analysis. Some forms of hate crime and state crimes involve projection, serving to alleviate psychic discomfort. Similarly, scapegoating in a post-9/11 society illuminates the frustration/aggression theory whereby members of an ingroup displace their bigoted aggression onto an outgroup. Although it is difficult to determine whether those scapegoaters suffer from an authoritarian personality, there is considerable social and cultural evidence to suggest that post-9/11 America has become noticeably more authoritarian, supporting political leaders who talk tough and "kick ass," both at home and abroad. The struggle over civil liberties and human rights in the war on terror is an important topic that shall be examined further elsewhere in this work.

Scapegoating in the war on terror also contributes to disconcerting degrees of social solidarity, reinforcing a "we versus them" mentality; from that standpoint, hate crimes and state crimes, along with war crimes, torture, and prisoner abuse tend to be ignored, excused, or justified. Those developments bring to light the emergence of cultural denial whereby large segments of society fail to recognize or oppose violence directed at innocent victims who are singled out solely because of their ethnic and religious differences. That form of blaming ought not to be decontextualized from a risk society, considering sites of anxiety that include an undifferentiated fear of crime, terrorism, and economic insecurity compounded by racial, ethnic, and religious tensions. Blaming and scapegoating have become key features in a culture of control in which harsh criminal penalties serve potent expressive functions, responding to public outrage over crime (see Mead 1964). With those phenomena in clear view, it is not surprising that there is relatively little American dissent to its government's use of the enemy combatant designation along with other detention measures codified in the Patriot Act. These issues, too, are subject to greater discussion in forthcoming chapters.

The criminology of the other thrives in the war on terror because it builds on stereotyping Arab and Muslim men as possible terrorists, reminiscent of derogatory ethnic and religious images dating back to the Crusades of the eleventh century (Said 1997, 1978). Also taking cues from the criminology of the other, the war on terror concentrates on the *terrorist* problem rather than the *terrorism* problem, thereby neglecting the sources and causes of political violence. Compounding that problem, the Bush administration has failed to recognize that Al Qaeda is now a global Islamic insurgency, rather than a conventional terrorist organization, therefore presenting a different form of threat. That argument is put forth by many scholars and experts, including former chief of the CIA's Osama bin Laden unit, Michael Scheuer, who is author of the book *Imperial Hubris: Why The West is Losing the War on Terror* (2004; see Danner 2005). Scheuer insists that the U.S. government "doesn't respect the threat" because most officials still regard Al Qaeda as a terrorist outfit that can be defeated by arresting or killing its operatives one at a time

(Risen 2004, A18). Taking exception to Bush's claim that the United States is waging success in the war on terror because two-thirds of the Al Qaeda leadership has been killed or captured, Scheuer contends that that figure is misleading since it refers to terrorist leaders who were in place as of September 11, 2001. "I think Al Qaeda has suffered substantially since 9/11, and it may have slowed down its operations, but to take the two-thirds number as a yardstick is a fantasy. To say that they have only one-third of their leadership left is misleading. That is looking at it from a law enforcement perspective. They pay a lot of attention to leadership succession, and so one of the main tenets of Al Qaeda is to train people to succeed leaders who are trained or killed (Scheuer quoted in Risen 2004, A18).

Scheuer points out that the difference between fighting a terrorist group rather than an insurgency is one of scope. The actual size of the insurgency is difficult to gauge because the war on terror as currently implemented adheres to a rigid law enforcement model rather than an informed paradigm aimed at understanding the nature of political violence. From that perspective, Scheuer and others such as Richard Clarke (2004) have been critical of the Bush administration's invasion of Iraq not only because it has diverted attention and resources away from the real war on terror but because it has also inflamed anti-American sentiment around the Arab world. Consequently, the war in Iraq has become a recruiting bonanza for Al Qaeda and other terrorist offshoots (Scheuer 2004).

Finally, borrowing from Mary Douglas, the criminology of the other as an extension of scapegoating also benefits from mystical thought styles. The criminology of the other creates a good versus bad dichotomy that is so compelling that it overrides a right versus wrong morality. As is elaborated in later chapters, American culture continues to adopt an "ends justifies the means" attitude toward the war on terror, including the wars in Iraq and Afghanistan. In doing so, public criticism of hate and state crimes is forced to swim against a tide of mainstream indifference.

Conclusion

In his sweeping book, *Scapegoats: Transferring Blame,* Tom Douglas concludes that scapegoating is one of the most universally found forms of individual and group behavior. Douglas reminds us that even though modern scapegoating has shed much its ancient commitment to religion, "modern man is still a creature who implicitly believes in mystical forces of some kind" (1995, 191). Joseph Campbell (1973) similarly points to myths as an essential part of humanity's equipment. For numerous reasons—cultural, political, psychological, and sociological—scapegoating persists in modern life because it serves a very basic human need. Attila Pok of the Hungarian Academy of Sciences has examined atonement, sacrifice, and scapegoating in modern Eastern and Central Europe. Applying enforced attribution theory whereby political blame becomes institutionalized, Pok observes: "Part of human nature is such that both individuals and groups want clear-cut, monocausal explanations of all events. However, this is, in most cases, impossible as historians know only all too well. Therefore, finding a scapegoat is often the easiest solution of the dilemma"(1999, 533–534). Pok goes on to note that in authoritarian/totalitarian nations "social tensions are created by the curtailment of individual rights and by a vague feeling of insecurity, of being in danger"(1999, 534). By comparison, similar tensions, insecurities, and fears are prominent in post-9/11 America, all of which contribute to scapegoating.

Whereas displaced aggression in the form of hate crimes is the subject of a forthcoming chapter, it is fitting here that we acknowledge similar consequences. Blending the work of Girard (1986) and Elias (1994) with a host of other social theorists, Irish penologist, Barry Vaughan delineates three functions of scapegoating: "It unites a faltering civic society by invoking a common threat (Mead 1964); it deflects attention away from the genuine causes of insecurity and hence prevents the fatalism incipient in an individualistic society (Douglas 1986); and it anchors the value of objects whose worth has been muddied by a continual process of revaluation" (2002, 205).

In closing, this chapter set out to survey various aspects of the scapegoating phenomenon. While reviewing its historical origins, key psychological theories of scapegoating were explored, distinguishing between explanations implying conscious intent and those suggesting unconscious impulse. Merging psychological and sociological viewpoints with cultural theory further advances a multidisciplinary approach to scapegoating, especially since it has become a chief dimension in the war on terror. More to the point for this analysis, a broad interpretation of scapegoating improves critical criminology by situating blame in a larger social context, encompassing the culture of control and the criminology of the other. As we shall examine further in the following chapter, those developments in a post-9/11 society have clear implications to the exclusive society and visions of social control (Cohen 1985; Young 1999).

CHAPTER FOUR

Crusading Against Terror

The United States is the only thing standing between tyranny and the rest of the world now. We saved Europe from Hitlerism and now we're saving the rest of the world from fundamentalist Muslims who will do anything to get where they want to go—even kill children.

—Carol Hanle, quoted in A. Hannaford,
"What's not to love about Bush?" *The Guardian Weekly,* 2004

Airports scrupulously apply the same laughable ineffective airport harassment to Suzy Chapstick as to Muslim hijackers. It is preposterous to assume every passenger is a potential crazed homicidal maniac. We know who the homicidal maniacs are. They are the one cheering and dancing right now. We should invade their countries, kill their leaders and convert them to Christianity.

—Ann Coulter, "This is war," *Ann Coulter Archive,* 2001

James Carroll, in his timely book *Crusade: Chronicles of an Unjust War* (2004a), puts into perspective significant events in the new millennium. We are reminded that as year 2000 approached there was growing anxiety over possibly abrupt changes in the world. The so-called Y2K problem loomed large on the consciousness of people across the globe. At a practical level there was technological anxiety over whether computers would collectively fail to adjust for the new numerical date, forcing a massive shut down. Virtually everything even remotely reliant on computers would be adversely affected, from automatic money machines to air traffic controlling. At a higher level of consciousness, all of those problems—and many more unforeseen ones—seemed cosmically linked to powerful mystical forces. Mainstream society appeared to have abandoned its secular bearings, giving into the symptoms of a millennium fever, imbued with a sense of dread and danger reminiscent of a medieval superstition. Even intelligent and rational people, including Carroll himself, stocked up on bottled water and withdrew large sums of cash in preparation for the global standstill.

> Of course, the mystical date came and went, the computers did fine, airplanes flew and the world went back to normal. Then came September 11, 2001, the millennial catastrophe—just a little late. Airplanes fell from the sky, thousands died and an entirely new kind of horror gripped the human imagination. Time, too, played its role, but time as warped by television, which created a global simultaneity, turning the whole human race into a witness, as the awful events were endlessly replayed, as if those bodies leaping from the Twin Towers would never hit the ground. Nightmare in broad daylight. New York's World Trade Center collapsed not just onto the surrounding streets but into the hearts of every person with access to CNN. (Carroll 2003b, 14)

As Americans watched and waited for President Bush to characterize his course of action in the wake of 9/11, he spoke spontaneously—without the aid of advisors or speechwriters—saying that the war on terror would be a crusade. Carroll says that upon hearing the crusade remark he slipped into a moment of vertigo, thinking that Bush had used that word out of a sense of ineptitude. As a Roman Catholic, Carroll explains with a feeling for history that he harbors some strong regrets over the Crusades that proved to be a set of world-historic crimes. Thousands of years before Iraqi "insurgents" shocked the public by decapitating hostages on television, Christian crusaders severed the heads of Muslim fighters. As Carroll's vertigo lifted, he realized that Bush's reference to the war on terror as a crusade was "an accidental probing of unintended but nevertheless real meaning" (2004b, 14; 2002).

This chapter explores the crusade against terror by taking into account the sociology of religion, especially as it interacts with politics and government. For years scholars have demonstrated the importance of forming a sophisticated understanding of religion. "The possible consequences of religion are matters in which both the supporters of religion and its detractors have a stake. The role of religion in promoting democracy, its part in stimulating violence, whether it nurtures the family or promotes bigotry . . . are all questions that continue to be debated" (Wuthnow 2004, 216; see Berger 1967; Wuthnow and Evans 2001). The discussion tracks the recent journey of America's newfound love for conservative Christianity and the roads leading to the White House where social policy, in particular counterterrorism, continues to bear the imprint of mystical forces. Regrettably, those developments have figured prominently in campaigns that cast Islam in a negative light, reproducing prejudice and bigotry (Mamdani 2004; Said 1997, 1979). The chapter closes with a critical look at the apocalyptic imagination and the way it escalates the spiral of violence committed by terrorists as well as by crusaders determined to extinguish evil.

A Nation Gets Religion

As explored in the previous chapter on the origin of scapegoating, anthropologists and sociologists approach the study of religion somewhat differently. Anthropologists tend to examine religion as it pertains to symbolism, myth, and ritual. Whereas sociologists value those insights, their focus often is directed at the ways in which religion influences social movements and social institutions, including politics. In his famous work, *The Religious Factor*, Gerhard Lenski predicted that socioreligious groups would eventually replace ethnic groups as the basic units in the system of status groups in American society (1961, 363). That forecast is not lost among contemporary sociologists. "In important ways, the growth of the so-called new religious right in recent years fits Lenski's model very well. In many ways, it goes farther than he imagined. Political and, more broadly, social activism join the actively religious not just from different Protestant denominations but also across the Protestant-Catholic divide. . . . Denomination matters less, but membership in the broad network of evangelicals works in many ways as Lenski suggested" (Calhoun 2004,

201). Surveys confirm that plurality. In 2000, a national study found that 66 percent of Americans agreed, on the one hand, that "Christianity is the best way to understand God," but, on the other hand, 66 percent also agreed that "all religions are equally good ways of knowing about God" (Wuthnow 2004, 213).

Whereas religiosity of all faiths is experiencing an upswing in American society, it is the fervor of evangelical and born-again Christians that draws much of the media attention. Those religious archconservatives seem ready to rumble with the seculars in the most recent round of the so-called culture war whereby their faith is more valuable than reason. In the war over America's morality, evangelical discourse has united with popular culture in ways that cast Jesus in a decidedly militant and macho light. This warrior Jesus is the central character in a series of apocalyptic novels titled *Left Behind*. In one of its works, *Glorious Appearing* (2003), authors Tim LaHaye and Jerry B. Jenkins depict the Second Coming of Christ as a prophetic action movie. With sensationalistic fire and brimstone, a muscular Jesus wreaks carnage on the unbelieving earthly world. Warrior Jesus is a cultural product of emergent evangelicalism, stirred with post-9/11 vengeance and a president who speaks of the godly purpose behind the invasion of Afghanistan and Iraq. As a darker, more martial Messiah, warrior Jesus is a stark contrast to the gentle, pacifist—even effeminate—Jesus who turned the other cheek. Ted Haggard of the National Association of Evangelicals says warrior Jesus is a healthy corrective, reminding people that the deity is judgmental as well as merciful: "The fear of God is a worthy emotion. In our stained-glass windows and our popular culture, Jesus is a kind of marshmallowy, Santa Claus Jesus, which is not at all in keeping with the gospels" (Kirkpatrick 2004a, 6).

Critics of the *Left Behind* series fault the authors for endorsing an exclusivistic interpretation of the Bible in which a returning Jesus slaughters everyone who is not a born-again Christian, most notably agnostics, Jews, Hindus, and Muslims. "If Saudi Arabians wrote an Islamic version of this series, we would furiously demand that sensible Muslims repudiate such hatemongering. We should hold ourselves to the same standard" (Kristof 2004, A23). Writers LaHaye and Jenkins stand firmly behind their words, insisting that they are not celebrating the decimation of non-Christians but merely revealing the painful reality of Scripture. "That's our crucible, an offensive and divisive message in an age of plurality and tolerance" (Kristof 2004, A23).

Although the separation of church and state is officially declared in American government, the two rarely stray far from one another. In his tour of the early republic in the 1830s, Alexis de Tocqueville (1835) marveled at the close alliance between religion and politics, producing a unique American brand of democracy. Nowadays, the merging of religion and politics is tightly wound. To say that religion played a pivotal role in the 2004 presidential election is an understatement. In June 2004, a *New York Times* poll found that 42 percent of those surveyed said they welcomed candidates discussing the role of religion in their lives. That figure is up from 22 percent in 1984 (Goodstein 2004). The rising acceptance of religion in campaigns is the expression of a social trend. Mark Silk, director of the Center for the Study of Religion in Public Life, adds: "It is the extent to which the evangelical voice has come back to American national politics, and the expectation since the 1980s that somehow it's a normal thing to talk about religion" (Goodstein 2004, sec. 4, 2).

Still, the Republican campaign went beyond a polite dialogue over religion, resorting to hardball intimidation tactics. Months before the election, the GOP acknowledged that it sent mass mailings to residents of Arkansas and West Virginia warning that "liberals" seek to ban the Bible, a maneuver intended to mobilize religious voters for Bush. The material featured images of the Bible labeled "banned" and a gay marriage proposal labeled "allowed." The mailings warned: "This will be Arkansas [or West Virginia] . . . if you don't vote." The Interfaith Alliance, a liberal religious group cried foul. Its spokesman Don Parker said the Republicans were "playing on people's fears and emotions" (Kirkpatrick 2004b, A22). Christine Iverson of the Republican National Committee offered no apologies: "When the Massachusetts Supreme Court sanctioned same-sex marriage and people in other states realized that they could be compelled to recognize those laws, same sex-marriage became an issue. These same activist judges also want to remove the words 'under God' from the Pledge of Allegiance" (Kirkpatrick 2004b, A22; 2005a).

Religious moderates weighed into the issue, underscoring the point that mainstream Christians were the real electoral force in the 2004 election and not the evangelicals. "Most Americans see morality more complexly. Many think a higher morality is found in Christ's command to help the needy, prevent war and pursue other humanitarian goals. Churchgoers of this sort aren't likely to believe childish allegations that Democrats want to ban the Bible" (*Charleston Gazette* [West Virginia] 2004, 16). Truth be told, President Bush was re-elected by a sweeping coalition of religious voters. For all the credit claimed by the evangelical wing of religious America, Bush owes his victory to conservative Catholics, mainline Protestants, Jews, and Mormons. Bush strategists set out to recruit voters from those religious groups who felt alienated and disrespected by a popular culture that trivializes religion. Moreover, conservatives of all religious stripes identified with the president's commitment to the trinity of social issues: abortion, same-sex marriage, and embryonic stem cell research (Goodstein and Yardley 2004, A22).

As the trinity of social issues gained popular currency, liberals seemed desperate to find a deeper interpretation of the Bush victory. That view quickly became known as the moral values explanation. Pollsters, however, wasted little time dispelling the myth of moral values. Andrew Kohut, president of the Pew Research Center cautioned against getting carried away with the emphasis on the moral values of voters: "It was a vote to some extent on values, but it was also a vote on John Kerry and how the America people felt about the way President Bush handled the war and the war on terror" (Goodstein and Yardley 2004, A22). Gary Langer, director of polling for ABC News, went further, citing serious methodological flaws in the exit poll question compounded by a dose of political spin. The Edison/Mitofsky (2004) survey reports that on issues that mattered most, moral values ranked first with 22 percent followed by economy/jobs (20%), terrorism (19%), Iraq (15%), health care (8%), taxes (5%), and education (4%) (Seelye 2004a, P4). Langer insists that the poll accurately reflected the exit poll data, but not reality since morals and values represent personal characteristics rather than discrete political issues. Consequently, the poorly devised exit poll produced misleading results. "Moral values is a grab bag: it may appeal to people who oppose abortion, gay marriage and stem cell research but because it's so broad, it pulls in others as well" (Langer 2004, A19). Langer also points out that the items economy/jobs, health care, education, and Iraq played in favor of Kerry while only terrorism and taxes favored Bush. "If you were a Bush supporter, and terrorism and taxes didn't inspire you, moral values was your place to go on the exit poll questionnaire" (Langer 2004, A19). Indeed, people who selected moral values on the poll voted for Bush by 80 percent. So how was it possible for such an important exit poll to become so poorly conceived? According to Langer, the exit poll was written by a committee whose members voted down his argument that moral values did not belong on the list. Langer nevertheless advocates research that identifies the intersection of religiosity, ideology, and politics because it serves as a staging ground for society's most pressing issues.

The White House of God

While virtually all U.S. presidents have invoked religion while serving in office, few have placed their faith at the center of their political persona as much as George W. Bush. His strident commitment to God echoes in virtually every major item on his administration's agenda, from faith-based initiatives to Iraq to the war on terrorism. The public, including those who voted for him and those who did not, other politicians (both Democrats and Republicans), the media, pundits, and scholars have all taken notice. Despite his failings, the Bush White House will occupy a unique place in presidential history in large part due to his unusually high degree of religiosity that cannot be separated from his way of managing national affairs (Woodward 2004).

Bush was born again while struggling against a mid-life crisis. His deep involvement in religion helped him overcome a drinking problem that was undermining his marriage. With his newfound faith, Bush put his personal—and political—life back together. On the day of his second inaugural as governor of Texas, Richard Land, a leader of the Southern Baptist Conference, recalls Bush saying to his close associates: "I believe that God wants me to be president." Adding, "We need commonsense judges who understand our rights were derived from God. And those are the kind of judges I intend to put on the bench" (Stanley 2004, E1; *Frontline* 2004). In 1993, Bush told a reporter that he believed that a person had to accept Christ to go to heaven, a disclosure that brought considerable criticism. Bush soon learned to be more diplomatic in discussing religion publicly. While on the 2000 presidential campaign, Bush said the he believed that schools should teach both creationism and evolution, but he refused to get baited as to which one he prefers (Suskind 2004; Wills 2003).

Political analysts generally agree that Bush's display of his faith is genuine but also calculated, intended to garner political support. Routinely, he quotes the Bible during speeches. In his inaugural address on January 21, 2001, Bush pontificated: "An angel still rides in the whirlwind and directs this storm." In the Books of Job and Ezekial, the whirlwind symbolizes a medium for the voice of God. Bush's references to good and evil increased noticeably since 9/11, implying the biblical dichotomy between Christ and Satan (Yourish 2003, 28). "We are in a conflict between good and evil, and America will call evil by its name" (Bush speech at West Point Commencement, June 1, 2002). "Freedom and fear, justice and cruelty have always been at war, and we know that God is not neutral between them" (Bush speech to Congress, September 20, 2001).

Bush appeals to religious voters across the Christian spectrum because he borrows from an array of theological and denominational ideas. His invocation of "Providence" and "God's will" resonate Calvinism but also expresses American civil religion linking the nation's purpose to those of a transcendent God, particularly during wartime (Bellah 1988, 1975; Fineman 2003). Altogether, those beliefs point to a sense of destiny. David Frum, former Bush speechwriter, recognizes that there is a fatalistic element. "If you are confident that there is a God that rules the world, you do your best, and things will work out" (Fineman 2003, 29). Bush's speeches since 9/11 are imbued with a distinct form of Calvinism. Just three days after September 11 at a memorial service at the National Cathedral in Washington, Bush pronounced: "Our responsibility to history is already clear: to answer these attacks and rid the world of evil" (Lifton 2003b, 12; Woodward 2004). Bush's claim that he was "called" to become president suggests a divine mandate. That form of messianism evokes the prophetic commissions of Hebrew scripture. In his 2003 State of the Union address, Bush said that the nation must go forth to "confound the designs of evil men" because "our calling, as a blessed country, is to make the world better"(Stam 2003, 27; see Marty 2003).

Bush's religiosity, especially since it seems to influence his governance, is subject to frequent and at times intense criticism. Theologian Juan Stam takes aim at Bush's cosmic vision, or ideology. Stam points out that as a fundamentalist, Bush relies on extreme individualism embodied in the metalanguage of evangelical code words called personal witness. While Bush has been effective in blending religion and politics, it is problematic in three theological areas: Manicheism, messianism, and the manipulation of prayer. Manicheism is the ancient notion dividing all of reality into two entities: Absolute Good and Absolute Evil. Centuries ago, the Christian church rejected Manicheism as heretical. After the attacks of 9/11, Bush declared: "This will be a monumental struggle between good versus evil, but good will prevail" (Stam 2003, 27). In search of a simple explanation for the terrorist strikes, Bush repeats the mantra: "There are people who hate freedom" (Stam 2003, 27). In other words, according to Stam, they are so evil that they abhor the good merely because it is good. "But if the terrorists hate freedom, why have they not attacked Canada, which in some respects is more democratic than the United States. Why is there not the same hatred for Switzerland, Holland, or Costa Rica" (Stam 2003, 27). Stam rails Bush for his heretical manipulation of religious language, his messianic claims of being the "chosen one," and his self-serving manipulation of prayer. "It is remarkable how closely Bush's discourse coincides with that of the false prophets of the Old Testament. While the true prophets proclaimed the sovereignty of Yahweh, the God of justice and love who judges nations and persons, the false prophets served Baal, who could be manipulated by the powerful" (Stam 2003, 27; see Singer 2004).

Aside from the theological criticism of Bush's faith, there are harsh charges that he uses the power of the White House to advance religious causes masked as social programs. In the late 1990s, during the last years of the Clinton presidency, the Christian right, including its standard bearer, the Christian Coalition, was on the verge of collapse. Gone were the days of Newt Gingerich and his campaign to use the federal government to advance the religious right. But with election of Bush in 2000, conservative Christians swung back into the political fold where it could once again influence public policies. That renewed social movement had virtually unobstructed access to tens of millions of dollars that could be funneled into the coffers of the Christian right's grassroots organizations. Critics say that Bush has turned his faith-based initiative into what Reverend Eugene Rivers of Boston calls "a financial watering hole for the right-wing evangelicals"(Kaplan 2004a, 20).

Conservative religious leader, Pat Robertson's Operation Blessing was one of the first organizations to receive a faith-based grant. The group was granted $500,000, renewable for three years, for a total of $1.5 million; the funds are to be used to offer technical assistance to smaller faith-based organizations so that they can compete for federal money of their own. Operation Blessing was granted funding despite having recently been investigated by the State of Virginia for misusing relief dollars to transport equipment for Robertson's for-profit diamond mining company. The faith-based initiative has been maligned by accusations that it is Christian-centric since no direct funding has been allocated to a single non-Christian religious outfit, whether Jewish. Buddhist, Sikh, or Muslim (Kaplan 2004a, 2004b). In the aftermath of the Katrina hurricane in 2005, the Federal Emergency Management Agency (FEMA) website directing charitable contributions prominently listed Robertson's Operation Blessing. According to IRS documents obtained by ABC News, Operation Blessing "has given more than half of its yearly cash donations to Mr. Robertson's Christian Broadcasting Network" (Rich 2005, 12).

Bush's chief political advisor, Karl Rove, picked up where Gingerich left off. Most notably he has transformed the sphere of social policy by stripping federal advisory positions of mainstream scientific, professional, and policy organizations and replaced them with ideologues possessing little or no expertise. When asked how he defined the Democratic base, Rove responded roughly: "Someone with a doctorate" (Kaplan 2004a, 21). Under the Bush/Rove regime, the American Medical Association no longer advises U.S. delegates to UN summits on children's issues; the role has been given to Concerned Women for America, a conservative body of religious Washington insiders. The screening of judicial nominees is currently conducted by the far-right Federalist Society, a procedure formerly carried out by the American Bar Association. Experts from the Center for AIDS Prevention Studies at the University of California, San Francisco no longer serve on the presidential AIDS advisory council; "they have been replaced by a former beauty queen who lectures on abstinence and an antigay evangelical barnstormer from Turning Point ministries" (Kaplan 2004a, 20; 2004b; also see Banerjee 2004; Jacoby, 2004).

Bush, due in large part to his evangelical values, enjoys considerable support from conservative Christian voters in the United States, but the role his faith plays in governance is viewed with skepticism from some Americans—and many people abroad. Even though he publicly praises Islam as a "religion of peace," "to many Muslims, especially Arabs, he looks sinister: a new Crusader, bent on retaking the East for Christendom" (Fineman 2003, 25). The image of Bush as a crusader along with a war on terror that profiles Muslims as terrorists and the invasion of Iraq contribute to a sense of wariness among Islamic people. "Evangelical missionaries don't hide their desire to convert Muslims to Christianity, even—if not especially in Baghdad. If one of the goals of ousting Saddam Hessein is to bring freedom of worship to an oppressed people, how can the president object?" (Fineman 2003, 30; Goodstein 2003).

Continuing the Campaign Against Islam

On September 16, 2001, just days after the attacks on the World Trade Center and the Pentagon, President Bush's vision of homeland security was taking form. When asked about the potential civil rights abuses in an emerging war on terror, Bush uttered a telltale word, crusade. "This is a new kind—a new kind of evil. And we understand. And the American people are beginning to understand. This crusade, this war on terrorism is going to take a while" (Suskind 2004, 50). Not much was made of the crusade remark among Americans who have grown accustomed to hearing political leaders engage in hyperbole and metaphors when speaking about getting things done, such as the war on poverty, the war on drugs, now the war on terrorism. However, in the global village—particularly in the Mid-East—the word crusade resonates, harking back to religious invaders driven by a sanctimonious need to convert Muslims to Christianity. Bush's handlers, after realizing that his crusade remark incensed Muslims, scrambled to perform damage control. White House spokesman, Ari Fleischer, spun into action: "I think what the president was saying was—had no intended consequences for anybody, Muslim or otherwise, other than to say that this is a broad cause that he is calling on America and the nations around the world to join" (Suskind 2004, 50).

But that was not the last time Bush invoked the word crusade in the war on terror; in February 2002, Bush repeated the crusade reference in a speech in Alaska. Making matters worse was the publicity over Lieutenant General William Boykin of the Army, deputy under secretary of the defense for intelligence and war-fighting support, who had delivered a series of fire and brimstone speeches to conservative religious groups. Decked out in full military uniform, Boykin told a group of evangelicals that Muslims worship an "idol" not "a real God." The general portrayed the American battle with Muslim radicals as a fight against "Satan," adding that militant Islamists sought to destroy America "because we're a Christian nation." In one speech, Boykin shared a war story from Somalia in which a Muslim fighter boasted that U.S. forces would not get him because he was protected by Allah. "Well, you know what I knew—that my God was bigger than his. I knew that my God was a real God, and his was an idol" (Reuters 2003, A7).

Boykin also delves into the Messianic, insisting that God selected Bush as president. "Why is this man in the White House? The majority of Americans did not vote for him. Why is he there? And I tell you this morning that he's in the White House because God put him there for a time such as this." In outlining America's fight with Islamic extremists, the general put forth: "The enemy is a spiritual enemy. He's called the principality of darkness. The enemy is a guy called Satan." The controversy thickened as Defense Secretary Donald H. Rumsfeld declined to criticize Boykin for his public remarks, pointing instead to the general's "outstanding military record." The Council on American-Islamic Relations took exception to Boykin's speeches, characterizing them as "bigoted." The group's executive director, Nihad Awad contends: "Putting a man with such extremist views in a critical policy-making position sends entirely the wrong message to a Muslim world that is already skeptical about America's motives and intentions" (Reuters 2003, A7). Yielding to enormous political pressure, Boykin issued a written apology for his remarks but that he had no intention of resigning (Jehl 2003, A6).

Hostility toward Muslims dates back to the crusades of the eleventh century when European powers organized waves of fighters intent on recovering Christian holy places in Palestine. More recently in the United States, the stereotyping of Muslims as terrorists was galvanized in 1979 when 52 Americans were held hostage in Iran for 444 days, The 1983 attack on American marine barracks in Lebanon, killing 240, and the 1993 blast at the World Trade Center, killing six and injuring more than 1,000, added to growing resentment and suspicion of Muslims. In the aftermath of the 1995 bombing of the federal building in Oklahoma City that killed 168, the *New York Post* editorialized: "Knowing that the car bomb indicates Middle Eastern terrorists at work, it's safe to assume that their goal is to promote free-floating fear and a measure of anarchy, thereby disrupting American life" (Naureckas 1995, 6). Similarly, *New York Times* columnist A. M. Rosenthal wrote: "Whatever we are doing to destroy Mideast terrorism, the chief terrorist threat against Americans has not been working" (Glassner 1999, xiii). Eventually, investigators determined that the explosion was not the handiwork of Muslim terrorists but that of Timothy McVey, a white U.S. citizen and former serviceman; nevertheless, Muslims had been negatively stereotyped as terrorists and threats to American national security (Council on American-Muslim Research Center 1995; Shaheen 1984).

In his widely acclaimed book, *Covering Islam: How the Media and the Experts Determine How We See the Rest of the World,* Edward Said discusses the social and cultural impact of those events, emphasizing that the media environment in the United States has become increasingly anti-Muslim (see also Mamdani 2004). On the day of the bombing of the federal building in Oklahoma City in 1995, Said writes that he received some twenty-five phone calls from major newspapers and news networks, "all of them acting on the assumption that since I was from and had written about the Middle East that I must know something more than most other people. The entirely factitious connection between Arabs, Muslims, and terrorism was never more forcefully made evident to me" (Said 1997, xiv; 1996). Said's writings on Islam—more precisely how the West views the East—demonstrate the ways in which language not only describes but also defines. The label "Islam," according to Said, either to explain or indiscriminately condemn "Islam" takes form as an attack. Moreover, self-appointed Western experts refer to "Islam" in such sweeping terms that it defies any enlightened and scholarly understanding of the subject given that the Islamic world includes billions of people and dozens of nations, societies, traditions, and languages. Such generalizations are what Said (1979) calls Orientalism. Instead of being introduced to scholarship, the public by way of the media is fed extravagant statements about Muslims, usually coupled with the term fundamentalism, thereby producing a perceptual shortcut that assumes the two are one in the same. "Given the tendency to reduce Islam to a handful of rules, stereotypes, and generalizations about faith, its founder, and all of its people, then the reinforcement of every negative fact associated with Islam—its violence, primitiveness, atavism, threatening qualities—is perpetuated. And all this without any serious effort at defining the term 'fundamentalism,' or giving precise meaning either to 'radicalism' or 'extremism,' or giving those phenomena some context" (Said 1997, xvi).

Said (1997) also finds fault in the American Academy of Arts and Sciences for publishing a massive five-volume study on "fundamentalism" in which the term is never coherently defined; consequently, the work stirs up feelings of alarm and consternation over perceived negative attributes of Muslims (see Lustick 1996). As the Cold War dissolved, the Soviet menace has been replaced with the putative threat of Islam. In 1996, the *New York Times* "Week in Review" headline declared "The Red Menace is Gone. But Here is Islam" (Sciolino 1996; see Esposito 1992). Zachary Karabell (1995, 39) exposes further the anti-Muslim bias in the media, issuing forceful negative images that influence how Westerners view Islam. "Ask American college students, in elite universities or elsewhere, what they think of when the word 'Muslim' is mentioned. The response is inevitably the same: gun-toting, bearded, fanatic terrorists hellbent on destroying the great enemy, the United States." Among the examples cited by Karabell is ABC's *20/20* news program that caricatured Islam as a crusading religion inculcating warriors of God; similarly, the well-respected *Frontline* series sponsored an investigative segment on the tentacles of Muslim terrorists that conjured fears of Islam (also see Emerson's PBS film *Jihad in America*). Of course, adding to the anti-Islam bias in the media are Hollywood movies (e.g., *True Lies, Delta Force, Indiana Jones*) that routinely cast Muslims as exotic villains. Those feature films serve to demonize and dehumanize Muslims in ways that portray them as "evil, violent, and above all, eminently killable" (Said 1997, xxvii; Mamdani 2004).

Said goes on to observe that the distortion of Islam in the media is not confined to marginal, patently crazy, or inconsequential writers on the

Middle East but rather well known and mainstream books (see Miller 1996; Viorst 1994) and magazines such as *The New Republic* and *The Atlantic,* the former owned by Martin Peretz, the latter by Morton Zuckerman, both of them ardent supporters of Israel (also see the body of writings by Bernard Lewis published in *The New York Review of Books, Commentary,* and *Foreign Affairs*). One of the most obvious pitfalls in the media's coverage of Islam is that reporters and many Western self-appointed experts do not read, speak, or understand languages indigenous to the Middle East. Revealing the inadequacies of such journalism in general and the work of Judith Miller in particular, Said notes:

> Writing about any other religion or part of the world Miller would be considered woefully unqualified. She tells us on numerous occasions that she has been involved with the Middle East as a professional for twenty-five years, yet she has no knowledge of either Arabic or Persian; she admits that wherever she goes she needs a translator whose accuracy or reliability she has no way of assessing. It would be impossible to be taken seriously as a reporter or expert on Russia, France, Germany, Latin America, perhaps in China and Japan, without knowing the requisite languages, but for "Islam" no linguistic knowledge seems to be necessary since what one is dealing with is considered to be a psychological deformation, not a "real" culture or religion. (1997, xxxvi)

In capturing the essence of Said's critique of the media and how it shapes popular—albeit Western—views of Islam, we return to the sociological facets of language. Said (1997, 1979) reminds us that language, or more precisely discourse, is a regulated system of producing knowledge. From that perspective, all knowledge is codified through a political and cultural filter that represents certain interests as well as collective fears and anxieties (see Chomsky 2003; Herman and Chomsky 1988). The campaign carried out by the U.S. government and American media that maligns Islam and treats Arabs and Muslims with suspicion has become a significant theme in the war on terror, especially since September 11. The tragic effects of that form of labeling are widespread and enduring. As we shall see in forthcoming chapters, the crusade against terror is a quasi-religious and political invention that contributes to an array of human rights abuses, including hate crimes, state crimes, and war crimes.

Conclusion

As this chapter suggests, post-9/11 America is so rife with religious and mystical thinking that it easily pervades government—and by extension the war on terror. Indeed, social anxiety over the risk of terrorism is expressed in simple but profound language, most recognizably in the word evil. Referring to terrorism as evil and terrorists as evildoers activates ancient defense mechanisms that not only marshal popular support but also drives legislation and crime control. That way of thinking about terrorism contributes to problems at two levels of society. At the policy level, such zeal leads to badly flawed counterterrorism tactics. On the cultural plane, it erodes intellectualism, a tradition dating back to the Enlightenment. "Seeing evil and goodness as transcendent polarities both reduces human beings to the status of spectators before a cosmic drama and makes them its permanent victims" (Carroll 2004c, 7; Morrow 2003). Popular and political notions of evil stoke the apocalyptic imagination, a national mindset that draws on the anxieties of living in a risk society in a post-9/11 world. Offering a critical look into culture, religion, and the war on terror, Robert Jay Lifton, author of *Superpower Syndrome: America's Apocalyptic Confrontation with the World* (2003a), writes:

> The apocalyptic imagination has spawned a new kind of violence at the beginning of the twenty-first century. We can, in fact, speak of a worldwide epidemic of violence aimed at massive destruction in the service of various visions of purification and renewal. In particular, we are experiencing what could be called an apocalyptic face-off between Islamist forces, overtly visionary in their willingness to kill and die for their religion, and American forces claiming to be restrained and reasonable but no less visionary in their projection of a cleansing warmaking and military power. Both sides are energized by versions of intense idealism: both see themselves as embarked on a mission of combating evil in order to redeem and renew the world; and both are ready to release untold levels of violence to achieve that purpose. (Lifton 2003b, 11)

The apocalyptic imagination produces an ironic war on terror insofar as it fuels rather than dampens violence. That cycle of violence is rotated faster as the America's excessive military response to Islamist attacks serves to inspire and recruit more terrorists and more attacks. Lifton

(2003b) argues that the war on terror is a sustained illusion and mythic cleansing—of terrorists, of evil, of our own fear.

This chapter allows us to view recent religious and political developments in the United States through the lens of culture. Accordingly, we are capable of visualizing a steep rise of evangelism and the pressure it exerts on government. However, rather than finding evidence of charitable grace—a value inherent in virtually all religions—we are witnessing a rigid, authoritarian, and anti-modern version of Christianity that stokes prejudice and bigotry. Those malevolent forces continue to drive campaigns against Islam, leaving ugly marks on the war on terror. In maintaining this critical theme, the next chapter takes a close look at hate crimes and backlash violence directed at Middle Easterners since September 11.

CHAPTER FIVE

Hate Crimes as Backlash Violence

The prevailing attitude toward the scapegoat is usually violence and this is often encouraged.

—Attila Pok, "Atonement and sacrifice: Scapegoats in modern Eastern and Central Europe," *East European Quarterly,* 1999

I stand for America all the way! I'm an American. Go ahead. Arrest me and let those terrorists run wild!

—Frank Roque, *We are not the enemy: Hate crimes against Arabs, Muslims, and those perceived to be Arab or Muslim after September 11,* Human Rights Watch 2002

George Orwell, in his futuristic novel, *1984,* describes a ritual labeled the "Daily Two Minutes of Hate." Fortifying vitriol and violence, the routine has a distinct communal dimension that facilitates collective and expressive punishment.

The horrible thing about the Two Minutes of Hate was not that one was obliged to act a part but, on the contrary, that it was impossible to avoid joining in. Within thirty seconds any pretense was always unnecessary. A hideous ecstasy of fear and vindictiveness, a desire to kill, to torture, to smash faces with a sledge-hammer seemed to flow through the whole people like an electrical current, turning one even against one's will into a grimacing, screaming lunatic. And yet the rage that one felt was an abstract, undirected emotion which could be switched from one subject to another like the flame of a blow lamp. (Orwell 1950, 16)

The impulsive hostility that Orwell describes projects a hatred that is not only intense but also flexible since it is capable of rotating from one target to another. In important ways, that idea reflects the conceptual inner workings of risk society theory insofar as hate crimes serve as a potent site of social anxiety. Violence motivated by hate, especially aimed at innocent victims, represents one of the most vivid manifestations of scapegoating.

On October 4, 2001, Mark Stroman shot and killed Vasudev Patel, a 49-year-old Indian and father of two, who was working at his convenience store in Mesquite, Texas. Stroman said that anger over the September 11 attacks caused him to attack any storeowner who appeared to be Muslim. "We're at war. I did what I had to do. I did it to retaliate" (*San Antonio Express-News* 2002, 1; see Tate 2001). Stroman was tried and convicted of capital murder for killing Patel and sentenced to death on April 3, 2002. For Stroman; however, it was not his only act of ethnoviolence in the wake of 9/11. Stroman shot Rais Uddin, blinding the gas station attendant. He also was responsible for the death of Waquar Hassan, a 46-year-old Pakistani father of four, who was killed on September 15, 2001, while cooking hamburgers at his Dallas grocery store. Stroman admitted to the homicide while being jailed for the Patel killing and his confession was introduced during the sentencing phase of his trial for the murder of Patel (Cooperman 2002; United Press International 2002).

While the recent wave of violence aimed at Middle Easterners (and South Asians) is propelled by tremendous outrage over the 9/11 terrorist attacks, it is also cued by a broader culture that often fails to condemn prejudice against Arabs and Muslims. Such hate crime is a social practice embedded in wider patterns of oppression and discrimination. In *Justice and the Politics of Difference,* Iris Marion Young (1990) identifies five "faces of oppression" that generally typify experiences of minority groups: exploitation (e.g., employment segregation); marginalization (e.g, impoverishment); powerlessness (e.g., underrepresentation in political office); cultural imperialism (e.g., demeaning stereotypes); and violence (e.g., hate crime). It is important to contextualize those "faces of oppression" in post-9/11 America since in tandem structural exclusions and cultural imaging render unpopular minorities susceptible to systemic ethnoviolence. "Specifically, ongoing patterns of marginalization and exclusion of Muslims and Arab Americans, together with their construction as the deviant Other provide the context for anti-Arab violence. The former makes them vulnerable targets, the latter makes them 'legitimate' targets" (Perry 2002, 9; see Hamm 1994a, 1994b).

This chapter looks critically into the nature of hate crimes, beginning with ethnoviolence precipitated by the attacks on the World Trade Center and the Pentagon and continuing to the present. So as to establish a broader social context involving that form of scapegoating, the chapter once again touches on the phenomenon of religious hostility then proceeds into a descriptive overview of hate crimes. So that we also may appreciate a deeper understanding of backlash violence, its conceptual and theoretical implications also are explored.[1]

Stoking Religious Hostility

As described in the previous chapter, the governmental response to the 9/11 strikes has emerged as a crusade against terror, a quasi-religious and political invention that casts a negative light onto Islam. Whereas General Boykin's outlandish speeches and Bush's own insinuating comments on proselytizing Muslims in the course of the war on terror are significant, there are other sources of religious hostility worth examining, especially since they, too, contribute to an ecology of hatred in post-9/11 America. Even though many political figures, including Bush himself, issued proclamations for tolerance and condemned backlash violence against Arabs and Muslims, there are notable exceptions. Imposing enormous suspicion onto followers of the Islamic faith, Representative C. Saxby Chambliss remarked to law enforcement officers in Georgia "just turn [the sheriff] loose and have him arrest every Muslim that crosses the state line" (*Washington Post* 2001a, 2; Sanders 2002). While such torrid remarks can be attributed to unfit elected officials with a zeal for pandering to public outrage over 9/11, the ring of hatred encircling Muslims and Arabs also is drawn by evangelicals, suggesting a deeper religious hostility.

Franklin Graham, son of the well-known Reverend Billy Graham, stoked religious hatred in an interview on NBC Nightly News after the September 11 attacks: "It wasn't Methodists flying into those buildings, and it wasn't Lutherans. It was an attack on this country by people of the Islamic faith" (Dowd 2003, WK9). Calling Islam "wicked, violent and not of the same God," Graham also caused waves when he said Muslims had failed to apologize adequately for the attacks and urged them to offer compensation to the victims (Eckstrom 2001, 1). Graham is well known for his evangelical view that "the true God is the God of the Bible, not the Koran" (Dowd 2003, WK9). The controversy does not end there. In 2003, the Pentagon invited Graham to deliver a homily at their Good Friday religious services despite objections from Muslim groups. The Pentagon spokeswoman, Victoria Clarke, said the military would not back off of its plans to allow Graham to speak: "It is a policy of openness and inclusiveness" (Marquis 2003, A10). Ibrahim Hooper of the Council on American-Islamic Relations rejected the Pentagon's explanation. "It sends entirely the wrong message in this country and around the world. This is a man who has repeatedly asserted that Islam is evil and it seems to convey a government endorsement, whether or not that is the case" (Marquis 2003, A10).

As anti-Islam sentiment flowed across the United States in the wake of 9/11, other religious conservatives piled on. Televangelist Pat Robertson maligned Islam, saying: "I have taken issue with our esteemed President in regard to his stand in saying Islam is a peaceful religion. . . . It's just not" (*Washington Post* 2002, 22). Robertson dismissed the prophet Muhammad as "an absolute wild-eyed fanatic, a robber and brigand" (Kristof 2003, A26). In an even harsher tone, former Southern Baptist President Jerry Vines told conventioneers at the June 2002 annual gathering of the Southern Baptist Convention that Muhammad was a "demon-possessed pedophile" (Shaidle 2001, 24; Ostling 2002).

To be sure, religious hostility toward Islam is more nuanced than the adolescent rantings issued by Boykin, Graham, Robertson, and Vines. The evangelical movement, especially its passion for born-again conversion, offers insight into the more subtle forms of animosity. In 2003, evangelical Christians from several states gathered in church fellowship hall in Grove City, Ohio, for an all-day seminar on how to woo Muslims away from Islam. The instructor advised the congregation to exhibit a kind demeanor when approaching Muslims, always exude love, charity and hospitality. It also helps to offer them copies of the New Testament as gifts. Many of those attending the meeting hoped to convert Muslims in the United States or on mission trips overseas. During much of the workshop, teachers encouraged friendly correspondence with potential converts; however, a PowerPoint presentation by one instructor included passages from the Koran that he said proved that Islam was regressive, fraudulent, and violent. "Here in the Koran, it says slay them, slay the infidels!" (Goodstein 2003a, A1).

The workshop in Grove City is evidence of a significant grassroots evangelical movement, demonstrating a growing interest in activities aimed at converting Muslims to Christianity. Arab International Ministries in Indianapolis claims to have trained 4,500 American Christians to proselytize Muslims; many of those certifications have been approved since 9/11. Whereas evangelicals have always held that all other religions are wrong, their recent momentum is notable for its vituperation. "They assert that while the vast majority of Muslims are not evil, they have been deceived by a diabolical religion based on flawed scripture that can never bring them salvation" (Goodstein 2003a, A23). In a dialectical way, the evangelical dictum to "love the sinner and hate the sin" produces a kind of "tough love" for Muslims. In doing so, such condescension breeds contempt and hatred. Although those recent developments might be viewed as relatively benign, especially compared to acts of brutal ethnoviolence, they are significant in large part because they contribute to a climate of distrust that enables hate crimes.

Hate Crimes in Post-9/11 America

In one of the clearest examples of scapegoating in the aftermath of 9/11, Arabs and Muslims in the United States—and those perceived to be Arab or Muslim, such as Sikhs and South Asians—have become targets of hate crime, including murder, beatings, arson, attacks on mosques, shootings, vehicular assaults, and verbal threats. "This violence was directed at people solely because they shared or were perceived as sharing the national background or religion of the hijackers and al-Qaeda members deemed responsible for attacking the World Trade Center and the Pentagon" (Human Rights Watch 2002a, 3; see World Conference Against Racism, Racial Discrimination, and Related Intolerance, Programme of Action [WCAR] 2002).

Whereas Arabs and Muslims have been victims of hate crimes in the United States for more than twenty years, the recent spike in backlash violence has the markings of hostility and rage that cannot be isolated from the events of September 11. That wave of hate crimes (or bias-motivated crimes) occurred throughout much of the United States. The FBI recorded a seventeen-fold increase in anti-Muslim crimes nationwide during 2001 (Federal Bureau of Investigation 2002). Officials in Chicago reported only four anti-Muslim or anti-Arab in year 2000 and during the three months after September 11 (2001) that figure soared to 51 (Chicago Police Department 2002). In Los Angeles County, there were 188 such hate crimes in 2001, up from 12 the previous year (Los Angeles County Commission on Human Relations 2002). The trend in hate crime also surfaced in Florida where the attorney general attributed the nearly 25 percent jump in the total number of hate crimes reported for 2001 to reactions to September 11 (Office of the Attorney General of Florida 2002). In its report, Human Rights Watch (2002a) cited more than 2,000 September 11-related backlash incidents.

> Hate crimes are a uniquely important and socially devastating kind of crime, however, that warrant enhanced public attention and action. What distinguishes a bias or hate crime from others is not the act itself—e.g. murder or assault—but the racial, ethnic, religious, gender, or sexual orientation animus that propels its commission. While typically directed at a particular individual—often randomly chosen—hate crimes are motivated by anger toward an entire community distinguished by specific shared characteristics. While the bias that motivates a hate crime may be unusual in its ferocity, it is rooted in a wider public climate of discrimination, fear, and intolerance against targeted communities, which may also be echoed in or enhanced by public policy. U.S. law as well as international human rights law single out hate crimes for particular attention precisely because of their broad social impact and their roots in discrimination and intolerance. (Human Rights Watch 2002a, 5–6; see International Covenant on Civil and Political Rights [ICCPR], article 26; International Convention on the Elimination of All Forms of Racial Discrimination [CERD], article 2)

Dating back to the Civil Rights Movement, there has been deep concern over violence motivated by bigotry and hatred. Legislation soon followed, either enhancing penalties for such crimes or identifying such offenses as distinct crimes under criminal code. The first law of its kind is the federal hate crimes statute passed in 1964 (18 U.S.C. 245 1964). The law criminalizes bias-motivated acts where the perpetrator attempts to stop the victim from engaging in one of six designated activities: (1) enrolling in or attending a public school; (2) participating in a service or facility provided by a state; (3) engaging in employment by any private or state employer;

(4) serving as a juror; (5) traveling in or using a facility of interstate commerce; and (6) enjoying the services of certain public establishments. Currently, all but five states sponsor hate crimes laws. Among the arguments favoring hate crimes legislation is that such statutes represent an expressed public affirmation of societal values committed to equality among all residents.

Literally minutes after the attack of the World Trade Center and Pentagon, Arabs and Muslims—as well as Sikhs—braced themselves for an impending backlash. Portentous messages flooded community email groups across the Internet.

> I'm sure we've all heard of the tragedy this morning. . . . Needless to say, we all realize that no Muslim in their right mind would condone such an action. I'm only writing to be sure you are all aware of the unavoidable atmosphere that will rise as a result of this attack: we're non-white, we're Arab . . . we're Muslims. . . . There will be some "serious" anti-Arab, anti-Muslim sentiment running rampant through this country. . . . So be careful, stay with your families, stay off the streets unnecessarily, and watch your fellow sisters and brothers. ("Bismillah" September 11, 2001)

For many Middle Easterners (and South Asians), their worst fears were realized as ethnoviolence spread rapidly throughout much of the United States. The worst recorded hate crimes occurred in the months immediately following 9/11. The Council on American-Islamic Relations (2002a) reports 1,717 incidents of backlash discrimination against Muslims from September 11, 2001 through February 2002 (Council on American-Islamic Relations 2002a). Acts motivated by hate ranged from vandalism and arson to verbal taunting, employment discrimination, and hassling at airports, to assault and murder.

At least three persons—and as many as seven—were murdered as a result of backlash violence. In addition to the killings of Vasudev Patel and Waquar Hassan, there is the murder of Bilbir Singh Sodhi, a 49-year-old turbaned Sikh and father of three. On September 15, 2002, while planting flowers at his gas station in Mesa, Arizona, Sodhi, was hit with three fatal gunshot wounds. His assailant, Frank Roque, who also allegedly fired into the home of an Afghani American and at two Lebanese gas station clerks, bragged in a local tavern, "kill the ragheads responsible for September 11" (Human Rights Watch 2002, 17). Other homicides also believed related to ethnoviolence in the wake of September 11 involve the victims Ali Almansoop, Abdo Ali Ahmed, Adel Karas, and Ali W. Ali (Human Rights Watch 2002a).

In the realm of assaults, the Council on American-Islamic Relations (2002b) documented hundreds of attacks and beatings in the first year following 9/11, some of them quite serious. Swaran Kaur Bhullar, a Sikh woman, was viciously attacked on September 30, 2001, in San Diego. While her car idled in traffic two men stabbed her twice in the head. Before attacking her, the men screamed, "This is what you get for what you've done to us!" and "I'm going to slash your throat." As another car approached the traffic light, the attackers sped off. Bhullar is convinced that she would have been killed had the other motorist not appeared. She was treated at a local hospital for two lacerations to her scalp. Local police and federal law enforcement officials have been unable to identify Bhullar's attackers (Human Rights Watch 2002, 20). The day after the attacks on New York City and Washington, Faiza Ejaz, a Pakistani woman, was standing outside a mall in Long Island, New York, when Adam Lang, a 76-year-old man, allegedly put his car into gear and started driving towards her. Ejaz was able to avoid being struck by the car by leaping out of the way and escaping into the mall. Lang then jumped out of his car and shouted that he was "doing this for my country" and was "going to kill her." Mall security agents seized Lang. Sergeant Robert Reecks, commander of the Suffolk County Bias Crimes Bureau, told reporters: "If she hadn't jumped out of the way, he would have run right over her"(Burson 2001, 12). Lang was charged with first-degree reckless endangerment, which includes an enhanced penalty since the offense was determined to be bias-motivated.

Places of worship, most notably mosques, also are key targets of hate crimes. During the first week after 9/11, one survey reported more than 100 biased attacks, including property damage, vandalism, arson, and gunshots. Understandably, attendance at places of worship declined dramatically during that period due to a climate of fear and intimidation (South Asian American Leaders of Tomorrow 2002). In addition to numerous violent and criminal acts apparently motivated by 9/11 rage, there is mounting evidence of other forms of hostility especially in the form of discrimination. The federal agency charged with enforcing federal employment discrimination laws, U.S. Equal Employment Opportunity Commission (EEOC), received 488 complaints of September 11-related employment discrimination in an eight-month period following the attacks. More than 300 of those complaints involved persons being unfairly terminated from their jobs (Equal Employment Opportunity Commission 2002; see Robbins 2004). During roughly the same period, the U.S. Department of Transportation (DOT) investigated 111 September 11-related complaints from airline passengers who claimed that they were singled out at security screenings due to their ethnic or religious appearance. Similarly, the DOT investigated 31 incidents in which persons complained they were barred altogether from boarding airplanes because of their ethnic or religious appearance (Wan 2002).

Reactions to the 9/11 attacks in the form of hate crimes and related hostilities have had an enduring impact on American society in general and its victims in particular. In the year following September 11, polls tracked the accumulating negative effects on Muslims living in the United States. The Council on American-Islamic Relations (2002c) found that of the nearly 1,000 Muslim Americans surveyed 48 percent felt that their lives had changed for the worse since 9/11. Moreover, 57 percent reported experiencing some act of bias or discrimination, ranging from disparaging remarks for being Muslim to in some instances being victim of a hate crime. Suggesting a lasting imprint from 9/11, anger and hate crimes directed at Middle Easterners and South Asians continued in the years following (Lueck 2004a; *New York Times* 2004a; Solomon 2003a). Indeed, the U.S. invasion of Iraq in 2003 and related events also have increased ethnic and religious hostility (Janofsky 2003). In summer 2004, when photographs were televised of the body of American Paul M. Johnson, Jr. who was beheaded after being taken hostage by terrorists in Saudi Arabia, neighbors of his sister in Little Egg Harbor Township, New Jersey, posted a sign in their front yard reading:

> Last night my heart was filled with love and prayers, but today it is filled with hatred. Last night I was not a racist, but today, I feel racism toward Islamic beliefs.
>
> Last night Islamics had a chance to speak up for Paul Johnson but today it was too late.
>
> Today Islamics better wake up and start thinking about tomorrow. (George and Santora 2004, 16)

As will be discussed in the next section, backlash violence in post-9/11 America has profound implications to the cultural and social order of the nation.

Social Context of Ethnic Hatred

So that we continue to draw connections among an array of concepts, it is useful to reiterate the flow of ideas examined in the previous chapters. Thus far, it has been acknowledged that perceived threats to individual and collective security inherent in a risk society have become a significant site of anxiety. That tension, aggravated by events such as the 9/11 attacks, produces forms of scapegoating that are easily recognizable as hate crimes. To situate these developments and concepts we turn to a major source of insight on this subject, namely Jock Young's *The Exclusive Society: Social Exclusion, Crime, and Difference in Modern Society* (1999). That important book greatly enhances our understanding of precipitous changes in a post-September 11 society. Young, much like others who have written on the subject of anxiety in late modernity (i.e., the last third of the twentieth century to the present), recognizes that we live at a time when we feel both material insecurity and ontological precariousness which become fertile soil for projection and moralism. "Social blame and recrimination ricochets throughout the social structure: single mothers, the underclass, blacks, new age travelers, junkies, crackheads—the needle spins and points to some vulnerable section of the community to whom we can apportion blame, and who can be demonized" (Young 1999, vii).

Within that framework, Young elaborates on the mechanism of scapegoating as a means of informal social control to maintain an exclusive society (also see Cohen 1985). Still, scapegoating by its very nature targets "the other," a person or group that is perceived as being not only different from "us" but potentially threatening to "our" society. Especially when "the other" is different in terms of race, ethnicity, and religion, blame for social problems and crises is simple to allocate and easy to justify (see Kearney 1999; Miller and Schamess 2000). Scapegoating and hate crimes are facilitated further by demonization, a process that casts "the other" into an evil light. Therefore, violence aimed at "them" is considered legitimate because it serves to defend the eternal Good (see Katz, 1988). "The demonization process taken to its extreme *allows* the perpetuation of atrocities . . . it permits behavior against others quite outside what is considered normal civilized behavior" (Young 1999, 112). Such hostility and violence are sometimes difficult to discourage since being bolstered by a series of techniques of neutralization, most notably, blaming the victim (Sykes and Matza 1957).

Stanley Cohen delves into the dynamics of such blaming by identifying the rationales and vocabularies of scapegoating, such as "they started it," "they had it coming," "they got what they deserved," and "violence is the only language they understand" (1995, 79; 2001). Denial of the victim is a phenomenon reinforced by three social psychological processes. First, dehumanization, particularly reflected in ethnic and racial slurs (e.g., sand niggers), disparages victims by repudiating their humanity, making them less eligible for compassion or empathy. Second, condescension allows victims to be portrayed as inferior, uncivilized, and irrational. Condescending views of Islam, and its followers, perpetuated by evangelicals bent on converting them to Christianity are particularly noteworthy in post-9/11 America. Third, distancing allows the dominant group to ignore the presence of others; in failing to recognize victims' existence, their pain and suffering are kept under the social radar. Governments that are unwilling to keep track of and prosecute crimes motivated by hate, according to critics, appear to be committed to distancing (Human Rights Watch 2002a).

The social context of scapegoating also is made clearer by attending to cultural shifts and identity politics that have thrown into question the historical parallel of privilege and whiteness. In their efforts to be included—and to participate—in American society, racial and ethnic minorities pose a threat to hegemonic cultural identities, producing for the dominant white group considerable anxiety over insecurity and in some cases leading to hostility (Perry 2002, 2003a; Winant 1997). "Trying to renegotiate a new American national identity and culture that no longer has the certainty of fixed race, class and gender categories create change, confusion and often violence. When people are wronged, they can use violence as a weapon; thus the degree of violence can be linked to the issue of a changing American national identity" (Anderson and Collins 1995, 361).

Because crimes motivated by hatred are generally committed by males—mirroring the prevailing pattern of violence—addressing issues of gender are central to understanding ethnoviolence in a post-9/11 society. Barbara Perry explains that perpetrators of ethnoviolence are responding to threats to their gender, race, and national identity since they realize that their whiteness no longer guarantees them status and security. "Consequently, many white men experience a sense of displacement and dispossession relative to people of color. This imagery of 'white-man-as-victim' provides an ideological rationale for recreating people of color as legitimate victims" (Perry 2002, 7). From the viewpoint of those unleashing ethnoviolence, their actions are believed to be justified because especially in the wake of 9/11 they are protecting "their" country—the "homeland"—from the threat of outsiders. Indeed, Katz (1988) reminds us that the defense of the eternal Good also extends to the protections of perceived property rights and national boundaries. Nationalistic and jingoistic statements used to justify hate crime figure prominently since they point to the significance of political identity. To repeat, the statement by Frank Roque, after being apprehended for the killing of Balbir Singh Sodhi, resonates symbolically: "I stand for America all the way! I'm an American. Go ahead. Arrest me and let those terrorists run wild!" (Human Rights Watch 2002a, 17). Compounding intolerance is the sense that Muslims do not "belong" in America, a prevalent theme accompanying ethnoviolence and vandalism like that against a San Francisco store owned by an Iraqi: "Arab, go home" (Council on American-Islamic Relations 2002a; see Abraham 1994; Moore 1995).

The dynamic of "othering" abounds in post-9/11 America. Indeed, the attacks on the World Trade Center and the Pentagon serve to sharpen an otherwise vague notion of "them," attracting greater scrutiny to otherwise undifferentiated "Middle Easterners." By doing so, they have quickly emerged as the "usual suspects" eligible for suspicion, blame, and persecution. Politics over racial and ethnic classification play a vital role in that form of "othering" since Middle Easterners are often considered "white but not quite" (Suleiman 1999; see Haddad 1998; McCarus 1994). In his research on ethnic archetypes and the Arab images, Stockton (1994) discovered several "assigned image themes" that contribute to popular—albeit Western—stereotypes of Arabs:

1. Sexual depravity (e.g., harems and belly dancers)
2. Creature analogies (e.g., vermin, camels)
3. Physiological and psychological traits (e.g., unappealing physical characteristics, fanaticism, vengeance)
4. Savage leaders (e.g., warmongers)
5. Deceit (in business and politics)
6. Secret power (e.g., use of oil wealth to manipulate others, especially the West)
7. Terrorism

Although we shall explore the racialization of terror in the next chapter, especially as it informs profiling, it is important to mention here that Western stereotyping of Middle Easterners as inferior elevates the dominant white group to a putative level of superiority. From their perch on top of their own socially constructed—and self-serving—hierarchy some whites are prone to violent scapegoating while relying on their privileged social position to justify ethnoviolence. That dynamic sheds a critical light onto how power intersects with race/ethnicity. Furthermore, stereotyping adheres to an essentialist paradigm based on the mistaken belief that "differences" among racial and ethnic groups are rooted in indisputably inscribed traits (I. Young 1990; J. Young 1999). Hence, pseudo-Darwinian views—along with scientific racism—circulate freely with little interference (see Gould 1981). In her analysis, Perry cites a near perfect illustration of that way of thinking about evolution, nationalism, and terrorism:

> Similarly, cartoon imagery—intended to be humorous—exploits decidedly "unfunny" stereotypes. A striking example emerged in the aftermath of the September 11 attacks. It pictures an evolutionary line up, in which a crazed-looking, wild-eyed, bearded "Middle Easterner" is just one step above apes. Moreover, he is pictured as a step behind Uncle Sam, plunging a knife into his back. Again, this highlights the untrustworthy character of the Middle Easterner, while simultaneously reaffirming the terrorist stereotype. (Perry 2003a, 187: see Shaheen 1999)

This segment of the chapter presents a conceptual and theoretical overlay from which ethnic hostility and crimes motivated by hatred can be more richly interpreted. Moreover, it strives to link those tangible developments with various social forces inherent in a risk society, all of which contribute to collective anxiety and feelings of insecurity or what Jock Young (1999) calls the ontological precariousness of late modernity. The dynamics of "othering" compounded by specific stereotypes disparaging Middle Easterners prepared the stage for intense backlash violence unleashed in the wake of September 11.

Conclusion

For Arabs, Muslims, Middle Easterners, South Asians and "others" casually lumped together into the same ethnic group, the horrific events of September 11 have brought greater meaning to each of the "faces of oppression," namely exploitation, marginalization, powerlessness, cultural imperialism, and especially violence in the form of hate crime (Young 1990). In examining more closely the nature of oppression and backlash violence in post-9/11 America, this chapter investigated several facets of hatred. We began with a critical look at religious hostility aimed at Islam by evangelicals harboring an agenda for conversion, a form of oppression that is difficult to separate from the larger effects of cultural imperialism. Whereas that type of condescension ought not be equated with hate crimes, it does—along with dehumanization and distancing—set into motion social psychological dynamics that facilitate ethnoviolence (see Cohen 1995, 2001).

Crimes motivated by prejudice in the wake of 9/11 ranged from property damage and bigoted graffiti to serious assaults and homicide. Such hostility was not only expressed by criminal perpetrators but also by employers and service industries including airlines which exercised their own brand of oppression by discriminating against persons of Middle Eastern or of a similar "foreign" background. Those hostilities are found to be widespread as more than half of the Muslim-Americans in a survey experienced some form of negative bias; moreover, nearly half of those polled felt that their lives had changed for the worse since September 11 (The Council on American-Islamic Relations 2002c). The social context of hostility is significant, especially since it allows us to understand hate crimes as a site of social anxiety. As Jock Young (1999) and Stanley Cohen (1985) point out, such pernicious forms of scapegoating operate as key mechanisms of informal social control that maintains an exclusive society in which issues of race, ethnicity, class, and gender figure prominently (see Connell 1987; Fine, Weise, and Addelston 1997; Winant 1997).

As shall be discussed in greater detail in forthcoming chapters, those hostilities are not limited to angry individuals or small groups of bullies determined to ventilate their post-9/11 frustration on relatively powerless victims. Rather, the state and various government agencies also engage in policies—part and parcel to the war on terror—driven by parallel forms of prejudice. Institutional discrimination is found most notably in ethnic profiling, leading to disappearances, arbitrary—and indefinite—detention, and deportation. In the realm of state crimes and war crimes, the "faces of oppression" also appear in prisoner abuse, torture, and in homicide (Dow 2004; Hersh 2004; Parenti 2004). In bridging these phenomena, bias-related crimes occur within an enabling environment whereby disparaging views of Arabs and Muslims are cued by government officials and their institutions. State complicity and its "mixed messages" in post-9/11 America serves to connect the dots between hate crimes, state crimes, and an array of civil liberties and human rights violations (Abraham 1994; Perry 2003a, 2003b). Joshua Salaam of the Council on American-Islamic Relations wonders about how discriminatory government practices, most significantly profiling, resonate in the public mind: "Most people are probably asking, 'If government doesn't trust these people, why should I?" (Human Rights Watch 2002a, 26).

CHAPTER SIX

Profiling and Detention in Post-9/11 America

It is also clear the scope of racial profiling in America has expanded greatly since 9/11. Today "driving while black or brown" has been joined by "worshipping while Muslim," "walking while South Asian," and "flying while Middle Eastern."

—Benjamin Jealous, "Profiles of the Profiled," *Amnesty International: The Magazine of Amnesty International USA,* 2004

If I see someone [who] comes in that's got a diaper on his head and a fan belt wrapped around the diaper on his head, that guy needs to be pulled over."

—U.S. Congressman, John Cooksey, quoted in J. McKinney, "Cooksey: Expect racial profiling," *Advocate,* 2001.

Since the 1970s, the criminal justice apparatus in United States has undergone significantly punitive transformations. Evidenced by a commitment to such hard-line tactics as mass imprisonment, there is widespread recognition of a culture of control whereby conservative measures continue to gain considerable political and popular support

(Garland 2002, 2001; Welch 2005a, 2004d). The events surrounding September 11 have not only reinforced a culture of control in America but also played a key role in methods involving profiling and detention. However, as we shall see in this chapter, such practices disproportionately target innocent persons, raising questions of scapegoating. The prevailing pattern in profiling and detention in the war on terror is that such policies and practices unfairly—and unjustly—net Middle Easterners and South Asians who are not involved in terrorism. With that realization in mind, there is good reason to believe that the state and its law enforcement agencies are displacing aggression onto less powerful people who have become increasingly unpopular since 9/11.

Consider for instance, the case of Anser Mehmood, just one of literally thousands of Kafkaesque ordeals brought on by the government. On October 3, 2001, Mehmood, a 42-year-old truck driver, was resting in his home in Bayonne, New Jersey, a working-class town in the shadows of New York City. When the doorbell rang, he opened the door to find some 30 FBI agents surrounding his house. The agents searched his home and then informed him that the FBI had cleared him but that the INS would want to meet with him for overstaying his business visa when he entered the country in 1994. Still, the FBI assured him that an immigration judge would look favorably on his case because he owned property and a business, and paid taxes. The next day Mehmood was escorted to a federal building in Manhattan where he stayed overnight; contrary to what the FBI told him, he did not see a judge. Rather he was met by Border Patrol agents who chained his hands and feet and loaded him into a van with four other Muslim men. Mehmood was transported to the Metropolitan Detention Center in Brooklyn where he was yanked from the vehicle by a jail guard and slammed into a wall, bloodying his lip. The guard angrily announced to him: "You are here as a World Trade Center suspect" (Rohde 2003, A9). During the first two weeks of a four-month solitary confinement, Mehmood was stuck in a communication blackout, unable to contact his family, his lawyer, or a judge. Nor would he receive any word as to why he was being held.

Eventually, Mehmood and several others were deported to Pakistan where they are stranded between nations and cultures. The men are visibly out of place. Many Pakistanis see them as victims of an anti-Muslim witchhunt while others view them as traitors to their home country where anti-Americanism is on the rise. Mehmood complained bitterly that he and others had been unfairly marked for detention and deportation because they were Muslims (see American Civil Liberties Union 2004).

"America should apply the laws of the Constitution to everybody all over the world, not just to Christians and Jews" (Rohde 2003, A9). His lawyer agrees: "We have the presumption of innocence turned on its head. Muslim males are presumed to be involved in terrorism and are held there until they are cleared." Likewise, Anthony Romero, executive director of the American Civil Liberties Union, added: "The individual cases are the tip of the iceberg. Essentially, the I.N.S. and FBI targeted Pakistanis, Muslims, Arabs and others for greater scrutiny because of their national origin and religion" (Rohde 2003, A9; see Dow 2004; Stevenson 2003).

This chapter carefully explores institutional ethnic profiling, especially the special registration program in which immigration authorities and the FBI interviewed more than 82,000 foreign nationals residing in the United States. Despite its sweeping nature, the program failed to discover any leads or links to terrorism. Equally puzzling from a policy—and human rights—standpoint is the government's brazen misuse of detention whereby thousands of Middle Easterners and South Asians have been rounded up arbitrarily and placed behind bars where many have been subject to abuse and denied basic rights including access to legal counsel. Alongside these developments, the chapter also examines the controversy of detaining asylum seekers, providing another compelling example of inappropriate and ineffective policymaking in the war on terror.

Scapegoating and Ethnic Profiling

As described in the previous chapter, hostilities and hate crime against Middle Easterners and South Asians surged in the wake of 9/11. Regrettably, acts of scapegoating and racial profiling also have been committed by law enforcement officers, the National Guard, and transportation security personnel. Sher J.B. Singh, an Indian Sikh and a U.S. citizen was removed from an Amtrak train in Providence (Rhode Island), handcuffed, and held for seven hours because, according to Singh, he wore a turban. Singh said the police and federal agents who questioned him knew nothing about the religion, the world's fifth largest. After the police searched the train, the agents told Singh they could not leave without taking someone into detention. "They were telling me they would let me go by the next day" (Glaberson 2001, EV2). After some officers taunted him because of his turban, Singh said they asked him general questions about Sikhism and never appeared to think he had any connection to terrorism. Some of those who have been questioned say the law enforcement officials have acknowledged that they were under pressure to hold people even if there was little reason to suspect them (Gross and Livingston 2002; Welch 2002a, 2005b).

At the Minneapolis airport, Dr. Jasjit S. Ahluwalia, an American Sikh and chairman of the department of preventative medicine at the University of Kansas School of Medicine, was stopped by a member of the National Guard who ordered him to remove his turban. Ahluwalia, who had already passed through a metal detector and been scanned by a hand-held wand, was stunned by the request: "It is such an inappropriate question. It's like saying, Can I look under your bra?" Numerous Sikhs have reported that since the September 11 attacks they had been targeted by airport police and security workers. More than two dozen Sikhs have filed complaints with anti-discrimination groups, asserting that they were forced to remove their turbans in public areas, a violation of their religious obligation never to reveal their hair in public. Muslim women similarly have been ordered by airport security to remove their headscarves, also a violation of their faith. Kareem Shora, a legal advisor for the American-Arab committee remarked: "This isn't even profiling. This is just outright discrimination and bigotry" (Goodstein 2001, B6).

Ziad Asali, president of the American-Arab Anti-Discrimination Committee, issued the following statement days following the attacks on the World Trade Center and the Pentagon:

> Unfortunately, as grief gives way to understandable anger, a pattern of collective blame and scapegoating against Arab Americans and Muslims seems to be emerging even before the culpability of any single individual has been established. Even if persons with connections to the Arab world or the Islamic faith prove to have had a hand in this outrage, there can be no reason or excuse for collective blame against any ethnic or religious community. Already we have received numerous disturbing reports of violent attacks, threats and harassment against Arab Americans and Muslims in many parts of the country and the pattern seems to be growing. As a result Arab Americans, in addition to feeling the intense depths of pain and anger at this attack we share with all our fellow citizens, are feeling deep anxiety about becoming the targets of anger from other Americans. We appeal to all Americans to bear in mind that crimes are the responsibility of the individuals who committed them, not ethnic or religious groups. (ADC Press Release 2001, EV1–2)

Fear of being trapped in the government's sweep for terrorists, immigration lawyers across the United States are instructing their clients to carry their documents with them at all times. Compounding their anxiety, immigrants have been warned that immigration laws that were once rarely enforced begin to take hold. Some immigration attorneys have said that, while the Immigration and Naturalization Service (INS) already enjoys broad powers to question, detain, and use secret evidence in prosecuting immigrants, they are concerned that the INS is now looking at the letter of the law and using it as a pretext to pick people up for questioning. Although it is technically a federal misdemeanor for immigrants not to carry their papers, the violation rarely called for a detention before September 11. David Leopold, an immigration attorney, acknowledged growing concern among his clients: "The key word is fear. Right now, for the first time, immigrants really feel their vulnerability. It's a scary time for them" (Kirchgaessner 2001, EV1).

In response to the attacks of September 11, the FBI and the INS immediately embarked on a sweeping process that involved the questioning of thousands of persons who might have information about terrorist activity (Welch 2004a, 2004b). While the search for information was frequently haphazard and random, Middle Eastern males (and those who appeared to be such) became profiled in the course of the investigation. In its report, *Presumption of Guilt: Human Rights Abuses of Post-September 11th Detainees* (2002b), Human Rights Watch discovered a growing use of profiling on the basis of nationality, religion, and gender. Being a male Muslim non-citizen from certain countries was viewed as a basis for suspicious behavior. Those cases suggest that where Muslim men from certain countries were involved, law enforcement agents presumed some sort of a connection with or knowledge of terrorism until investigations could subsequently prove otherwise. The questioning led to the arrest and detention of as many as 1,200 non-citizens, although the precise number is unknown due to the Justice Department's unwillingness to divulge such information. Of those arrested, 752 were charged not with terror-related crimes but with immigration violations (e.g., overstaying a visa).

Using nationality, religion, and gender as a proxy for suspicion is not only unfair to the millions of law-abiding Muslim immigrants from Middle Eastern and South Asian countries, it may also be an ineffective law enforcement technique. The U.S. government has not charged a single one of the thousand-plus individuals detained after September 11 for crime related to terrorism. Such targeting has also antagonized the very immigrant and religious communities whose cooperation with law enforcement agencies could produce important leads for the investigation. (Human Rights Watch 2002b, 12)

It should also be noted that a series of cases in which there is more substantive evidence of links to acts of terror clearly demonstrate that a national origin terrorist profile is flawed. Most notably, Zacarias Moussaoui, the so-called "twentieth" hijacker, is a French citizen. The "shoe bomber," Richard Reid, is a British citizen. José Padilla (aka Abdullah Al Muhajir), the alleged "dirty bomber," is a U.S. citizen of Puerto Rican descent (Welch 2004b, 2003b).

As the Justice Department vastly widened the scope of an investigation that had yielded no direct links to the September 11 terrorist attacks (see Chapter 8), civil libertarians and other critics accused the government of engaging in wanton racial profiling that may scare away people who might be able to help (Butterfield 2001). In response to the Justice Department's plan to interrogate thousands of men that it believes might have information about the terrorist attacks, James Zogby, executive director of the Arab American Institute, said: "The kind of broad net-casting that was done right after September 11 may have been excusable, but at this point there has to be a better way of conducting this investigation" (Farragher and Cullen 2001, EV1). Hussein Ibish, spokesman for the American-Arab Anti-Discrimination Committee in Washington was critical of the investigation: "This notion that all people of this category are red flags for scrutiny just stigmatizes young Arab men. It suggests that we're starting to rely increasingly on a crude type of stereotyping in our police work. And it encourages the public to find people of this description suspicious" (Farragher and Cullen 2001, EV2). Attorney General Ashcroft defended his tactics, insisting that the unconventional warfare triggered by the terrorist attacks calls for unconventional law enforcement methods. Terrorism experts flatly disagreed. Criminology professor Edith Flynn of Northeastern University said the government's tactics suggest how little hard evidence the authorities have to proceed with in their attempts to prevent another terrorist attack. Flynn also questioned whether profiling would work, "unless you have well-schooled questioners who could detect untruthfulness. Because of the inherent cultural differences, I really wonder how effective it will be" (Farragher and Cullen 2001, EV3). Whereas immigration rights' groups favor a thorough investigation, they are concerned that the Justice Department's net is so broad it will inevitably ensnare men who are afraid to refuse to speak to federal officials out of fear of legal consequences. "It is inherently intimidating for an individual, especially one who has just arrived in this country, to be questioned by the FBI," said Lucas Guttentag of the American Civil Liberties Union. "It is not at all clear what the consequences of not talking to them would be, and whether the next knock on the door would come from the immigration service" (Farragher and Cullen 2001, EV3).

Special Registration Program

Despite objections from civil liberties and human rights organizations, the Department of Justice expanded its use of profiling in the war on terror by introducing a special registration program in December 2002.The directive, intended to produce vital information about terrorist activity, was aimed at all non-immigrant male visitors who are over the age of 16 and entered the United States before September 30, 2002. Specifically, special registration applied to those males from countries that, according to the U.S. government, have links to terrorism, including 12 North African and Middle Eastern countries plus North Korea, affecting more than 82,000 students, tourists, businessmen, and relatives. Those who attended special registration were required to complete a personal information form, then be fingerprinted, photographed, and interviewed by the FBI. Justice Department spokesman Jorge Martinez believes that this information is necessary intelligence for the war against terrorism. "These people are considered a high risk," he said. "The goal of the system is to know who is coming in and out, and that they are in fact doing what they said they would do" (Gourevitch 2003, EV2).

In the first few months of special registration, the Justice Department had failed to discover any links to terrorism, raising questions of its effectiveness. Initially, about 1,000 people were detained but only 15 were charged with a criminal violation and none was charged with a terrorism-related crime. Most of those detained were in violation of immigration laws, most commonly overstaying their visas in hopes of finding a job and eventually adjusting their status to legal resident. From its start, the program was confusing for registrants and the immigration service, suggesting that the initiative was poorly planned. The Justice Department neglected to issue a press release or post information on its website until 10 days before the first deadline; that explains why many foreign nationals did not know they had to register and were subsequently arrested for showing up late. In another mishap, an Arabic rendering of the rules was embarrassingly mistranslated to say individuals under the age of 16 rather than over the age of 16 (Gourevitch 2003, EV3).

Many immigration officials and immigration lawyers are perplexed over the precise meaning of the law. The special registration program states that "foreign citizens and nationals" must register; but the language of the requirements does not clearly define the difference between a "citizen" and a "national," or even what a "national" is. The only available guidance is a phrase from a 50-year-old statute that defines a "national" as "a person owing permanent allegiance to a state" other than the United States. Even Justice Department spokesman Jorge Martinez did not know how to define "national" (Gourevitch 2003, EV3). Due to the confusion, several foreign nationals not covered by the program (e.g., Canada, Liberia, and Norway) showed up to register. Immigration officials did not know how to know how to interpret the procedures, so they arrested them. Similarly, two Canadian citizens, who were born in Iran but emigrated when they were children, were detained for several days. They were in the United States on work visas for the high-tech industry, and had appeared at an INS office uncertain whether they were required to register. The special registration program also created problems for the INS, an agency already strained by other operations in the war on terror. INS employees complained that they received very little special training; moreover, they frequently had to work overtime to process the thousands of registrants. The Arlington (Virginia) immigration office became so inundated with registrants that it had to send many to the Dulles International Airport office for processing.

One of the most controversial incidents occurred in Los Angeles where more than 400 foreign nationals who appeared for registration were handcuffed and detained. Soheila Jonoubi, a Los Angeles-based attorney representing several of the men, said that the detainees spent the next several days (and in some cases weeks) in custody. Many of them were stripped searched, verbally accosted, deprived of food and water, bedding and adequate clothing, and denied information as to why they were being detained. The Justice Department reported that the men were detained because their visas had expired; after completing background checks, all but 20 were released. Still, many of those detained held legal immigration status and were waiting to receive work permits that had been delayed by the INS due to a backlog in processing a high volume of applications (Talvi 2003a, 2003b).

Whereas the registration of more than 82,000 foreign nationals failed to uncover any major links to terrorism, the Justice Department moved forward with plans to deport as many as 13,000 Arab and Muslim men whose legal immigration status had expired. Many of the men had hoped for leniency since they had cooperated fully with the program. Detentions coupled with deportations have sent shock waves through immigrant communities across the nation, producing heightened fear. Many Middle Eastern men and their families—many of whom are U.S. citizens—fled the country, particularly to Canada where they intend to apply for political asylum (Cardwell 2003; Elliott 2003).

Those developments bring to light the significance of human rights in the realm of immigration, criminal justice, and the war on terror. Still, government officials stationed in the Department of Homeland Security (DHS) and the Bureau of Immigration and Customs Enforcement (BICE, the newly re-organized INS) point to the need for national security. Jim Chaparro, acting director for interior enforcement at the DHS, emphasizes: "We need to focus our enforcement on the biggest threats. If a loophole can be exploited by an immigrant, it can also be exploited by a terrorist" (Swarms 2003, A9). Civil liberties and human rights groups denounce the government for using the immigration system as a weapon in the war on terror. Similarly, they complain about selective enforcement since the government focuses on immigrants from Arab and Muslim nations while ignoring similar violations by those from Mexico and Central America.

The overall logic of implementing special registration as a program in the war on terror raises serious doubts among criminologists and legal scholars. Why would a terrorist risk detection and detention by appearing before the special registration program, especially since the exhaustive procedure involves fingerprinting, photographing, and interrogation by FBI agents? "And if intelligence officials are right that Al Qaeda sleepers generally lead quiet, unremarkable lives in conformity with legal requirements, the INS would have no way of knowing even if an Al Qaeda member *were* to walk in" (Cole 2003, 5). Moreover, experts point out that deportation is among the worse anti-terrorism maneuvers. According to David Cole, professor of law at Georgetown University, "The last thing you want to do with a real terrorist is send him abroad . . . What we want to do is charge him and lock him up. Which, of course, would also spare the innocent thousands caught in the middle" (Gourevitch 2003, EV5; see Cole and Dempsey 2002; Welch 2003b).

Even government agencies have weighed into the debate over the utility of the special registration program. The General Accounting Office (2003a) issued a report that left many questions unanswered as to the value of the project. That study included interviews with officers, many of whom expressed doubts over the usefulness of registration in the campaign against terrorism. Still, the Justice Department defended the special registration program. "To date, the program has not been a complete waste of effort," replied Jorge Martinez who points out that it has led to the arrest of "a wife beater, narcotics dealer and very serious violent offenders" (Gourevitch 2003, EV6). To which critic Alex Gourevitch countered: "But that isn't exactly the same as catching terrorists. And if what we really want is to catch wife beaters, narcotics dealers and violent offenders, the Justice Department should simply require everyone in America to show up and register" (2003, EV6). Likewise, James W. Ziglar, who was commissioner of the INS before it was subsumed into the Department of Homeland Security also remained critical of the registration program when the Justice Department proposed it. Ziglar told his boss, Attorney General Ashcroft, that he thought it was unlikely that terrorists would voluntarily submit to intensive scrutiny: "The question was, "What are we going to get for all this?. . . . As expected we got nothing out of it. To my knowledge, not one actual terrorist was identified. But what we did get was a lot of bad publicity, litigation and disruption in our relationships with immigrant communities and countries that we needed help from in the war on terror" (Swarns 2004a, A26). Indeed, it stands to reason that when one is looking for a needle in a haystack, the last thing one needs is more hay.

To reiterate, issues of profiling and human rights figure prominently in the war on terror, producing an array of contradictions that undermine efforts to detect terrorist activity. "The racist component to these directives is hard to overlook. The escalation of selective registration, detention and deportation of immigrants has taken the form of a large, very poorly guided fishing expedition. One of the great ironies of this kind of social control is that it erodes the cooperation of these immigrant communities. When a government embarks on a fishing expedition like this one, they're admitting that they don't have a lot of clues to begin with" (Welch quoted in Talvi 2003a, 3).

Organizations, such as the American Civil Liberties Union and the Center for Constitutional Rights, disagree with the government's position that in order to fight effectively the war on terror, people must surrender some of their freedoms. That reasoning marks a false paradigm insofar as national security is not predicated on diminishing civil liberties. Mass detention produced by the special registration program is dysfunctional and ineffective. Former executive director of the ACLU, Ira Glasser, reminds us that: "No one can be made safe by arresting the wrong people. In focusing on them [wrong targets], the government certainly violated their civil rights but, more important to most Americans, abandoned public safety as well" (2003, WK12).

In a major development in June 2003, President Bush announced guidelines barring federal agents from relying on race or ethnicity in their investigation. One exception to that policy, however, is terrorism, allowing agents to use race and ethnicity aimed at identifying terrorist threats. Officials in the immigration service will continue to require visitors from Middle Eastern nations to undergo registration and special scrutiny. Civil rights groups swiftly denounced the policy since it perpetuates stereotyping and provides authorities with legal justification to single out Arabs, Muslims, and others who may fall under suspicion. The initiative also falls short of what Bush claimed to do about racial profiling. In a February 2001 national address, Bush declared that racial profiling was "wrong, and we will end it in America" (Lichtblau 2003a, A1). Ibrahim Hooper of the Council on American-Islamic Relations also complained about the policy, especially in light of a recent government report criticizing the Justice Department for rounding up and detaining hundreds of Middle Eastern men following the 9/11 attacks. As we shall see in the next segment, the misuse of detention prompts serious questions over the penal features of the war on terror.[1]

Misuse of Detention

In addition to problems posed by profiling—evident in its special registration program—the government continues to face similar charges of human rights violations, especially in the realm of detention. Shortly after the Justice Department began its post-9/11 sweeps and roundups, allegations surfaced involving arbitrary detention, abuse of detainees, and a host of other procedural infractions. Civil liberties and human rights organizations issued stern warnings to the government that, despite the unique circumstances caused by the attacks on the Pentagon and the World Trade Center, such abuses would not be tolerated. Ignoring those concerns, the Bush administration abruptly announced a major expansion of its power to detain immigrants suspected of crimes, including plans that would allow the Justice Department to detain indefinitely legal and illegal immigrants. (Previously, the Department faced a 24-hour deadline on whether to release detained immigrants or charge them with a crime, or with violating the terms of their visa.)

Given the Kafkaesque nature of indefinite detention, civil liberties advocates swiftly condemned the plan. David Martin, a law professor at the University of Virginia and a former general counsel of the INS, said, "There's definitely a civil liberties concern" in the new regulations. "I don't want to be alarmist about this. If we're talking about adding an additional 12 hours or 24 hours to detention, I don't think that's a problem. But if we are holding people for weeks and weeks, then I think there will be close scrutiny" (Shenon and Toner 2001, EV2). Just months before the September 11 attacks, the U.S. Supreme Court ruled against the government's use of indefinite detention of illegal immigrants, even when their homeland refuses to accept their deportation (*Zadvydas v. Underdown* 1999). After much wrangling over the civil liberties issues contained in the new anti-terrorism legislation, the Patriot Act was passed by Congress. Although the statute expanded the powers of the Department of Justice and the INS, it limited the length of detention to seven days before the government must charge the detainee of a crime. Once charged under the new law, however, detainees found to be engaged in terrorist activities can be held for six months (Rovella 2001).

The Justice Department forged ahead with its broad powers, including the government's new rule to listen in on conversations between inmates and their lawyers—in effect suspending the Sixth Amendment right to effective counsel. Rachel King of the ALCU said the rule set a "terrifying precedent"; it's "very scary," adding: "It's nothing short of a police state" (Reuters 2001b, EV1). Robert Hirshon, president of the American Bar Association, concurred, saying his group was "deeply troubled" by the rule because it ran "squarely afoul" of the U.S. Constitution and impinged on the right to counsel (Reuters 2001b, EV1). Members of Congress also were distressed by the new rule. Senator Patrick Leahy (D-Vt.), chairman of the Senate Judiciary Committee, stated in a letter to Ashcroft that the new policy raised grave concerns: "I am deeply troubled at what appears to be an executive effort to exercise new powers without judicial scrutiny or statutory authorization" (Reuters 2001b, EV2). Those new rules further empower an agency that already enjoys considerable authority. "Under immigration law, the Justice Department is both ac-

cuser and judge, with its Immigration and Naturalization Service serving
as police and prosecutor and its Executive Office for Immigration Review
running special courts that decide whether resident aliens should be detained or deported. INS agents need no warrant to arrest noncitizens,
and immigration courts don't provide lawyers for indigent suspects"
(Bravin, Fields, Adams, and Wartzman 2001, EV1).

Professor David Martin elaborates on the government's use of power:
"There may not be evidence right now to hold someone on a criminal
charge." But with immigration charges, it often is "very easy to demonstrate a violation" of immigration law, allowing officials to deport or detain suspects (Bravin, Fields, Adams, and Wartzman 2001, EV1).

As the government rounded up and detained more than 1,200 immigrants and foreign nationals, many concerned citizens took notice, most
notably those who had previously suffered similar forms of detention.
Janice Mirikitani, San Francisco's poet laureate, said that when she read
that the government is seeking the power to detain immigrants considered suspect and saw polls showing that Americans support racial profiling she felt a horrible sense of déjà vu. "Oh, no. Not again. For me, and
other Japanese-Americans, what we immediately felt was great concern
about what could happen to Afghan-Americans or Arab-Americans. It
made us want to speak out and say, 'Never again'" (Nieves 2001, EV1).
Mirikitani, age 59, was an infant when she was imprisoned by the federal
government. Her entire family—both sets of grandparents, eight aunts,
her parents, all American citizens—was rounded up after the Japanese
attack on Pearl Harbor, herded into freight trains and dumped in re-
mote camps ringed with barbed wire, where they spent three and a half
years during World War II. Fear and war hysteria led to the imprisonment
of 120,000 Japanese-Americans, nearly all from the West Coast (as well as
nearly 11,000 Germans and German-Americans and 2,000 Italians) who
were considered possible allies of the nation's enemies, even though
many of those imprisoned had sons and husbands serving in combat for
the United States (Nieves 2001, EV1).

Several groups released reports documenting serious violations of
civil liberties and human rights (American Civil Liberties Union 2001;
Amnesty International 2003a; 2003b; Lawyers Committee for Human
Rights 2003). Chief among the complaints among civil liberties and immigration attorneys is that the government, in waging its war on terror,
misuses immigration law to circumvent its obligations under the criminal justice system. Moreover, the Department of Justice has established

new immigration policies and procedures that undermine previously existing safeguards against arbitrary detention by the immigration authorities. Those violations are catalogued into three key areas: arbitrary detention, mistreatment of detainees, and abusive interrogations (Human Rights Watch 2002b). Moreover, each of those problems was exacerbated by the government's reliance on secrecy whereby the Department of Justice refused to release information concerning the persons being detained (see Chapter 8).

Arbitrary Detention

Civil liberties and human rights groups remind us that physical liberty is a fundamental human right affirmed in international law and in the U.S. Constitution contained in the due process clauses of the Fifth and Fourteenth Amendments. Correspondingly, arbitrary detention violates that right. "An individual who is arbitrarily detained is rendered defenseless by the coercive power of the state. While arbitrary detention is a hallmark of repressive regimes, democratic governments are not immune to the temptations of violating the right to liberty" (Human Rights Watch 2002b, 46; Amnesty International 2003a). Regrettably many detainees swept up during the early phase of the post-9/11 investigation were subjected to arbitrary detention and held for lengthy periods of time. Such violations were not merely inadvertent due to the confusion surrounding the events of September 11. Rather, arbitrary detention became a systematic tool in the Justice Department's campaign against terror under which new procedural rules had been created. Those rules provided greater power to the government and undermined earlier existing protections for detainees. As noted previously, the new rules enabled the government to use immigration detention as a form of preventative detention for criminal procedures even though it lacked evidence that detainees were flight risks or presented a danger to the community (Lawyers Committee for Human Rights 2003).

In line with the U.S. Constitution as well as international human rights law, all persons, citizen or non-citizen, have the right to be represented by legal counsel after being deprived of liberty for alleged criminal or immigration law violations. Human Rights Watch (2002b) discovered that "special interest" detainees (those the government suspected of being involved in terrorism-related activity) were questioned in custody as part of a criminal investigation, even though they were subsequently charged with immigration violations. Many of those detainees were interrogated by FBI and INS agents concerning criminal matters as well as their immigration status. Immigration attorneys complain that the government relies on administrative proceedings under the immigration law as a proxy to detain and interrogate terrorism suspects without affording them the rights and protections that the U.S. criminal system provides. Among those safeguards is the right to have a lawyer present during custodial interrogations, including free legal counsel if necessary (Cole 2003b; Cole and Dempsey 2002).

Mistreatment of Detainees

With emotions running high after the attacks on the Pentagon and the World Trade Center, detainees feared reprisals from corrections officers and prisoners who might subject them to a form of violence that can best be described as scapegoating (Welch 2003a, 2003b). In some instances, those fears were realized. Human rights advocates report numerous incidents in which detainees were subject to physical and verbal abuse by staff and inmates (Amnesty International 2003a, 2003b; Human Rights Watch 2003, 2002b). In one particular case, Osama Awadallah, a lawful permanent resident of the United States and a citizen of Jordan, was held as a material witness for 83 days during which he experienced a series of humiliating and physically abusive incidents. While at the San Bernardino County jail (California) corrections officers forced Awadallah to strip naked before a female officer. At one point, an officer twisted his arm, forcing him to bow, and pushed his face to the floor. After being transferred to a federal facility in Oklahoma City, a corrections officer hurled shoes at his head and face, cursed at him, and issued insulting remarks about his religion.

Later, Awadallah was shackled in leg irons and flown to New York City and while in transit U.S. marshals threatened to get his brother and cursed the Arabs. At the Metropolitan Correctional Center he was confined to a room so cold that his body turned blue. Physical abuse continued as one corrections officer caused his hand to bleed by pushing him into a door and a wall while he was handcuffed. The same guard also kicked his leg shackles and pulled him by the hair to force him to face an American flag. In another incident, marshals kicked him and threatened to kill him. After being detained for nearly three months, Awadallah was released on bond. A government investigation corroborated the physical mistreatment. His attorney has filed a complaint on his behalf (Human Rights Watch 2002b; see Amnesty International 2003a).

Weeks after September 11, ample evidence surfaced of abuse and mistreatment against those detained, prompting concern among human rights advocates:

> In Mississippi, a 20-year-old student from Pakistan reported that he was stripped and beaten in his cell by other inmates while jail guards failed to intervene and denied him proper medical care.
>
> In New York, prosecutors are investigating an Egyptian detainee's courtroom allegations of abuse by a guard, and the Israeli Consulate is concerned about five Israeli men who say they were blindfolded, handcuffed in their cells, and forced to take lie detector tests.
>
> In three Midwestern states, U.S. immigration officials cut off all visits and phone calls for detainees for a full week after the attacks, a directive that officials now say was mishandled.
>
> And in Texas, a man from Saudi Arabia initially was denied an attorney and was deprived of a mattress, a blanket, a drinking cup and a clock to tell him when to recite his Muslim prayers, his lawyer said. (Serrano 2001a, EV1; 2001b)

Such mistreatment amounts to scapegoating since it appears unlikely that any of those detainees played a role in the attacks on the Pentagon or World Trade Center; none of them were held as material witnesses and two had been released. The government's initial dragnet failed to link the vast majority of those detained to the terrorism investigation. Most of those who were swept up were charged on immigration violations, most commonly overstaying their visas. Attorney General Ashcroft insisted that there had been no wholesale abuse of detainees, even as four more cases surfaced in which young men allegedly were kept from their attorneys and confined in jails without proper food or protection. The new cases, in Florida and Pennsylvania, include a Pakistani man who lost 20 pounds while being detained along side suspected murderers and other violent offenders, and a teenage Iraqi whose family said he came to America to escape one repressive regime and now fears he may have found another (Serrano 2001b).

One of the more tragic incidents amid the sweep for terrorists involved Muhammad Rafiq Butt who was found dead at the Hudson County Correctional Center in New Jersey. Butt, a native of Pakistan, had been arrested for being in the country illegally, one of hundreds who had been picked up on the basis of tips from an anxious public. An autopsy revealed that Butt, 55, whose one-year stay in the United States seems to have been hapless from the very start, had coronary disease and died of a heart attack. His death forced the INS to do something it had not had to do during the 33 days it had him in custody: talk about him publicly and explain the circumstances behind his arrest, detention, and death. It was finally revealed to the public that Butt had been picked up after a bad tip to the FBI from the pastor of a church near his home in South Ozone Park, Queens. His only violation was overstaying his visitor visa. It took the government a day to determine that it had no interest in him for its investigation into terrorism. "He chose to appear at his deportation hearing without a lawyer, even though he spoke virtually no English and had little education. From jail, he made no calls to his relatives, nor to the Pakistani Consulate in New York" (Sengupta 2001a, EV1–2).

According to the *International Covenant on Civil and Political Rights* (Article 10), "all persons deprived of their liberty shall be treated with humanity and with respect for their inherent dignity of the human person." Correspondingly, the ICCPR forbids cruel, inhuman or degrading treatment or punishment. In the aftermath of 9/11, human rights advocates complained that INS detainees were subjected to abuse and inadequate conditions of confinement even though they were not accused of criminal conduct, much less convicted of it. Simply put, from the early stages of the investigation on, those detainees were treated as if they were convicted terrorists, locked down in solitary confinement where they were rarely allowed to leave their cells for weeks and sometimes months. Additionally, they were subjected to extraordinarily strict security measures that prevented them communicating with their families and attorneys. Even worse, some were victims of verbal and physical abuse, refused adequate medical attention, and housed with suspected or convicted criminals (Human Rights Watch 2002b; Welch 2002a, 2002b).

Abusive Interrogations

Adding to the controversy over the mistreatment of detainees held in connection with the September 11 attacks is the issue of torture. An experienced FBI agent involved in the investigation, in discussing the use of torture, is quoted as saying, "It could get to that spot where we could go to pressure" (*Washington Post* 2001b, 25). Similarly, Robert Litt, a former Justice Department official, arguing that while torture ought not be "authorized," perhaps it could be used in an "emergency," as long as the person who tortures then presents himself to "take the consequences" (Williams 2001, 11). Those views appear to have some public support; a recent CNN poll revealed that 45 percent would not object to torturing someone if it would provide information about terrorism (Williams 2001). Journalists and human rights groups quickly responded. "We trust that the Bush administration is not seriously considering torture . . . [still] Ashcroft has been careless with the Constitution when it comes to the treatment of people arrested in the wake of September 11, raising fears he will be similarly careless when it comes to using the broad new investigative powers recently granted him by Congress" (*New York Times* 2001, A22; see Millett 1994). Amnesty International (2001) also condemned the use of torture and remains concerned over the well-being of detainees especially in light of numerous reports that many of those arrested in the wake of the attacks were denied prompt access to lawyers or relatives. Moreover, questions about the mistreatment of detainees have yet to be fully answered because the government refuses to disclose such information to the public. Understandably, a policy of mass detention shrouded in secrecy and confusion has greatly distressed human rights and civil liberties advocates.

As matter of procedure, the right to have an attorney present during custodial interrogations serves to prevent coercive interrogations. But as evident in the 9/11 round-ups, detainees were not only denied access to attorneys, but also were subjected to abusive treatment. Both the U.S. Constitution and *Principle 21 of the United Nations Body of Principle for the Protection of All Persons under Any Form of Detention or Imprisonment* specifically prohibit abusive interrogations since such mistreatment impairs a person's judgment and capacity to make decisions. Abusive interrogations likewise produce false confessions.

Consider the case of Abdallah Higazy, a 30-year-old Egyptian graduate student with a valid visa, who was detained as a material witness on December 17, 2001. A pilot's radio had allegedly been found in the New York City hotel room where he had stayed on September 11. Higazy was placed in solitary confinement at the Metropolitan Correctional Center (MCC) in Manhattan. Eager to establish his innocence, Higazy volunteered to take a polygraph examination. He then was subjected to a grueling five-hour interrogation during which he was not given a break, food, or drink. Due to some unusual restrictions concocted by the Justice Department, Higazy's attorney was forced to remain outside the interrogation room, unable to advise his client. Higazy reported that from the beginning of the interrogation, the agents threatened him and his family. Yielding to intense emotional and physical fatigue as a result of the abusive interrogation, Higazy eventually said that the radio belonged to him. The Justice Department charged Higazy with lying to the FBI, but three days later an American pilot went to the hotel to claim the radio. Charges against Higazy were dropped and after one month in solitary confinement, he was dumped from the MCC into the streets of New York City wearing a prison uniform and given three dollars for subway fare. Months later, Ronald Ferry, the former hotel security guard who found the pilot's radio, admitted that he had fabricated the story accusing Higazy. Ferry was sentenced to six months of weekends in prison for lying to the FBI. He admitted that he knew that the device was not in a safe belonging to Higazy. Ferry, a former police officer, said that he lied during a "time of patriotism, and I'm very, very sorry." The judge said that his conduct was "wrongly motivated by prejudicial stereotypes, misguided patriotism or false heroism" (Human Rights Watch 2002b, 39; see Weiser 2002).

The 2003 Inspector General's Report

As discussed throughout the chapter, much of the criticism over the government's handling of the war on terror has been delivered by human rights and civil liberties organizations relying on their own investigations. In June 2003, that body of knowledge was greatly expanded by the government itself, particularly in a report released by Glenn A. Fine, the inspector general at the Department of Justice. Civil liberties and human rights advocates hailed the report especially since it confirmed their complaints that the Justice Department's approach to the war on terror was fraught with abuse. The report concluded that the government's round-up of hundreds of illegal immigrants in the aftermath of 9/11 was a mistake since it forced many people with no connection to terrorism to languish behind bars in unduly harsh conditions. The inspector general found that even some of the lawyers in the Justice Department expressed concerns about the legality of its tactics only to be overridden by senior administrators. Suggesting that the Justice Department had cast too wide a net in the fight against terrorism, the report was critical of FBI officials, particularly in New York City, who made little attempt to distinguish between immigrants who had possible ties to terrorism and those swept up by chance in the investigation. Shanaz Mohammed, 39, who was held in Brooklyn for eight months on an immigration violation before being deported to Trinidad in 2002, responded to the report: "It feels good to have someone saying that we shouldn't have had to go through all that we did. I think America overreacted a great deal by singling out Arab-named men like myself. We were all looked at as terrorists. We were abused" (Lichtblau 2003b, A1; U.S. Department of Justice 2003a, 2003b; von Zielbauer 2003a).

Since the Justice Department has maintained a policy of secrecy concerning arrests and detentions, the report was noted for its openness, offering to the public the most detailed portrait to date of who was held, the delays many faced in being charged or gaining access to a lawyer, and the abuse that some faced in jail. William F. Schulz, executive director of Amnesty International USA, said that the inspector general's office "should be applauded for releasing a report that isn't just a whitewash of the government's actions" (Lichtblau 2003b, A18). Figures cited in the report show that a total of 762 undocumented immigrants were detained in the weeks and months after the attacks on the Pentagon and the World Trade Center; none have been charged as terrorists and most others have been deported (see American Civil Liberties Union, 2004). The report validated complaints that the 84 detainees housed at the Metropolitan Detention Center in Brooklyn faced a pattern of physical and verbal abuse from some corrections officers. Videotapes, which investigators discovered after being told by prison employees that the tapes no longer existed, showed staff members slamming chained detainees into walls and twisting their elbows. In one episode captured on videotape, a guard was seen ramming a detainees face into a T-shirt taped to a wall. The shirt featured a U.S. flag and the words "These Colors Don't Run." The detainees were also subjected to unduly harsh detention policies, including a highly restrictive, 23-hour lockdown. Detainees also were handcuffed, placed in leg irons and heavy chains any time they moved outside their cells (U.S. Department of Justice 2003a, 2003b; von Zielbauer 2003a).

Compounding their isolation, detainees were limited to a single phone call per week and due to a communication blackout, families of some inmates in the Brooklyn facility were told their relatives were not housed there. The report faulted the Justice Department for not processing suspects more rapidly, a procedure that would have determined who should remain in detention while releasing others. In sum, the findings "confirm our long-held view that civil liberties and the rights of immigrants were trampled in the aftermath of 9/11," said Anthony D.

Romero, executive director of the ACLU (Lichtblau 2003b, A18; see Liptak 2003a; *New York Times* 2003b).

Despite strong evidence of civil rights violations contained in the report, Justice Department officials defended themselves saying that they believed they had acted within the law in pursuing terrorist suspects. Barbara Comstock, a spokeswoman for the department announced: "We make no apologies for finding every legal way possible to protect the American public from further terrorist attacks" (Lichtblau 2003b, A1). Despite their disagreements with some of the report's conclusions, Justice Department officials said that they have already adopted some of the 21 recommendations made by the inspector general, including one to develop clearer criteria for the processing of such detentions. Other areas of improvement encompass procedures that would ensure a timely clearance process, better training of staff on the treatment of detainees, and better oversight of the conditions of confinement (see Welch 2002b, 2000b).

Detaining Asylum Seekers

The crackdown on undocumented immigrants and foreigners also extends to another vulnerable subset of the immigrant population, namely, asylum seekers. Along with an undifferentiated fear of terrorism, crime, and non-white immigrants, there is growing suspicion that under existing asylum proceedings: "People would show up, ask for asylum and then "disappear, and of course stay in this country indefinitely" (Congressman Lamar Smith, R-Tex, quoted in Tulsky 2000a, EV3). However, experts insist that using asylum seeking as a means of gaining entry to the United States is a tremendously high risk for terrorists because all asylum applicants are fingerprinted, thoroughly interrogated, and face the prospect of months or years in detention (Amnesty International 2003b).

Between September 11, 2001, and December 2003, more than 15,300 asylum seekers were detained at U.S. airports and borders. From the port of entry, asylum seekers are transported to jail often in handcuffs, and usually without any clear understanding of why they are being detained. In detention, once they pass a screening interview, asylum seekers are legally eligible to be paroled if they satisfy the Department of Homeland Security (DHS) parole criteria (i.e., community ties, no risk to the community, and that identity can be established). However, in practice, even asylum seekers who meet those criteria remain in detention (*Asylum Protection News 22* 2004). Immigration officials too often ignore or selectively apply the parole criteria, which exist only in guideline form rather than formal regulations. Compounding matters, when an asylum seeker's parole request is denied by DHS officials, they have no meaningful recourse; they cannot appeal the decision to an independent authority, or even an immigration judge (*Asylum Protection News 21* 2003; Jones 2003; Lawyers Committee for Human Rights 2004). Since the attacks of September 11, other strict measures have been established that adversely affect asylum seekers in the United States, including *Operation Liberty Shield* and the *Blanket Detention Order of 2003*.

Human rights advocates are appalled by a recent program officially titled *Operation Liberty Shield,* which was initiated by the DHS on the eve of the war with Iraq. That program requires detention of asylum seekers from 33 countries where Al Qaeda has been known to operate. Under *Operation Liberty Shield,* even asylum seekers who did not raise any suspicion of security or flight risks were slated for detention for the duration of their asylum proceedings (estimated by the Department to be six months or significantly longer if the case was appealed). Consequently, many of them would be deprived of a meaningful opportunity to request release through parole (Lawyers Committee for Human Rights 2004).

Adding to the government's escalating war on terror, Attorney General John Ashcroft issued a profoundly significant measure on April 17, 2003. Under that directive, illegal immigrants, including asylum seekers, can be held indefinitely without bond if their cases present national security concerns. Ashcroft firmly stated: "Such national security considerations clearly constitute a reasonable foundation for the exercise of my discretion to deny release on bond" (Anderson 2003, EV-1). Whereas the *Blanket Detention Order* is framed as being necessary for maintaining national security, the actual case involves a Haitian asylum seeker, David Joseph. The DHS, the agency that now has authority over most immigration matters, sought the opinion of the Attorney General after the Board of Immigration Appeals upheld a judge's decision to release Joseph on $2,500 bond. Ashcroft argued: "National security would be threatened if the release triggered a huge wave of immigrants to attempt to reach U.S. shores. That would overtax the already-strained Coast Guard, Border Patrol and other agencies that are busy trying to thwart terror attacks" (Anderson 2003, EV-1). The State Department weighed into the controversy, stated that Haiti has become a staging point for non-Haitians considered security threats (i.e., Pakistanis and Palestinians) to enter the United States, a claim widely disputed by immigration and national security experts (see Welch 2004c; Welch and Schuster 2005a, 2005b).

Whereas most of the immigration issues have been transferred to the DHS, the measure promises to centralize further the power of the attorney general in the area of asylum seeking. Human rights groups and immigration attorneys swiftly opposed the blanket detention order. Amnesty International denounced Ashcroft's ruling to hold groups of asylum seekers and other noncitizens in detention indefinitely, noting that the provision extends to those who pose no danger to the United States. "To suggest that all Haitian asylum seekers pose a threat to U.S. national security, as Attorney General Ashcroft has done, strains credulity and makes a mockery of our immigration system," said Amnesty International USA's executive director, Bill Schulz. "Ordering asylum-seekers to remain locked up simply because of their nationality is tantamount to discrimination and a violation of international standards" (Amnesty International 2003, EV1). Human rights organizations acknowledge the U.S. government's obligation to protect national security against terrorism and support legitimate means of doing so. Still, the blanket detention policy violates international standards specifying that the detention of asylum seekers be limited to exceptional cases under law. Furthermore, governments have the burden of demonstrating the need for detaining asylum seekers in prompt and fair individualized hearings before a judicial or similar authority. The current detention policies and practices retreat from the historical practice of protecting asylum seekers. "This sends a message to the people who are victims of human rights abuses that we are going to put you into detention if you come from the very countries that the U.S. has identified—that President Bush has identified—as having torture chambers and committing egregious human rights abuse," said Bill Frelick, director of the refugee program for Amnesty International USA (Shenon 2003a, A22).

In his book, *Folk Devils and Moral Panics,* Cohen speculates that more anonymous, or "nameless," folk devils will emerge in the years come. That forecast is especially relevant to asylum seekers whose actual identity and biography are commonly obscured from public consciousness. As a result, "social policies once regarded as abnormal—incarcerating hundreds of asylum seekers in detention centers—run as punitive transit camps by private companies for profit—are seen as being normal, rational and conventional" (Cohen 2002, xxxiv; see Molenaar and Neufeld 2003). Cohen writes in reference to moral panic over asylum seekers in the UK where the phenomenon is characteristically noisy insofar as there is considerable public outrage over the issue. By contrast, the controversy over asylum seekers in the United States occurs below the public radar, spreading quietly among government officials and bureaucrats who dictate and administer detention policies (Welch 2004c; Welch and Schuster 2005).

Conclusion

In the 1920s, W. I. Thomas (1923) observed that whatever people believe to be real, will be real in its consequences. Since then sociologists have concentrated on the significance of popular perceptions and their effects on society (Best 1999; Glassner 1999). Moral panic is indicative of turbulent societal reaction to social problems, particularly those producing a disaster mentality in which there is a widespread belief that society is endangered. As a result, there is a sense of urgency to do something now or else society will suffer even graver consequences later, compelling social policy to undergo significant transformation in a rash attempt to diffuse the putative threat (Cohen 2002). Those social constructions provoke intense public hostility and condemnation aimed at a particular group; correspondingly, they strengthen the social control apparatus with more criminal justice legislation that produces more penalties, police, and prisons (Welch 2005b; Welch, Fenwick, and Roberts 1997).

Altogether the USA Patriot Act (2001), the Antiterrorism and Effective Death Penalty Act (1996), and Illegal Immigration Reform and Immigrant Responsibility Act (1996) continue to produce a host of violations against civil liberties and human rights (see Chapter 8). Moreover, the enforcement of those statutes is patterned along predictable lines of race and ethnicity that criminalize foreigners and immigrants of color. Anti-terrorist tactics are driven by stereotypes depicting Middle Eastern people as threats to national security. As Anthony D. Romero, of the ACLU, notes, "The war on terror has quickly turned into a war on immigrants" (Liptak 2003, A18). As to be discussed in upcoming chapters, civil liberties organizations take exception to the government's claim that in order to fight effectively the war on terror, citizens must surrender some of their freedoms. That reasoning marks a false paradigm insofar as national security does not rest on diminishing civil liberties. Mass detention produced by the special registration program is dysfunctional and counterproductive. The public and political leaders ought to be cautious not to overreact to the tragic events of September 11 (Cole 2003; Cole and Dempsey 2002). Drawing on lessons from social constructionism and moral panic, it is important to contain fear of terrorism and anxiety over national security so as not to undermine fair and just treatment of immigrants, refugees, and asylum seekers.

CHAPTER SEVEN

State Crimes in the War on Terror

Man desires a world where good and evil can be clearly distinguished, for he has an innate and irrepressible desire to judge before he understands.
—Milan Kundera, *The Unbearable Lightness of Being,* 1984

Scapegoating, stereotyping, profiling, and typifying people belonging to these [marginalized] groups is far easier for the state because of broad asymmetries of power. It is therefore not surprising that galvanizing support for unethical and illegal practices and policies against these groups is not difficult for the state.
—David Kauzlarich, Rick Matthews, and William Miller,
"Toward a victimology of state crime," *Critical Criminology,* 2001

Events following September 11 have greatly compounded problems in a post-9/11 world, most notably the misguided military actions by the U.S. government. In the span of a few short years, America has gone from being viewed with tremendous sympathy to being despised around much of the globe, in large part due to the invasion of Iraq, along with a host of illegal and unjust tactics in the war on terror (Knowlton 2005). For the United States as an unrivaled superpower, the attacks on 9/11 merely hardened an already strong sense of entitlement; therefore, the war on terrorism represents an impulse to undo violently the humiliation of September 11. By emphasizing the term war, counterterrorism policies and practices have become increasingly militarized, marking a sharp transition from the figurative to the literal. According to Lifton: "War then becomes heroic, even mythic, a task that must be carried out for the defense of one's nation, to sustain its special historical destiny and the immortality of its people" (2003b, 12; Hedges 2002; Katz 1988).

Critical criminologists frequently interpret governmental responses to crime in ways that highlight belligerent state policies aimed at reducing perceived threats: the war on crime, the war on drugs, and, of course, the war on terror (Pepinsky 1991; Quinney 2000; Welch, Bryan, Wolff 1999; Welch 2003a). Contributing to those observations, Gregg Barak (2005, 2003, 1991) reminds us of the significance of warmaking criminology, a phenomenon that figures prominently not only in American domestic criminal justice but also in its campaigns abroad, particularly actions that produce state crimes. There are varied definitions of state crimes, most notably those referring to governmental crime, political crime, and state-organized crime. Nevertheless it is generally agreed that such violations constitute "illegal, socially injurious [harmful], or unjust acts which are committed for the benefit of a state or its agencies, and not for the personal gain of some individual agent of the state" (Kauzlarich, Matthews, and Miller 2001, 175; see Chambliss 1989; Friedrichs 1998; Ross 2000a, 2000b). That understanding of state crime clearly lends itself to an array of legal and human rights atrocities along with numerous abuses of power (see Kramer and Michalowski 2005).

Beyond taking a purely descriptive approach by which one documents the extent of state crimes in the war on terror, a critical analysis of warmaking criminology brings to light the rituals of adversarialism. As Barak writes: "Adversarial rituals are used by cultures to bind anger and accusation, defamation and humiliation, subjugation and victory. The value of these rituals is that they sustain hostility in structured and predictable ways. These rituals do something else as well: they represent collective clichés or ways of avoiding possibilities of real dialogue and real change" (2005, 145). Such adversarial rituals are coercive in nature, manifesting in four distinct sets: killing, undermining, deprecation, and denial (see

Fellman 1998). War perhaps is the most extreme version of the killing ritual, given the scope and scale of that form of lethal violence. Undermining refers to the range of insulting and offensive tactics intended to frighten and intimidate, complemented by the ritual of deprecation in which images project aggressors as superior to their victims. Finally, denial is a particularly potent ritual since it relies on blaming the "other," which in turn justifies violence by aggressors who see themselves as innocent or merely "defending the eternal good" (Katz 1988).

Reflecting on criminological research after September 11, Mark Hamm proposes "terrorism has become an instrument for clarifying criminology's own purposes" (2005, 245; 2002). This chapter sets out to demonstrate that it is also important to track governmental responses to terrorism, especially those policies and practices leading to state crimes. Here the discussion concentrates on four interrelated areas of America's war on terror: the invasion of Iraq, prison scandals in Iraq and Afghanistan, the controversy over unlawful enemy combatants held at Guantanamo Bay, and the use of torture. As we shall see, many of those governmental tactics involve scapegoating since they seem to have more to do with displacing aggression, or "kicking ass," than maintaining public safety and national security. Implications to the risk society perspective abound, especially given the preponderance of blaming and skirting accountability. Indeed, a hot potato continues to make the rounds as greater evidence of government malfeasance surfaces, adding to an emerging culture of impunity in which state—and military—officials go unpunished for their participation in an array of state crimes.

Illegal War in Iraq

The U.S. invasion of Iraq marks a troubling juncture where the fog of war slips deeper into the fog of terror, creating a host of uncertainties compounded by shifting rationales for the occupation. For years, the Bush team issued an onslaught of claims pronouncing a link between Saddam Hussein and the attacks of September 11, thereby attempting to justify the war in Iraq. However, given the lack of evidence needed to support its position—most significantly the absence of weapons of mass destruction—the White House began to back pedal, even insisting "that it had never made such an assertion—only that there were ties, however, murky, between Iraq and Al-Qaeda" (*New York Times* 2004b, 4). A brief retrospective of what the White House said, nevertheless, tells quite a different story. President Bush has proven to be one of the most prolific mythmakers in this regard.

Saddam Hussein is a threat because he is dealing with Al Qaeda." (Bush, Washington press conference, November 7, 2002)

Iraq sent bomb-making and document forgery experts to work with Al Qaeda. Iraq has also provided Al Qaeda with chemical and biological weapons training. (Bush, speech: "World can rise to this moment, February 6, 2003)

The liberation of Iraq is a crucial advance in the campaign against terror. We've removed an ally of Al Qaeda." (Bush, Announcement that major combat in Iraq is over, May 1, 2003)

The battle of Iraq is one victory in the war on terror that began on September 11, 2001. (Bush, Announcement that major combat in Iraq is over, May 1, 2003)

The reason I keep insisting that there was a relationship between Iraq and Saddam and Al Qaeda is because there was a relationship between Iraq and Al Qaeda." (Bush, Statement after cabinet meeting, June 17, 2004)

Likewise, Vice President Cheney played the party line: "I continue to believe, I think there's overwhelming evidence that there was a connection between Al Qaeda and the Iraqi government" (Cheney, National Public Radio interview, January 22, 2004). Adding to a greater sense of urgency, Secretary of State Colin Powell announced: "The more we wait, the more chance there is for this dictator [Hussein] with clear ties to terrorist groups, including Al Qaeda, to pass a weapon, share a technology or use these weapons again" (Powell, Remarks at the World Economic Forum, January 26, 2003). In a similar tone, National Security Advisor, Condoleezza Rice, stated: "And what we do not want is the day when Saddam Hussein decides that he's had enough of dealing with sanctions . . . and it's time to end it on his terms by transferring one of these weapons, just a little vial of something to a terrorist" (Rice, interview on "Face the Nation," March 9, 2003).[1]

Despite widespread—albeit waning—support for the war, criticism of American militarism has remained persistent and probing (*International*

Herald Tribune 2005). Former vice president Al Gore fiercely attacked Bush, saying he "betrayed this country! He played on our fears. He took America on an ill-conceived foreign adventure dangerous to our troops, an adventure preordained and planned before 9/11 ever took place" (Seelye 2004b, A18). At a higher level of abstraction, however, editors at the *Nation* draw crucial attention to the semantics of the war on terror, arguing that "there can be no war on terrorism, since terrorism involves a *tactic,* not an organization or state" (*Nation* 2004, 3). That observation sheds light on the tragic realities of the war in Iraq brought on by the colossal mistakes, missteps, and miscalculations at the hands of the neo-conservatives who push for greater militarism. "[The neocons] said Saddam had WMDs. He didn't. They said he was in league with Osama bin Laden. He wasn't. They predicted that no major postwar insurgency in Iraq would occur. It did. They said there would be a wave of pro-Americanism in the Middle East and the world if the United States acted boldly and unilaterally. Instead, there was a regional and global wave of anti-Americanism (Lind 2004, 23). Those events and developments weigh heavily in evaluating the legality of the war in Iraq, thereby, lending greater precision to unveiling state crimes that contribute to the destruction of large swaths of people and property. In search of evidence that the Bush administration abused its power and misled the world as to why it was invading Iraq, the so-called 10 Downing Street memo offers crucial information. That secret British document reported on July 23, 2002, that Bush had decided to "remove Saddam, through military action," suggesting that the White House was intent on war with Iraq earlier than it acknowledged (Jehl 2005, A10). Controversial books by Richard Clarke (2004), former counterterrorism advisor, and about Paul H. O'Neill (see Suskind 2004), former treasury secretary, also have indicated that Bush had decided to invade Iraq by summer of 2002; hence, the British memo provides additional validation of those assertions. In the House of Representatives, 89 Democrats contacted the White House to determine whether the memo accurately reported the administration's thinking at the time, eight months before the invasion of Iraq. John Conyers, Jr. (D-Mich.), top Democrat on the House Judiciary Committee said the British memo "raises troubling new questions regarding the legal justification for the war as well as the integrity of your own administration" (Jehl 2005a, A10).

The British memo reveals that Sir Richard Dearlove, chief of Britain's Secret Intelligence Service, reporting back from talks in Washington, had told other senior British officials that Bush "wanted to remove" Hussein "through military action justified by the conjunction of terrorism and

W.M.D" (weapons of mass destruction). "But the intelligence and facts were being fixed around the policy" (Jehl 2005a, A10). The issue over the legality of war has attracted a wide range of critics, including John L. Allen, Jr., the Vatican correspondent for the *National Catholic Reporter* who writes: "The Bush administration argues that when it has intelligence about imminent threats to the United States, it has the right to strike first. The Vatican insists that a single nation-state never has this right. Only the United Nations can authorize military action to disarm an aggressor, to ensure that disarmament is the real objective rather than a particular country's political or commercial interests" (Allen 2004, A27). Still, the words of Secretary General of the United Nations Kofi Annan caused the greatest stir when he said that he believed that the war was "illegal" and not valid under international law terms. "Well, I'm one of those who believe that there should have been a second resolution [because] it was up to the Security Council to approve or determine" what the "consequences should be" for Iraq's non-compliance with earlier resolutions. "I have stated that it was not in conformity with the Security Council—with the U.N. Charter." Reiterating his pointed, Annan said: "It was illegal, if you wish. From our point of view and from the charter point of view it was illegal" (Tyler 2004b, A11).

Lord Goldsmith, British attorney general, publicly stated that his government was acting legally in backing military action. "But his private advice to Mr. Blair may have also expressed reservations about the legality of the war" (Tyler 2004b, A11). Whereas Blair held the position that regime change justified the invasion, Goldsmith insisted that it did not constitute a legal cause of war. Compounding matters, Admiral Sir Michael Boyce, Britain's senior commander at the start of the war, expressed worries that he might have faced prosecution at the International Criminal Court for joining the invasion (Cowell 2005). In a partly declassified letter of resignation, Elizabeth Wilmshurst, a deputy legal adviser to the British Foreign Office, protested on the eve of the invasion that the incursion was not authorized by Resolution 1441 and would be a "crime of aggression" (*Nation* 2005a, 8; see Hinds 2005).

That perspective is shared by others, including some American soldiers who have faced combat in Iraq. Camilo Mejia of the Florida National Guard argued: "This is an immoral, unjust and illegal war. The whole thing is based on lies. There are no weapons of mass destruction and there was no link with terrorism. It's about oil, reconstruction contracts and controlling the Middle East" (Parenti 2004, 202). Ralph Nadar, the independent candidate for president in 2004, condemned Bush as a "messianic militant" who should be impeached for pushing the nation into a war in Iraq "based on false pretenses." Nadar contends that Bush's actions rise to the level of high crimes and misdemeanors, adding that "the founding fathers did not want the declaration of war in the hands of one man." At the center of Nadar's criticism is his insistence that Bush hyped the threat to draw popular support for more militaristic policies in order to generate military contracts for corporations with close links to the White House (Lueck 2004b, A21).[2] Concerns over the legality of the war in Iraq also have surfaced in the federal judiciary. In a trial against four anti-war demonstrators who engaged in what the authorities call an act of unlawful civil disobedience, the defendants were cited for contempt for violating "the judge's order not to mention that in their view the war is illegal according to international law" (York 2005, B3).

The war in Iraq, indeed, has proven costly in both financial and human terms. By mid-year 2005, the price of the war exceeded $200 billion with the passage of the $82 billion emergency war-spending bill (Kirkpatrick 2005c, A5.) Thus far, there seems to be little satisfaction in those expenditures and critics have cited numerous incidents of financial waste (*Nation* 2005b; Parenti 2004). Even the Inspector General's office reported millions of dollars in unaccounted-for reconstruction funds. Specifically, American officials in a mad rush to initiate building projects in Iraq did not keep required records on the spending of $89.4 million in cash and cannot account at all for another $7.2 million. "They also rushed, critics charge, to spend Iraqi money entrusted to the Americans before 2004 when the new Iraq government took charge of it. The evidence of sloppy controls is of international concern because the Americans were using funds under authority from the United Nations that required strict accounting" (Eckholm 2005, A16).

Keeping tabs on the human death toll has been equally frustrating but one thing is clear—it is the Iraqi civilians who bear the brunt of the war (Howard 2005). Figures of civilian casualties are fiercely debated. In late 2004, a new study by a research team at the Bloomberg School of Public Health at Johns Hopkins in Baltimore estimated 100,000 civilians have died in Iraq as a direct or indirect consequence of the March 2004 United States-led invasion (Rosenthall 2004, A8).[3] American servicemen and women also account for a growing list of casualties. By the middle of May 2006, more than 2,440 have been killed in the line of duty. Especially considering the extremely difficult circumstances inherent in war, the vast majority of American soldiers have conducted themselves in accord with the rules of engagement (Parenti 2004; Wright 2004a, 2004b). However, human rights advocates have tracked incidents in which there is reason to believe that war crimes may have occurred. For example, international law experts said that U.S. soldiers might have committed a war crime on November 11, 2004, when they sent fleeing Iraqi civilians back into Falluja. Citing several articles of the Geneva Conventions, they said that established laws of war require military forces to protect civilians as refugees and must not return them to a combat zone. Jordan Paust, a law professor at the University of Houston and former army prosecutor, said: "This is highly problematical conduct in terms of exposing people to grave danger by returning them to an area where fighting is going on." Similarly, James Ross, senior legal advisor to Human Rights Watch, noted: "If that's what happened, it would be a war crime" (Janofsky 2004, A8.). Nevertheless, because the United States refuses to participate in the International Criminal Court, it is unclear whether American troops could be held accountable (see Kramer and Michalowski 2005).

In one of the many battles over Falluja, there remain questions concerning the U.S. bombing of the Central Health Center on November 9, 2004. Whereas the U.S. military has dismissed accounts of the health center bombing as unsubstantiated, Dr. Samil al-Jumaili who was working at the center at the time of the incident said that American warplanes dropped three bombs on the clinic where approximately 60 patients were being treated, many of whom had serious injuries from previous U.S. aerial bombings and attacks. Dr. al-Jumaili reported that 35 patients were killed in the airstrike, including two girls and three boys under the age of ten. He said, fifteen medics, four nurses, and five support staff also died after the entire health center—a protected institution under international law—collapsed on the patients. According to James Ross, Human Rights Watch, "The onus would be on the U.S. government to demonstrate that the hospital was being used for military purposes and that its response was proportionate. Even if there were snipers there it would never justify destroying the hospital" (Schuman 2004, 5–6). The Association of Humanitarian Lawyers has petitioned the Inter-American Commission on Human Rights of the Organization of American States to investigate the incident.[4]

The legality of other acts of violence also has been called into question. Consider the well-publicized incident in which a U.S. marine shot and killed an unarmed and wounded Iraqi prisoner, unaware that he was being videotaped by an NBC News cameraman Kevin Sites. No weapons were visible inside the Falluja mosque where the shooting occurred (on November 13, 2004) and the wounded Iraqi made no sudden or threatening moves before being shot (Glanz and Wong 2004, A13; see www.kevinsites.net). As footage of the killing aired internationally, provoking intense anger across the Middle East, the marine was removed from the battlefield for questioning. Ross of Human Rights Watch noted: "Obviously the shooting of an incapacitated detainee is a fundamental violation of the Law of Armed Conflict" (Schmitt 2004, A12).

The execution of wounded, unarmed combatants, violates Article 3 of the Geneva Convention Relative to the Treatment of Prisoners of War, that states in part that "persons taking no active part in the hostilities, including members of armed forces who have laid down their arms and those placed hors de combat by sickness, wounds, detention, or any other cause shall in all circumstances be treated humanely." Even to those unfamiliar with the Geneva Conventions, it seems obvious from the mosque video that a war crime was committed. The response from the administration and military was unusually swift. Ambassador to Iraq John Negroponte expressed his regrets to Prime Minister Ayad Allawi and vowed that "the individual in question will be dealt with," and his commanders issued a statement promising to investigate what they called "an allegation of the unlawful use of force in the death of an enemy combatant" (Wright 2004a, 22).

In 2005, Captain Rogelio Mayulet, a U.S. Army tank company commander, was freed after a court martial, although he was dismissed from the Army, for what he called a "mercy killing." Mayulet had faced ten years in prison after being guilty of assault with intent to commit voluntary manslaughter; instead he was sentenced with dismissal from the armed services and there would be no confinement time. Prosecutors had pressed for conviction on a more serious charge of assault with intent to commit murder, which carries a maximum 20-year prison term. The "mercy killing" defense was used in the cases of two other American soldiers convicted in December (2004) and January (2005) of murdering an Iraqi teenager (*New York Times* 2005c, A5). Also that year, Army Staff Sergeant Shane Werst was acquitted of murder in the death of an unarmed Iraqi he said he had shot to save a fellow soldier; he had faced a maximum sentence of life in prison without parole. Werst and a fellow soldier had entered a house with the victim in search of weapons. After shooting him, Werst said he fired the Iraqi's pistol into a couch and instructed another soldier to put the man's fingerprints on it. Werst testified he had been scared because he had never shot anyone before. The prosecutor said the story did not make sense. "If this is a legitimate kill, if this follows the rules of engagement, why in the world would he have to create a lie?" (*New York Times* 2005d, A18).

Similarly, Second Lieutenant Ilario Pantano was cleared of criminal wrongdoing in a murder case of two Iraqis who were shot in the back with as many as 60 rounds of ammunition. On April 15, 2004, Pantano unloaded two magazines from an M-16 rifle then left a sign reading "No Better Friend-No Worse Enemy" as a warning to other Iraqis to stay away from the insurgency, a message that was likened to a "head stake." Pantano claims that it was an act of self-defense. The hearing officer wrote in a report that Pantano used poor judgment in the incident but his behavior did not constitute a crime" (DeSantis 2005a, A10; see www .defendthedefenders.org). Major General Richard A. Huck, commander of the Second Marine Division, found that evidence presented at a later hearing did not support accusations of premeditated murder (DeSantis 2005b, A18).

In the midst of warfare, many servicemen constantly debate the morality of their violence. A sergeant told reporter Evan Wright that he had consulted with his priest about killing. "The priest had told him it was all right to kill for his government as long as he didn't enjoy it." By the time the unit reached the outer sections of Baghdad, the sergeant was certain he had killed at least four men. Later reflecting on "slaying dragons," he reconsidered what his priest told him about killing. "Where the fuck did Jesus say it's OK to kill people for your government? Any priest who tells me that has got no credibility." In another interview with Wright, a soldier conceded: "If we did half the shit back home we've done here, we'd be in prison" (Wright 2004a, 24).

Abu Ghraib Prisoner Abuse Scandal

In late 2002, the *Washington Post* published detailed accounts of American intelligence officers who had resorted to abuse and torture of detainees held at Bagram Air Force base in Afghanistan (Priest and Gellman 2002). Even though the story appeared front page, it generated little public or political interest. Then some 15 months later, the horrors of Abu Ghraib were exposed. A significant difference between the two otherwise similar reports of abuse and torture was the availability of explicit photographs. Within days of the breaking story, graphic visual evidence circulated around the globe. Pictures of nude Iraqi prisoners taunted by dogs, simulating sex acts, and stacked in human pyramids confirmed suspicions that the U.S. military was operating outside the orbit of international law, relying on abuse and torture to extract information or merely as a means of punishment and humiliation (Hersh 2004). Writer Susan Sontag examined the incidents at Abu Ghraib within a broader historical context. "Rape and pain inflicted on the genitals are among the most common forms of torture. Not just in Nazi concentration camps and in Abu Ghraib when it was run by Saddam Hussein. Americans, too, have done and do them when they are told or made to feel, that those over them they have absolute power deserve to be humiliated, tormented. They do them when they are led to believe that the people they are torturing belong to an inferior race or religion" (2004, 28).

Images at Abu Ghraib are remarkably similar to pictures snapped at public lynchings in the American South during the 1880s through the 1930s, typically featuring a naked mutilated body of a black man dangling from a tree. In the foreground of those pictures are townspeople milling about, or like the MPs at Abu Ghraib, grinning and pointing. Again the dynamic of scapegoating is clearly evident. "The lynching photographs were souvenirs of a collective action whose participants felt perfectly justified in what they had done" (Sontag 2004, 27). Indeed, the Abu Ghraib photographs were not taken to conceal the events but to document and share them, becoming trophies or as author Luc Sante (2004) observed in the age of accessible technology, "Here's-me-at-war.jpeg." It is that casualness in the face of abuse and torture that is disconcerting. Sontag compares American soldiers in Iraq to tourists, or as Defense Secretary Donald Rumsfeld put it: "running around with digital cameras and taking these unbelievable photographs and passing them off, against the law, to the media, to our surprise" (Sontag 2004, 42).

The photographs not only verify torture and abuse but also shame the U.S. government, its military, and Americans themselves. Perhaps that is the reason why there was so much concern to control the spin of the scandal. The government and military quickly unleashed the standard "bad apples" explanation to counter the realization that the extensive use of abuse and torture was systemic (*New York Times* 2004c). Adding to the long-term controversy over Abu Ghraib is the realization that those human rights abuses would be blamed solely on a handful of reservists featured in the photographs and not on high-level military officers. In light of that particular trajectory of blaming, there is reason to believe that the Pentagon along with the White House is perpetuating a culture of impunity in which ranking military leadership and key policy makers are immune from accountability and punishment. "Under Commander in Chief, George W. Bush, the notion of command accountability has been discarded. In Mr. Bush's world of war, it's the grunts who take the heat. Punishment is reserved for the people at the bottom. The people who foul up at the top get promoted. There was no wholesale crackdown on criminal behavior" (Herbert 2005a, A25).

The "few bad apples" explanation of Abu Ghraib has retained steady currency even as the scandal makes its way through a series of commissions, none of which are independent from the Defense Department. For example, the Church report, based on an investigation by Vice Admiral Albert Church III, concluded that only the lowest-ranking soldiers are to be held accountable, not their commanders or civilian overseers. Critics, however, note that it selectively ignores Bush's declaration that terrorists are not covered by the Geneva Conventions and that Iraq is part of the war against terror. The Church commission also ignored Rumsfeld's approval of interrogation techniques for Guantanamo Bay that violate Geneva Conventions and it glossed over the way military attorneys who were ordered to ignore their own legal opinions and instead adhere to Justice Department memos on how to make torture appear legal (Greenberg and Dratel 2005; Danner 2004). The Church report said, "none of the pictured abuses at Abu Ghraib bear any resemblance to approved policies at any level, in any theatre." Admiral Church and his investigators must have missed the pictures of prisoners in hoods, forced into stress positions and threatened by dogs. All of those techniques were approved at one time or another by military officials, including Mr. Rumsfeld. Curiously though, another investigation by former defense secretary, James Schlesinger, reported "both institutional and personal responsibility at higher levels" for Abu Ghraib. But the panel declined to name names. "Who will? Not the Pentagon, clearly" (*New York Times* 2005e, A22). The Senate Armed Services Committee plans additional hearings, but that's inadequate. Human rights advocates insist that Congress should open a serious investigation, but to date lawmakers have shown little interest (see Harbury 2005).

In a more recent acknowledgment of the degree of detainee abuse occurring in Iraq before and even during the Abu Ghraib investigation, three former members of the Army's elite 82nd Airborne Division say soldiers in their battalion at Camp Mercury near Falluja routinely beat and abused prisoners to help gather intelligence on the insurgency and to amuse themselves. One of the sources is Captain Ian Fishback, who presented some of his allegations in letters to top aides of two senior

Republicans. Fishback approached the Senators' offices only after he tried to report the allegations to his superiors for 17 months (Human Rights Watch 2005; Schmitt 2005). One sergeant said he was a guard and acknowledged abusing some prisoners at the direction of military intelligence personnel. Detainees were also stacked in human pyramids (fully clothed) and forced to hold five-gallon water jugs with outstretched arms or do jumping jacks until they lost consciousness. "We would give them blows to the head, chest, legs and stomach, and pull them down, kick dirt on them. This happened every day." The sergeant continued: "Some days we would just get bored, so we would have everyone sit in a corner and then make them get in a pyramid. This was before Abu Ghraib but just like it. We did it for amusement." (Schmitt 2005, A1, A6). The sergeant stated that he said he had acted under orders from military intelligence personnel to soften up detainees, whom the unit called PUCs (Persons Under Control) to make them more cooperative during formal interviews. "They wanted intel. As long as no PUCs came up dead, it happened." He added, "We kept it to broken arms and legs and shit." In one disclosure, a sergeant said he had seen a soldier break open a chemical light stick and beat the detainees with it. "That made them glow in the dark, which was real funny, but it burned their eyes, and their skin was irritated real bad" (Human Rights Watch 2005, 2).

> Soldiers referred to abusive techniques as "smoking" or "fucking" detainees, who are known as "PUCs," or Persons Under Control. "Smoking a PUC" referred to exhausting detainees with physical exercises (sometimes to the point of unconsciousness) or forcing detainees to hold painful positions. "Fucking a PUC" detainees referred to beating or torturing them severely. The soldiers said that Military Intelligence personnel regularly instructed soldiers to "smoke" detainees before interrogations.

> One sergeant told Human Rights Watch: "Everyone in camp knew if you wanted to work out your frustration you show up at the PUC tent. In a way it was sport . . . One day [a sergeant] shows up and tells a PUC to grab a pole. He told him to bend over and broke the guy's leg with a mini Louisville Slugger, a metal bat." (Human Rights Watch 2005, 2)

Even after the Abu Ghraib scandal became public, "We still did it, but we were careful," (Schmitt 2005, A6). Human Rights Watch (2005) pointed out that those accounts show that abuses resulted from civilian and military failures of leadership and confusion about interrogation standards and the application of the Geneva Conventions. Moreover, they contradict claims by the Bush team that detainee abuses by U.S. military abroad have been infrequent, exceptional, and unrelated to policy.

Prisoner Abuse in Afghanistan

The Pentagon persistently claims that prisoner abuse is not systemic or widespread but rather confined to a rowdy weekend at Abu Ghraib. Mounting evidence, however, demonstrates a very different reality. Reports from the war in Afghanistan indicate that some forms of abuse are more of a result of formal—and informal—policy in the war on terror (Human Rights Watch 2004; Priest and Gellman 2002; Rohde 2004). Consider the following incident:

> Even as the young Afghan man was dying before them, his American jailers continued to torment him. The prisoner, a slight, 22-year-old taxi driver known only as Dilawar, was hauled from his cell at the detention center in Bagram, Afghanistan, at around 2 A.M. to answer questions about a rocket attack on an American base. When he arrived in the interrogation room, an interpreter who was present said, his legs were bouncing uncontrollably in the plastic chair and his hands were numb. He had been chained by the wrists to the top of his cell for much of the previous four days.

> Within days after the two deaths in December 2002, military coroners determined that both had been caused by "blunt force trauma" to the legs. Soon after, soldiers and others at Bagram told the investigators that military guards had repeatedly struck both men in the thighs while they were shackled and that one had also been mistreated by military interrogators. (Golden and Van Natta 2005a, A12)

Even in the face of autopsy findings of homicide and statements by soldiers that two prisoners died after being struck by guards, military investigators initially recommended closing the case without bringing any criminal charges. The Army's Criminal Investigation Command reported to its superiors that it could not determine precisely who was responsible for the detainees' injuries and military lawyers concurred. "I could never see any criminal intent on the part of the M.P.s to cause the detainee to die," one of the lawyers, Maj. Jeff A. Bovarnick, told investigators, referring to one of the deaths. "We believed the M.P.'s story, that this was the most combative detainee ever" (Golden and Van Natta 2005b, A18.). The decision to close the case was among a series of apparent missteps in an Army inquiry that ultimately took nearly two years to complete but eventually resulted in criminal charges against seven soldiers. Documents indicate that crucial witnesses were not interviewed, reports and memos disappeared, and key pieces of evidence were mishandled. As the case was made public, in large part due to tireless investigative journalism, the *New York Times* commented: "President Bush said the other day that the world should see his administration's handling of the abuses at Abu Ghraib prison as a model of transparency and accountability. He said those responsible were being systematically punished, regardless of rank. It made for a nice Oval Office photo-op on a Friday morning. Unfortunately, none of it is true (*New York Times* 2005f, A18).

The horrific story of the deaths at Bagram confirms that what happened at Abu Ghraib was no aberration, but rather is part of a prevailing pattern. It shows the deep impact of the initial decision by Bush administrators that they were not going to observe the Geneva Conventions, or even U.S. law, for detainees captured in anti-terrorist operations. As the investigative file on Bagram reveals, mistreatment of prisoners was routine: "shackling them to the ceilings of their cells, depriving them of sleep, kicking and hitting them, sexually humiliating them and threatening them with guard dogs—the very same behavior later repeated in Iraq" (*New York Times* 2005f, A18.). Further evidence of systematic abusive tactics is the use of the "common peroneal strike," referring to a blow to the side of the leg just above the knee that can cause severe damage. The taxi driver, Dilawar, died after "blunt force injuries to the lower extremities" stopped his heart, according to the autopsy report (*New York Times* 2005f, A18; see Davey 2005; Weisman 2005).

Unlawful Enemy Combatants and Guantanamo Bay

Another controversial invention in the war on terror is the designation of unlawful enemy combatant. With that tactic at its disposal, the executive branch of the U.S. government claims to have the broad and robust authority to imprison individuals—including its citizens—even away from the battlefield. An appeals court, however, ruled in December 2003 that President Bush had exceeded his constitutional authority in detaining Jose Padilla, an American citizen whom the government contends is linked to Al Qaeda. Padilla stands accused of planning to detonate a radioactive "dirty bomb" in the United States and although he has not been formally charged, he remains imprisoned and virtually incommunicado in a South Carolina military brig. Whereas the Padilla case focuses on U.S. citizens captured off the battlefield, the debate over the government's pursuit of enemy combatants has far-reaching international significance. At the crux of the issue is Guantanamo Bay, located on the southeast tip of Cuba, where the United States has leased a compound for a military installation for more than 100 years. There the U.S. military holds more than 600 unlawful enemy combatants, many them captured in Afghanistan in the early phases of its war on terror following September 11. The U.S. government insists the detainees are terrorists affiliated with the Taliban or Al Qaeda and pose an imminent threat to national security. On those grounds, the United States contends that it has the authority to detain them indefinitely and some selected detainees are subject to military tribunals, not civilian criminal courts (Lewis 2004a).

Following years of intense legal wrangling, the U.S. Supreme Court in 2004 ruled on three overlapping cases challenging the government's authority over enemy combatants, including the use of indefinite detention and refusal to allow them access to federal courts. Declaring that "a state of war is not a blank check for the president," the High Court ruled that those deemed enemy combatants both in the United States and at Guantanamo Bay have the right to contest their detention before a judge or other neutral decision maker (Greenhouse 2004b, A1). In the case of Yasser Esam Hamdi, a U.S. citizen seized abroad, the court decided (8-1, Clarence Thomas dissenting) that his two-year detention at Guantanamo Bay either had been invalid from the beginning or had become so for statutory or constitutional reasons. Moreover, Hamdi has the right to use federal courts to argue that he is being held illegally (*Hamdi v. Rumsfeld*). In two other cases (*Rasul v. Bush and United States*), filed on behalf of 16 detainees at Guantanamo Bay, the Court also ruled (6-3) that noncitizens apprehended overseas during military operations could not be held without access to American courts. Finally, the Court concluded that it would not offer a ruling on *Rumsfeld v. Padilla*. The justices determined that Padilla had filed his case in the wrong court in New York and should refile his challenge in Federal District Court in South Carolina where he is being held.

Those rulings, however, did not end the legal battles over how the Bush administration applies the unlawful enemy combatant designation. In late 2004, federal judge Joyce Hens Green was still interested in scanning the limits of presidential power to detain enemy combatants and whether the White House satisfied the requirement laid out in the June (2004) U.S. Supreme Court decision to provide a justification for their detention acceptable to federal courts. In court, Green introduced a hypothetical case to Brian Boyle, a Justice Department lawyer: Could the president of the United States imprison "a little old lady from Switzerland" as an enemy combatant if she donated to a charity not knowing that her money was eventually used to finance the activities of Qaeda terrorists? After a long pause, Boyle responded: "Possibly." He then went on to explain that the enemy combatant definition "is not limited to someone who carries a weapon." Especially, given the global reach of the enemy combatant definition, Green pressed Boyle about the temporal scope of the war on terror and the application of the powers under the enemy combatant order: "When will they end?" To which Boyle said, "I wish I could give you an answer" (Lewis 2004b, A36.) There are other complications in the enemy combatant designation. Joseph Margulies, one of the lawyers who brought the case to Judge Green, said that the Combatant Status Review Tribunals "make a mockery of the commitment to due process" because the detainees cannot review much of the evidence against them because it is classified. Furthermore, most of the evidence used to justify the designation of someone as an enemy combatant is based on statements of the detainee himself, and such disclosures might have been obtained by torture (Lewis 2004b, A36).

In her decision, Green ruled against the Bush team, declaring that the detainees at Guantanamo Bay were clearly entitled to have federal courts examine whether they had been lawfully detained. Moreover, the judge also deemed unconstitutional the Combatant Status Review Tribunals; among other concerns she questioned whether some of the information used against detainees was obtained by torture and thus unreliable. Green concluded that the president overstepped his authority when he said Taliban fighters captured in Afghanistan were not entitled to the protection of the Geneva Conventions (Lewis 2005b). Also in 2005, Harry F. Floyd, a federal judge in South Carolina ruled the Bush had greatly overreached his authority by detaining Jose Padilla as an enemy combatant for nearly three years (since June 2002) without filing criminal charges. Floyd ordered the government to release Padilla within 45 days but left time for the Bush administration to file an appeal (Lewis 2005b, A14). However, in another major development, a three-judge panel of the U.S. Circuit Court of Appeals for the District of Columbia ruled unanimously that the Bush administration could resume tribunals at Guantánamo Bay which had been abruptly halted by a federal district judge in Washington, D.C. The appeals court said Congress had given the president all the authority he needed in a resolution passed just after September 11, 2001. The decision marks an enormous victory for the White House which had been charged with overstepping its powers.

Adding to the legal controversies over the enemy combatant designation, human rights organizations criticize the institutional conditions at Guantanamo Bay, issuing allegations of torture, abuse, and mistreatment against detainees. Former detainees have told the press that American soldiers at Guantanamo Bay beat and humiliated them, even holding guns to their heads during interrogations. Ex-detainees have said that some of those being held were chained and shackled for up to 15 hours at a time, fed food rations that were 10 years expired, and given foul water to drink. One prisoner reported that he was beaten after refusing to be injected with an unknown substance (Lewis 2004a; Tyler 2004; Waldman 2004). In May 2005, a high-level military investigation into accusations of detainee abuse at Guantanamo Bay concluded that "several prisoners were mistreated or humiliated, perhaps illegally, as a result of efforts to devise innovative methods to gain information," including acts in which female interrogators forcibly squeezed male prisoners' genitals (Lewis and Schmitt 2005, 35.) In memorandums that were never meant to be disclosed publicly, the FBI reported it had witnessed questionable interrogation methods. One agent observed: "On a couple of occasions, I entered interview rooms to find a detainee chained hand and foot in a fetal position to the floor, with no chair, food or water. Most times they had urinated or defecated on themselves and had been left there for 18, 24 hours or more" (A. Lewis 2005, EV1).

The abuse of detainee Mohamed al-Kahtani, a Saudi suspected of being the planned 20th hijacker on September 11, 2001, was logged in great detail. Kahtani was interrogated for as long as 20 hours at a stretch, and at one point he was put on an intravenous drip and given 3½ bags of fluid. Upon his request to urinate, guards told him to do so in his pants, which he did. FBI agents, reporting on the mistreatment of Kahtani, said a dog was used "in an aggressive manner to intimidate" him. According to the log, Kahtani's interrogator told him that he needed to learn, like a dog, to show respect: "Began teaching detainee lessons such as stay, come and bark to elevate his social status to that of a dog. Detainee became very agitated" (A. Lewis 2005, EV1).

Mistreatment of detainees is forbidden by three sources of law: the Geneva Conventions, the United Nations Convention Against Torture, and the Uniform Code of Military Justice that make cruelty, oppression, or maltreatment of prisoners a crime. Even armed services lawyers worried that some tactics might violate the Uniform Code and federal criminal statutes, exposing interrogators to prosecution. A Pentagon memorandum, obtained by ABC News, said a meeting of top military lawyers on March 8, 2003, concluded that "we need a presidential letter" approving controversial methods, to give interrogators immunity (A. Lewis 2005, EV1). Reports of abuse are consistent with those prepared by the International Red Cross and Physicians for Human Rights that state, "since at least 2002, the United States has been engaged in systematic psychological torture" at Guantanamo Bay (Lewis and Schmitt 2005, 35).

Critics argue that most of the more than 600 prisoners at Guantanamo Bay are not terrorists or unlawful enemy combatants. Rather, they are victims of bad luck to have been caught up on the chaotic aftermath of war during the fall of the Taliban (Lewis 2004b). Curiously, more than 100 detainees have been released, raising doubts over the U.S. government's claim that it is holding only the worst of the worst. Among those released after more than a year of confinement are three juveniles as young as 12 years of age. They were suspected of belonging to the Taliban even though they were not captured on the battlefield or carrying weapons. Other youths remain in custody at Guantanamo Bay and the U.S. military continues to capture and detain juveniles with scant justification (Gall 2004; Golden and Van Natta 2004).

Torture in the War on Terror

In December 2002, nearly a year and a half before the Abu Ghraib prison scandal broke in the media, Dana Priest and Barton Gellman for the *Washington Post* unveiled a front-page story involving questionable interrogation tactics used on terrorism suspects held by American authorities in secret overseas facilities. The story offers evidence that stress and duress techniques have become part and parcel to the war on terror.

Journalists describe clandestine detention units located in U.S.-occupied Bagram air base in Afghanistan where metal shipping containers hold those believed to be high level Al Qaeda operatives and Taliban commanders. Detainees who refuse to cooperate with CIA interrogators are sometimes kept standing or kneeling for hours, in black hoods or spray-painted goggles. Often detainees are forced into awkward, painful positions and deprived of sleep with a 24-hour bombardment of lights. "Those who cooperate are rewarded with creature comforts, interrogators whose methods include feigned friendship, respect, cultural sensitivity and, in some cases, money. Some who do not cooperate are turned over—'rendered,' in official parlance—to foreign intelligence services whose practice of torture has been documented by the U.S. government and human rights organizations" (Priest and Gellman 2002, A1).

Whereas the American government publicly denounces the use of torture, each of the current national security officials interviewed by the *Washington Post* defended the use of violence against captives as just and necessary. Moreover, they expressed confidence that the American public would back them. According to one official who has supervised the capture and transfer of accused terrorists: "If you don't violate someone's human rights some of the time, you probably aren't doing your job. I don't think we want to be promoting a view of zero tolerance on this. That was the whole problem for a long time with the CIA" (Priest and Gellman 2002, A1). Apparently, there seems to be considerable public support for torture. A CNN poll revealed that 45 percent of those surveyed would not object to having someone tortured if it would provide information about terrorism (Williams 2001). Dana Priest, one of the *Washington Post* reporters who exposed the use of torture, was asked why there's been so little follow-up in the rest of the media. "It's hard," Priest explained, "to keep a story going when there's no outrage, as in Congress—where there have been no calls for hearings" (Hentoff 2003a, 33).

Nevertheless, when the *Washington Post* story broke, human rights organizations wasted little time in confronting the government. Ken Roth, executive director of Human Rights Watch, responded to torture allegations by sending a firmly worded letter to the White House, insisting that the Bush administration must promptly investigate and address allegations of torture of suspected Al Qaeda detainees or risk criminal prosecution. Roth continued saying that he was "deeply concerned" by allegations made in the *Washington Post* that detainees had been subjected to torture or other forms of mistreatment while in U.S. custody in Afghanistan or while held by U.S. allies. "Torture is always prohibited under any circumstances," said Roth. "U.S. officials who take part in torture, authorize it, or even close their eyes to it, can be prosecuted by courts anywhere in the world" (Roth 2002, 1).

Aside from the psychological satisfaction that scapegoating delivers for those involved in — or endorsing — that form of displaced aggression, torture is ineffective and in the long run undermines legitimacy for a government striving to protect itself by any means necessary. "As a tool for collecting information, moreover, torture is notoriously ineffective (since people in pain have the unfortunate habit of lying to make it stop) and has done little to solve long-term security threats" (Press 2003, 16). Adding to the controversy, there is recent debate over the precise definition of torture. At the international level, the widely accepted definition is clearly laid out in *Article 1* of the *Convention Against Torture and Other Cruel, Inhuman or Degrading Treatment or Punishment* (1984):

> [T]he term "torture" means any act by which severe pain or suffering, whether physical or mental, is intentionally inflicted on a person for such purposes of obtaining from him or a third person information or a confession, punishing him for an act he or a third person has committed or is suspected of having committed, or intimidating or coercing him or a third person, or for any reason based on discrimination of any kind, when such pain or suffering is inflicted by or at the instigation of or with the consent or acquiescence of a public official or other person acting in an official capacity. It does not include pain or suffering arising only from, inherent in or incidental to lawful sanctions.

Since 9/11, however, the White House has developed it's own interpretation of the Convention Against Torture, raising grave concerns that political operatives are deliberately weakening the document that the United States ratified in 1994. In a memorandum by Jay S. Bybee, assistant attorney general for Alberto R. Gonzales, then White House Counsel and current attorney general, altered the meaning of the long-standing Convention Against Torture by arguing: "Physical pain amounting to torture must be equivalent in intensity to the pain accompanying serious injury, such as organ failure, impairment of bodily function, or even death" (Gonzales 2002; see Greenberg and Dratel 2005, 172; Danner 2004). Efforts by the White House to sidestep its obligations under the Convention Against Torture, in addition to the International Covenant on Civil and Political Rights ICCPR ratified in 1992 and key federal statutes that prohibit torture, worry the human rights community. Compounding matters, several government officials have publicly revealed that they endorse interrogation tactics that squarely fit into the ambit of torture. While being questioned by the Senate, Porter J. Goss, director of the CIA, was confronted by Senator John McCain (R-AZ) who had spent five years as a prisoner of war in Vietnam. When McCain asked Goss about the CIA's reported use of "waterboarding," in which a prisoner is made to believe that he will drown, Goss replied only that the approach fell into "an area of what I will call professional interrogation techniques" (Jehl 2005b, A11; see Herbert 2005b).

Events surrounding the capture and prosecution of John Walker Lindh, the so-called "American Taliban," suggest that the U.S. government not only engages in torture but goes to great lengths to conceal such violations. Persons close to the case believe that Lindh had been tortured. On June 12, 2002, in an evidence suppression hearing concerning the confession he had signed, Lindh was poised to "tell under oath, about how he signed the document only after being tortured for days by US soldiers." A federal district judge indicated he would allow Lindh, at trial, to put on the stand military officers and even Guantanamo detainees who were witnesses to or participated in his alleged abuse. The Pentagon communicated to the Justice Department that it wanted the suppression hearing blocked. Michael Chertoff, who was then head of the Justice Department's criminal division (and is now the director of Homeland Security), had the prosecution offer a deal. "All serious charges against Lindh—terrorism, attempted murder, conspiracy to kill Americans, etc.—would be dropped and he could plead guilty just to the technical charges of 'providing assistance' to an 'enemy of the U.S.' and of 'carrying a weapon.'" Eventually, Lindh accepted a stiff 20-year sentence but that was half of what he faced if convicted on two minor charges alone. As part of the deal, Lindh signed a statement swearing that he had "not been intentionally mistreated" by his captors and waiving any future right to claim mistreatment or torture. Chertoff also attached a "special administrative measure," essentially a gag order, barring Lindh from talking about his experience for the duration of this sentence" (Lindorff 2005, 6).

Other incidents of torture have been officially documented. In 2003, two army officers were handed career-ending punishments for staging mock executions of Iraqi prisoners. Mock executions, in which a prisoner is made to believe that his death is imminent, are clearly prohibited by the Army as a form of torture. In one of those cases, a U.S. captain, "took an Iraqi welder out to the desert and had him dig his own grave before staging an attempt to shoot him." The captain—who had been cited in a similar act of mock execution—was court-martialed, convicted of aggravated assault and battery and sentenced to 45 days' confinement and loss of $12,000 in pay (*New York Times* 2005g, A10). With the exception of a mere handful of cases in which U.S. soldiers are prosecuted for violating rules banning torture, there remain questions as to the extent of such cruelties and how involved are officials connected to the White House and the Pentagon, particularly in the realm of extraordinary renditions in which detainees are outsourced to a third party for purposes of torture.

In 1998, Congress passed legislation declaring that it is "the policy of the United States not to expel, extradite, or otherwise effect the involuntary return of any person to a country in which there are substantial grounds for believing the person would be in danger of being subjected to torture, regardless of whether that person is physically in the United States" (Mayer 2005, EV2). Despite clear prohibitions against such renderings, there is mounting evidence that the Bush administration has frequently and systematically violated the law (*New York Times* 2005h; Scheuer 2005; Shane, Grey, and Williams 2005). David Cole, professor of law at Georgetown University, opined: "We spent $73 million investigating President Clinton's affair with a White House intern and Whitewater, but we are unwilling even to empower an unbiased investigator to look into widespread allegations of torture and cruel, inhuman, and degrading treatment of hundreds of prisoners" (2005, 4; see Gearty 2005; Harbury 2005).

Conclusion

This chapter offers a close and critical look at several interlocking state crimes in the war on terror. Since 9/11, the U.S. government has launched a major war that is not only illegal but also continues to contribute to human rights violations on a mass scale, disproportionately affecting civilians. Among the drifting rationales that attempt to justify the American invasion and occupation of Iraq is the claim that the Pentagon is taking the war on terror to the terrorists. Terrorism experts, however, insist that the war in Iraq has worsened matters (Scheuer 2004; Clarke 2004, Danner 2005). Both the National Intelligence Council and the CIA, have determined that "the war in Iraq could provide an important training ground for terrorists, and the key factors behind terrorism show no signs of abating over the next 15 years" (Jehl 2005c, 4). Likewise, the prisoner abuse and torture scandals in Iraq and Afghanistan alongside the controversies at Guantanamo Bay have severely damaged the moral authority of the U.S. government, making it more difficult to recruit the degree of international cooperation necessary to contain terrorism.

Critical criminology provides a valuable framework to analyze state crimes in the war on terror, bridging existing international and domestic laws that prohibit detainee mistreatment and torture with deeper observations on the nature of unlawful government intervention. As the prevailing response to terrorism, war-making criminology not only perpetuates political violence but also sabotages basic principles of social justice that would otherwise improve prospects for peace. In that vein, Gregg Barak reminds us that a "codependent marriage" has developed between adversarial elites in the executive, legislative, and corporate suites of a state like the USA and in the various cells and extremist networks of terrorist organizations like Al Qaeda. In other words, as both seek to destroy each other, they may also find each other useful in the promotion of their own ends (2005, 135).

As the next chapters further demonstrate, the war on terror represents a massive government enterprise that is fraught with error and contradiction, producing measures that fail to protect the public and national security. Key among those developments is a pattern of scapegoating in which certain ethnic and religious groups are directly and indirectly blamed for September 11. Such realizations are important to recognize in light of critical criminology's interest in developing a victimology of state crime, which reaches beyond domestic populations to international ones as well (Kauzlarich et al. 2001; see Hamm 2005; Kramer and Michalowski 2005).

CHAPTER EIGHT

Claiming Effectiveness

Our investigators, sent after dangerous terrorists, came back with a motley crew of hapless innocents and people who had said and done stupid things but were hardly a threat to the nation's security.

—*New York Times,* 2004

You hear that there's more than 1,000 detainees, and if these cases are any example, you have to wonder if they're just locking people up to make it look like they are getting somewhere on their investigation.

—Attorney David Leopold, quoted in T. Lewin and A. L. Cowan,
"Dozens of Israeli Jews are being kept in federal detention,"
New York Times, 2001

A logical and reasonable method of assessing what works in counterterrorism is to examine recent outcomes of policies and practices, particularly in the realm of law enforcement and prosecution. In doing so, tangible evidence is uncovered, forming a basis for reality checks that assist in determining overall effectiveness (Welch 2004d). That approach to evaluation also invites close scrutiny into problems and errors, especially when the mistakes are so egregious that they erode public confidence in government and its capacity to protect citizens from threats of terrorism. Recent moves by some law enforcement officials have been nothing less than embarrassing, domestically and abroad. In the days following the March 11, 2004 train bombing in Madrid that killed 191 people and injured more than 2,000, Spanish authorities reached out to the FBI for assistance in identifying a set of fingerprints found on a plastic bag full of detonators. With near breakneck speed, the FBI claimed confidently that it had a match to the digital copy of the fingerprints, leading to the arrest and detention of a Portland-area immigration lawyer, Brandon Mayfield.

Fourteen days later, Mayfield was freed. Even as Spanish authorities raised deep questions about the FBI's fingerprint assessment, the Bureau had characterized the match as "100 percent." Unsealed court records indicate that the FBI never bothered to examine the original print while in Madrid on April 21 and pushed forward with an aggressive investigation of Mayfield, a 37-year-old Muslim convert who had previously represented a terrorism defendant in a custody case. Mayfield denies all FBI accusations that he had contact and associations with Islamic foundations that appear on a federal watch list. The government justified Mayfield's arrest on his attendance at a mosque that had been under FBI surveillance, a claim that infuriated Muslims grown tired of terrorist profiling campaigns aimed against them. "I'd be surprised if there's a mosque in the country that hasn't come under scrutiny these days. It has become the whole Kevin Bacon game—no Muslim is more than six degrees away from terrorism," said Ibrahim Hooper, spokesman for the Council on American-Islamic Relations (Kershaw and Lichtblau 2004a, A20; *New York Times* 2004e).

This chapter examines the war on terror as currently waged by the U.S. government. Unfortunately, there is a lot of bad news to report given the wealth of evidence pointing to seriously flawed operations along with poorly investigated cases. In contrast to the embarrassing no-fly incidents involving Mr. Islam (Cat Stevens) and Senator Kennedy, the consequences of many of the problems are not benign since those caught in the government's machinery suffer months—sometimes years—of detention in harsh conditions of confinement where they have been subject to harassment and abuse (Lipton 2005b). Moreover, in so many cases thus far, the suspects ultimately have been cleared of serious terrorism-related charges.

The purpose of the chapter is to provide straightforward evidence that the war on terror as waged by the Bush administration is not as effective as it claims. The discussion canvases numerous bungled and relatively insignificant cases that clearly do not live up to their billing as major achievements in fighting terrorism at home. Certainly, constraints on page length keep us from addressing all the problems undermining the war on terror[1]; nevertheless, several key cases, incidents, and developments offer ample opportunity to evaluate the general effectiveness of law enforcement and prosecution. The chapter concludes with more than just a passing thought that the current counterterrorist strategy—particularly at the helm of the Justice Department—contains many features resembling the failed war on drugs, offering a dreadful forecast as to where the war on terror is heading.

Bungled Cases in the War on Terror

Rather than delivering a resumé of well-investigated prosecutions of terror-related crimes, the war on terror, under the direction of Attorney General John Ashcroft, has produced "a mounting pile of bungled operations, ranging from merely inept to scandalously abusive, and military prisons filled with Afghans, Iraqis, and other Muslims who had committed no real offenses" (*New York Times* 2004d, A26). Indeed, Law professor David Cole, co-author of *Terrorism and the Constitution* (2002), reminds us that from 9/11 to year-end 2004, the Justice Department arrested and detained 5,000 persons but secured only one terrorist conviction, and that case, in Detroit, was overturned on appeal. While many of those arrests were accompanied by jolting press conferences intended to convince the public that the government was keeping us safe, the Justice Department understandably remains quiet as its suspects walk free (Cole 2004a).

The case in Detroit offers several tough lessons for the government. A month after September 11, Ashcroft heralded the arrests as the first of many successful takedowns of Al Qaeda. But even from the onset, that case was hobbled by nagging ambiguity. The Justice Department could not precisely identify what terrorist activity was being planned and never clearly linked the defendants to Al Qaeda, even though the government— bolstered by statements from President Bush—claimed to have thwarted "a sleeper operational combat cell" based in a dilapidated apartment. In lieu of compelling evidence of terrorist plans, prosecutors turned to what they called "casing materials" consisting of a pair of sketches and a videotape. The defense lawyers were never informed that other govern-ment terrorism experts did not consider those items to be "casing materi-als." Equally problematic, the government's expert witness, eager to gain a generous plea deal himself, later confessed to lying. After the appellate courts overruled the convictions, a much needed postmortum to look into what went wrong reveals key developments (*United States v. Koubriti* 2004, 2003).

A Justice Department internal memo obtained by the *New York Times* shows that prosecutors had their doubts from the beginning but pushed forward nevertheless. According to Barry Sabin, the department's coun-terterrorism chief: "We can charge this case with the hope that it will get better and the certainty that it will not get much worse" (Hakim and Lichtblau 2004, A1). The case, however, did get worse, leaving the Justice Department with a major public relations embarrassment. More than a year after the trial, the government repudiated its own case and found fault in virtually every aspect of its prosecution. Interestingly, the Jus-tice Department directed blame at its lead prosecutor, Richard G. Con-vertino, whom his superiors now call a "rogue lawyer." Nonetheless, top officials in the office of the Attorney General remained aware of Con-vertino's tactics during each step of the prosecution, from planning a strategy to preparing draft indictments to discussing how the defendants would be imprisoned (Hakim and Lichtblau 2004, A1).

The Detroit case was not only an example of overzealous prosecution but was marred further by numerous missteps and in-fighting at the De-partment of Justice. It strikes a blow to the Bush administration's preemp-tive strategy designed to disrupt terrorism plots before they can material-ize. Peter Margulies, professor of law at Rogers Williams University, said: "This case became a poster child for the Justice Department in the war on terrorism, and it had no institutional checks and balances in place to re-ally look hard at the evidence" (Hakim and Lichtblau, 2004, A32). Even a year after the arrests of Farouk Ali-Haimoud, Ahmed Hannan, Karim Koubriti, and Abdel Ilah Elmardoudi, the only charges that were filed against them were document fraud. Still, Ashcroft generated worldwide attention in a press conference on October 31, 2001, stating that the men were "suspected of having knowledge of the Sept. 11 attacks" before they happened. The statement spawned a significant round of news coverage but the claim was baseless; it also violated a gag order issued by the judge. The Justice Department retracted Ashcroft's statement two days later. Fol-lowing a nine-week trial, the government received a split decision. Two of the defendants were convicted of terrorism and document fraud charges and a third was convicted only of document fraud. The fourth, Ali-Haimoud was acquitted. Despite the relatively weak convictions, Ashcroft took center stage, hailing the verdict as "a clear message" that the government would "work diligently to detect, disrupt, and dismantle the activities of terrorist cells" (Hakim and Lichtblau 2004, A32).

On August 31, 2004, the Justice Department disclosed the findings of its court-ordered review of the Detroit case. The results were not pretty. Craig Morford, the U.S. attorney in Cleveland characterized the case as "a three legged stool" since it was built on shaky evidence and kept the defense in the dark over information that government possessed that could point to the innocence of the defendants. The prosecution, in the words of Morford, "created a record filled with misleading inferences" (Hakim and Lichtblau 2004, A32; Hakim 2004a). Terrorism charges against Hannan and Koubriti were dropped but the men remained in custody, facing a new trial on document fraud and deportation hearings. And in a move reeking of retaliation, Hannan and Koubriti also were charged with faking injuries in a 2001 car accident as part of a conspiracy to defraud an insurance company (*New York Times* 2004f, A37). During much of their detention, the defendants were kept in isolation for 23 hours a day, denied any reading materials, and verbally abused for being terrorist suspects. Koubriti said: "It was horrible, especially from some of the deputies—not all to be honest with you—I heard all sorts of stuff—devil worshipper, monster, go pray to your terrorist god" (Hakim 2004b, A16). Defense lawyer, James Thomas, insisted that someone in the government must be held accountable for the prosecution of the Detroit terrorism case: "To the extent these guys have been vindicated, maybe we should look at the people who bang that drum of fear. We as United States citizens were vulnerable to that fear, and it was played on fear" (Hakim and Lichtblau 2004, A32).

In another stinging defeat against the government in 2004, a federal jury in Boise, Idaho acquitted Sami Omar Al-Hussayen who prosecutors argued used his computer expertise to assist Muslim terrorists to raise funds and recruit followers. The case was significant in that it involved a key provision in the Patriot Act that makes it a crime to provide expert advice or assistance to terrorists. Prosecutors charged that Al-Hussayen, a doctoral candidate in computer science, developed websites that posted religious edicts justifying suicidal bombings. Al-Hussayen's denied accusations that he was involved in creating the material posted on websites, which his lawyer argued was protected by the First Amendment right to freedom of expression. The jury acquitted him on each of the three terrorism charges as well as one count of making a false statement and two counts of visa fraud. Jurors could not reach verdicts on three false-statement counts and five visa fraud counts, and a mistrial was declared on those charges. One juror, John Steger stated: "There was a lack of hard evidence. There was no clear-cut evidence that said he was a terrorist, so it was all on inference" (*New York Times* 2004g, A14). If convicted Al-Hussayen could have faced up to 15 years for each of the three terrorism charges, 25 years on each of the visa fraud charges, and 5 years on each charge of making false statements.

In January 2004, a federal judge in California ruled in a separate case that the provision of the Patriot Act under which Al-Hussayen was prosecuted violated First and Fifth Amendments; however, that ruling did not extend beyond the one case in California (*Humanitarian Law Project v. Ashcroft* 2004). In the California case, Judge Audrey B. Collins of the Federal District Court in Los Angeles ruled on behalf of humanitarian groups that planned to provide support to the nonviolent arms of two organizations designated as terrorist in Turkey and Sri Lanka. According to Judge Collins: "A woman who buys cookies at a bake sale outside her grocery store to support displaced Kurdish refugees to find new homes could be held liable" if the sale was sponsored by a group designated terrorist (Egan 2004, A16). The case against Al-Hussayen was eventually put to rest when the government agreed to throw out all remaining charges in return for his dropping an appeal of a deportation order (*New York Times* 2004h).

A case in Albany, New York, also brings to light other significant difficulties for prosecutors in terrorism-related trials, namely translations from foreign languages into English. Federal authorities arrested Yassin M. Aref and Mohammed M. Hossain after a year-long sting operation in which they were led to believe that a government informant was a terrorist recruiting the two men for an elaborate scheme involving laundering money from the sale of a shoulder-fire missile. The weapon was supposed to be used to strike a Pakistani diplomat in New York City. But early on, prosecutors acknowledged a possible flaw in a major piece of evidence. The Defense Department furnished prosecutors with a notebook listing Aref's name and address that was found in what the government said was a terrorist training camp in Western Iraq. The notebook written in Arabic included a message that allegedly referred to Aref as "commander." However, the word is Kurdish but written using the Arabic alphabet and might be inaccurately translated since the word for "commander" could also be interpreted as "brother." At the request of *The New York Times*, Nijyar Shemdin, U.S. representative for the Kurdistan Regional Government, reviewed the message and said he did not understand how a translation would arrive at the word "commander." Shemdin explained that Aref is referred to with the traditional honor, *kak*, which could mean brother or mister, depending on the degree of formality.

Aref's lawyer, Terence L. Kindlon, contended that the error was emblematic of what he saw as deeper problems with the government's case: "It looks to me like a two-bit frame-up. In 30 years of practicing law, I have come to expect high standards from government prosecutors. This thing is just shabby. I suspect that there is something political driving this" (Santora 2004, B8). Kindlon also reported that accusations against Aref, a Kurd, were false and that there was no independent verification that the note had been found in a terrorist training camp. His co-defendant, Hossain, became unwittingly involved after Aref asked him to bear witness to the transaction with the government informer. The conversations were videotaped and recorded; however, problems of accurate translation persist because their conversations with the informant were in Urdu as well as in Arabic and English (Santora 2004, B8).

The trial of Sheik Mohammed Ali Hassan al-Moayad in New York City also was plagued with problems for the prosecution, especially concerning its key witness, Mohamed Alanssi. That development greatly undermined the government's case and brings to light the dilemma of hiring paid informants in cracking alleged terrorist schemes. Alanssi is a former employee at the American Embassy in Yemen and was fired not once but twice, then left his country with a warrant out for his arrest. Still, federal authorities were willing to listen to him when he claimed that he could help them trap a major terrorist financier. In 2003, he arranged for a meeting in Frankfurt, Germany, with Sheik Mohammed Ali Hassan al-Moayad and an FBI agent posing as a former Black Panther interested in funneling millions of dollars to the jihad. Attorney General Ashcroft shared his enthusiasm for the case with lawmakers during a Congressional hearing in 2003, claiming that Sheik Moayad had donated $20 million for Osama bin Laden, much of it raised in Brooklyn. Looking back, it appears that the case against the Sheik was built heavily by Alanssi, a troubled man with a checkered past. Among his friends and associates, Alansi was well known for his appetite for fast cash, producing a long trail of unpaid bills and bounced checks. Once CI1, Alanssi's code name, secured his role as a paid informant for the FBI, he began demanding more dollars, often spinning sob stories about needing medication for his failing health.

> The question now casting a cloud over the case, lawyers say, is how much damage may have been done by the revelations about his past. Not the least of which is that the same prosecutors who were relying on Mr. Alanssi quietly filed federal charges against him when they learned that, despite having been paid $100,000 as an informer, he had continued writing bad checks. The bank fraud charges were filed in May [2004], while the internationally noted case in which he had been the main informer was moving toward trial. (Glaberson, Urbin, and Newman 2004, B4)

The secretly videotaped meeting in Frankfurt was planned in hopes that Sheik Moayad would make statements that could convince a jury that he "provided material support to terrorist organizations" as the charges eventually read. However, the session did not go particularly well since the Sheik appeared jittery and elusive as the supposed Black Panther pressed him for detailed information about future terrorist attacks on the United States. Asked if he knew of Islamic warriors in New York who might do battle against "the big Satan," Moayad replied, "We'll talk about this in its proper time" (Glaberson, Urbin, and Newman 2004, B4). The Sheik and his associate—and co-defendant—spoke Arabic and Alanssi translated to the FBI agent. But for all their planning, the tape recording was marred by several gaps. Defense attorneys argued that the gaps might have covered up statements made by the defendants "that may be extremely helpful to the defense" (Glaberson 2005a, B3).

For all those weaknesses with the case, nobody expected Alanssi's next move. On November 15, 2004, according to the police report: "a Middle Eastern man" approached a White House gate with a letter for President Bush. "After a conversation with Secret Service officers, the subject pulled a lighter from his jacket pocket and ignited his jacket" (Glaberson, Urbin, and Newman 2004, B4). Alanssi was hospitalized, suffering severe burns over 30 percent of his body. Despite that shocking incident, the trial of Sheik Moayad remained on schedule although prosecutors decided against having their star witness, Alanssi, testify. As the trial began, the case was pared-down considerably, barely resembling the big fish story spun by Ashcroft. Allegations about Al Qaeda and ties to bin Laden faded in importance, and U.S. attorneys did not mention the supposed $20 million delivery to bin Laden. Prosecutors focused on the Sheik's connections to

Hamas, a group the United States has designated as terrorist but also has charitable operations. One of the lawyers defending the Sheik told reporters: "This is a bad case that should be dropped. They know it should be dropped because they started it because of his alleged connections to bin Laden and they now know he has none" (Glaberson 2005b, B8). Jonathan Marks who represented the Sheik's assistant, Mohammed Mohsen Yahya Zayed, believes that the prosecutors were stuck with a case the promised more than it could deliver: "It is very important for the Bush administration to show that they are winning the war on terrorism. Attorney General Ashcroft billed this case as a case against a major financier of Al Qaeda. There is no evidence of that at all" (Glaberson 2005b, B8).

After a five-week trial featuring a series of dramatic developments, the jury found the Sheik and his assistant guilty of conspiring to support Al Qaeda and other charges. Federal prosecutors hailed the victory as an example of a successful campaign in the war on terror that applied traditional law enforcement methods to new targets. "Money is the lifeblood of terrorism," announced Roslynn Mauskopf, U.S. attorney (Glaberson 2005c, B6). By contrast, William H. Goodman, the Sheik's defense lawyer, told reporters: "This is a prosecution that was designed and carried out in a way that played upon the worst possible fears of the public," adding that the verdict was an injustice that "can only strengthen the evil people in this world to perpetuate more terrorism" (Glaberson 2005c: B6). The Sheik faces up to 75 years in prison and Zayed could be sentenced to serve up to 45 years.

Despite the apparent "victory" in the case against Sheik Moayad, there remain crucial legal tactics adopted by prosecutors that defense attorneys complain are unethical since they stray from their intended purpose. Consider, for example, the controversy over the misuse of the material witness statute. Rather than clearly determining probable cause—a requirement for detention—federal authorities resort to employing the material witness statute in cases where there is only mere suspicion of criminal activity however flimsy the evidence. Dating back to the early days of the republic, the government has used the material witness statute to ensure that individuals with important information about a crime do not disappear before testifying. But since 9/11, the government has interpreted that statute in a profoundly new way. In many instances involving suspected terrorist activity, material witnesses are not called on to testify against others but rather charged with crimes themselves. Material witnesses are not granted constitutional protections afforded criminal suspects. They are not informed of their Miranda rights, do not always have prompt access to lawyers, and are subjected to long—and harsh—detention. Federal authorities recognize the danger of misusing the material witness statute and insist that it must be applied judiciously. Still, legal experts contend that U.S. attorneys understate the magnitude of potential violations of due process. Ronald L. Carlson, law professor at the University of Georgia describes such a quandary in post-9/11 America: "The law was designed to hold Mr. A, the material witness, to testify about a crime committed by Mr. B, the suspect. Now they are locking up Mr. A as a material witness to the crime of Mr. A. The notion is 'we'll hold him until we develop probable cause to arrest him for a crime" (Liptak 2004a, A20).

Human Rights Watch (2004) together with the American Civil Liberties Union issued a study outlining the misuse of the material witness statute in the war on terror. The report shows that since September 11, fifty-seven people have been detained as material witnesses in a terrorism investigation. Of those, eighteen were charged with a crime unrelated to terrorism, seven were charged with a terrorism-related crime, and two were designated enemy combatants. Thirty of those material witnesses faced no criminal charges. Defense attorneys note that many material witnesses are detained even though they are willing to testify voluntarily but the government insists that many of them still pose a flight risk and must be held. There also remain ethnic and religious disparities evident in how the statute is applied since all but one of the fifty-seven detentions involved Muslims (Human Rights Watch 2004). "Now everyone who has any conceivable Middle Eastern tie is considered to be a flight risk. That's never been the case before. It's become a very popular device for rounding people up. It's a systemic weapon used against an ethnically identifiable group. It's a holding device," says Randall Hamud, an attorney representing three material witnesses (Liptak 2004a, A20).

Scanning recent cases brings to light some of the significant difficulties plaguing the government's pursuit of prosecuting defendants charged with terrorism and terrorism-related offenses (also see Landler 2004; *New York Times* 2004i). At the heart of much of the criticism aimed at the Justice Department is the leadership of Attorney General John Ashcroft, who stepped down from his post at the end of 2004. The record shows that Ashcroft expressed little interest in counterterrorism before the attacks of September 11. In fact, his May 2001 memo outlining the strategic priorities for the Department of Justice did not include an item on terrorism. When asked about that lack of formal interest in battling terrorism, Ashcroft snapped back at the 9/11 Commission by shifting blame—a hot potato—to the Clinton administration, along with a personal attack against one of the panelists, Jamie S. Gorelick, who worked in the Justice Department during the Clinton years (National Commission on Terrorist Attacks Upon the United States 2004). Observers note that Ashcroft employed two tactics to deflect criticism of his tactics in the war on terror, grandstanding and secrecy. In his farewell speech to his staff at the Justice Department, Ashcroft boldly proclaimed: "For three years, terrorists have not struck at American because you and people who work with you in this law enforcement community have not let them" (*Village Voice* 2004, 24).

Interestingly, when Jose Padilla, the so-called "dirty bomber" was arrested in May 2002 there was no public announcement by the Justice Department. However, on June 6, 2002, FBI agent Colleen Rowley unleashed damning testimony to Congress about failures in counterterrorism investigations in the year leading up to the attacks. Four days later, Ashcroft issued a dramatic press conferencing, announcing the capture of Padilla (Krugman 2004b). As the Justice Department braced itself for public grilling over its endorsement of abusive interrogation tactics and torture detailed in a department memo, Ashcroft called another press conference to announce the arrest of a Somali, whom the government contended had plans to bomb a shopping mall in Ohio (Johnston 2004). However, "there was no evidence of any confederates or weapons, or even a plot, but people in Ohio were treated to days of debate about whether it was safe to go shopping anymore" (*New York Times* 2004d, A26). From the beginning, columnist Paul Krugman remained skeptical of the arrest, accusing Ashcroft of grandstanding: "The timing was, I'm sure purely coincidental" (2004b: A23). When Ashcroft announced his resignation, the *New York Times* opined: "The next attorney general will have to tackle the great undiscussed failing of Mr. Ashcroft's Justice Department: its ineffectiveness. The investigation and prosecution of domestic terrorism cases have produced little since 9/11 except dismissed charges, misidentified suspects and minor convictions of minor figures" (*New York Times* 2004j, A32; see Hentoff 2004a).

In addition to hyping the war on terror, critics fault Ashcroft for his compulsive grip on secrecy. Throughout his tenure, Ashcroft frustrated civil liberties organizations, the media, and members of Congress with his unwillingness to share even basic information about who the government had taken into custody and why. As the following section illustrates, government secrecy poses grave threats to democracy and undermines the legitimacy of counterterrorism tactics.

Government Secrecy

Contributing to a host of problems driving bungled operations, ethnic profiling, and the misuse of detention is the government's policy of secrecy in its war on terror (Dow 2001). Months following the investigation of the attacks on the World Trade Center and the Pentagon, Attorney General Ashcroft repeatedly denied access to information about many of those in detention, including their names and current location. Such secrecy has been denounced by human rights and civil liberties advocates as well as by news organizations. Even some political leaders have complained that Ashcroft failed to explain adequately the need for those drastic measures. Kate Martin, director of the Center for National Security Studies, said: "The rounding up of hundreds of people secretly, secretly arresting them and putting them in jail where their families don't know where they are and not telling the public is unprecedented and extraordinary in this country"(Donohue 2001, EV1). Martin added: "This is frighteningly close to the practice of 'disappearing' people in Latin America" where secret detentions were carried out by totalitarian regimes (Williams 2001, 11). An attorney for three other men held in detention in San Diego likened their detention to the sweeps for communists and sympathizers during the Red Scare of the 1920s; he complained that he was not even told where his clients were being held and was not permitted to contact them (Fox 2001). Harvey Grossman of the ACLU added: "There's been nothing as massive as this since the day after Pearl Harbor, when they rounded up 700 Japanese immigrants and held them incommunicado and without charges for a protracted period" (*Chicago Tribune* 2001, EV2).

Reports that detainees have been subjected to solitary confinement without being criminally charged as well as being denied access to telephones and attorneys raises questions about whether detainees are being deprived of due process. Moreover, those deprivations clearly contradict assurances by the Department of Justice that everyone arrested since September 11 has access to counsel. Key members of Congress have begun to challenge the sweeps of aliens in search of terrorists. Seven Democrats, most notably a co-author of Ashcroft's anti-terror legislation, Senate Judiciary Committee Chairman Patrick Leahy (Vt.), and the only senator to vote against it, Russ Feingold (Wis.), requested from the attorney general detailed information on the more than 1,200 people detained since the terror attacks. Specifically, the lawmakers asked for the identity of all those detained, the charges against them, the basis for holding those cleared of connection to terrorism, and a list of all government requests to seal legal proceedings, along with the rationale for doing so. Lawmakers stated that while the officials "should aggressively investigate and prevent further attacks," they stressed the Justice Department's "responsibility to release sufficient information . . . to allow Congress and the American people to decide whether the department has acted appropriately and consistent with the Constitution" (Cohen 2001, EV1).

Similarly, human rights groups have railed the Justice Department for operating a war on terror behind a thick wall of secrecy, a tactic that "reflects a stunning disregard for the democratic principles of public transparency and accountability" (Human Rights Watch 2002b, 5; Lawyers Committee for Human Rights 2003; Welch 2004b). The government puts forth an effort to shield itself from public scrutiny by concealing information that is crucial to determining the extent to which its investigations have been conducted in accordance with the law. Civil liberties advocates also take strong exception to the government's attempt to silence criticism of its anti-terrorist efforts, most notably with Ashcroft's infamous statement to Congress: "To those who scare peace-loving people with phantoms of lost liberty, my message is this: your tactics only aid terrorists, for they erode our national unity and diminish our resolve. They give ammunition to America's enemies, and pause to America's friends. They encourage people of goodwill to remain silent in the face of evil" (Ashcroft 2003).

Legal experts strongly urge the government to amend its tactics in the war on terror so that its actions may be subject to public scrutiny, thus averting civil rights violations. Three areas of accountability are recommended. First, the Justice Department must release information about those it detains, including their names and location. Secret detentions such as those used by the Justice Department in its anti-terrorism campaign violate the *Declaration on the Protection of All Persons from Enforced Disappearances,* a non-binding resolution by the United Nations General Assembly in 1992. Second, independent monitoring groups must be granted unrestricted access to detention facilities so as to ensure that detainees are treated in a fair and humane manner. "Such scrutiny is particularly important when dealing with foreigners who for reasons of language, lack of political clout, difficulty retaining counsel, and unfamiliarity with the U.S. justice system may be more vulnerable to violations of these rights" (Human Rights Watch 2003, 23). Third, immigration proceedings must no longer be conducted in secrecy. Open hearings have been the practice at the INS for nearly 50 years, a tradition that is consistent with U.S. constitutional law (Cole 2003b; Cole and Dempsey 2002).

In a major blow to civil rights initiatives aimed at striking down the government's use of secret detention, a federal appeals court, in 2003, ruled 2-1 that the Justice Department was within its rights when it refused to release the names of the more than 700 people rounded up in the aftermath of the 9/11 attacks. The case stemmed from a campaign by civil liberties groups asserting that the Freedom of Information Act required the Justice Department to disclose the names of those detained on immigration charges. Moreover, such secrecy invites abuse since law enforcement officials are stripped of their accountability. The ruling will likely be appealed, setting the stage for another confrontation over secrecy and the war on terror.

In so many ways, Ashcroft's obsession with secrecy mirrors—and arguably stems from—the White House's overly guarded sense of political privacy, or what Vice President Dick Cheney calls a "zone of autonomy" (Greenhouse 2004a, 16). Whereas presidents and their staff have always worked in confidential circles outside the reach of public scrutiny, the degree to which the Bush administration operates in secret is unprecedented (*New York Times* 2003b; Phillips 2004). The following items are some significant examples of an executive lockdown on information about which citizens have the right to know. Nine days after taking office, Bush requested a study group to propose a national energy policy and appointed Cheney to head it. Despite complaints that corporations were driving energy policy behind closed doors, the panel operated in complete secrecy, offering recommendations to the president, which he accepted (Lewis 2003). In 2003, Bush signed an executive order that will delay the release of millions of government documents, making it easier for presidents and their administrations to keep historical records secret (Bumiller 2003; also see Stolberg and Lee 2004; Wiener 2004). In reconstructing post-war Iraq, corporations are caught in a classic Catch-22 since federal law requires all publicly traded companies to be forthcoming with investors about significant business developments. "The contracts, though, have been handled with such secrecy that many executives say they are wary of talking about their companies role for fear of alienating the agencies and thus losing out on the most ambitious reconstruction effort since the Marshall Plan in Europe after World War II" (Henriques 2003, C1).

As the National Commission on Terrorist Attacks Upon the United States worked strenuously to gather as much information on the attacks as possible, the White House stonewalled their investigation. The Bush administration initially opposed the formation of the panel but eventually caved in to public opinion. Bush said that although he and his staff were cooperating with the commission, he stopped short of handing over intelligence documents. The White House also refused to declassify a crucial 28-page chapter of a Congressional report that centers on accusations about Saudi Arabia's role in financing the hijackers (Johnston and Jehl 2003; see also O'Brien 2003). The 9/11 Commission, which had already issued a subpoena to the Federal Aviation Administration for withholding documents pertinent to its investigation, threatened legal action against the Bush administration (*International Herald Tribune* 2003a; *New York Times* 2003c). Eventually a deal was struck that allowed the Bush team to edit documents before releasing them to the commission. Two Democratic members of the 10-member bi-partisan panel objected, demanding that the commission have full access to the Oval Office summaries, known as Presidential Daily Briefs (PDBs). Those two panelists insist that the White House should not have been permitted to determine what is relevant to the investigation. Timothy J. Roemer, a Democrat from Indiana, said he was concerned that the commission was allowing the Bush administration to remove items that could be viewed as "smoking guns." The Family Steering Committee, a group led by many advocates who were most responsible for pressing Congress to create the Commission, released a statement criticizing the agreement to allow the White House to edit documents, saying that it would "prevent a full uncovering of the truth and is unacceptable" (Shenon 2003b, 24; *New York Times* 2004j).

The White House's penchant for secrecy most notably in the war on terror also extends to the FBI and the CIA. In 2003, the FBI opened an internal ethics investigation to find out whether its agents abused their authority by seizing from a news organization documents on international terrorism. The incident raises the prospect of serious First Amendment violations by government officials (Lichtblau 2003d). Although CIA Director George Tenet promised Congress that he would provide the names of agency officials responsible for one of the most glaring intelligence mistakes leading up to the 9/11 attacks, that disclosure has not been forthcoming. In a startling revelation, the CIA waited 20 months before placing on a federal watch list two suspected terrorists who served as hijackers. Congressional investigators reported: "Had the information about the two hijackers [Khalid al-Midhar and Nawaq Alhazmi] been promptly relayed to other agencies, the government might have been able to disrupt, limit or possibly even prevent the terrorist attacks" (Gerth 2003, A25; also see Jehl 2004a).

In his book, *Worse Than Watergate: The Secret Presidency of George W. Bush,* John Dean—former counsel to President Nixon—delivers harsh criticism at the White House for its unrelenting secrecy. While describing an array of events that expose in detail how the Bush administration has tightened its grip on the control of information, Dean puts forth a series of arguments condemning government secrecy: (1) secrecy is undemocratic; (2) secrecy threatens liberty; (3) secrecy precludes public accountability; (4) secrecy alienates; (5) secrecy negatively affects character; (6) secrecy is dangerous; (7) secrecy encourages incompetence (2004, 185–188). It is with the final caveat that we are reminded that when mistakes are easily concealed, there is little interest in operating carefully. Perhaps that is why the White House has waged a war against terror in which much of the government's activities are shrouded by secrecy. In doing so, the administration can cover up its mistakes and avoid having to play the blame game in which it would still resort to passing the hot potato (see Clymer 2003; Lott and Wyden 2004).

Lessons from the War on Drugs

The war on terror, even in its early stages, is strikingly similar to another sweeping criminal justice campaign, namely the war on drugs. Both strategies are intricately linked to race/ethnicity and produce an array of civil liberties violations, compounded by unnecessary detention and incarceration (Talvi 2003b; Welch 2005a, 2004a, 1999a). Equally important is evidence that raises serious concerns over effectiveness, alongside patterns of wasteful spending. While the war on drugs has succeeded in locking up unprecedented numbers of poor people who are disproportionately black or Latino, it has failed to reduce consumption of illegal and legal drugs (Husak 2002; Welch, Bryan, and Wolff 1999). Similar doubts suggest that the current campaign against terrorism also is capturing small fries rather than big fish.

Professor David Burnham, director of the Transactional Records Access Clearinghouse at Syracuse University, released a report showing that the war on terror and its reliance on ethnic profiling have produced small-scale success (TRAC 2003). That study found a large proportion of so-called terrorist prosecutions involve minor charges (e.g., document fraud, identification theft, threats, and immigration violations), resulting in jail sentences of only a few months. In the year after the attacks on the World Trade Center and Pentagon, prosecution of crimes connected with terrorism increased tenfold to 1,208 cases from 115 the previous year. But the sentences dropped significantly, from a median of nearly two years in 2001 to just two months in 2002. Senator Patrick Leahy weighed into the matter, saying: "It raises questions about whether too many resources are being tied up on minor cases that have nothing to do with terrorism" (Lichtblau 2003e, A16; see Lichtblau 2003f).

Contributing to growing skepticism, the General Accounting Office (2003) found that federal prosecutors inflated their success in terrorism-related convictions in 2002 by wrongly classifying almost half of them. Overall, 132 of the 288 convictions reported as international or domestic terrorism (or terrorism related hoaxes) were determined by investigators to have been wrongly classified (see *New York Times* 2003b). Similar problems have been discovered in New Jersey where prosecutors report handling 62 "international terrorism" indictments in 2002. However, all but two of those cases involved Middle Eastern students accused of hiring imposters to take standardized English exams for them. Nearly all of the accused students were released on bail pending trial while nine of them already have been convicted, fined between $250 and $1,000, and deported (Associated Press 2003b).

As has been the experience with the war on drugs, the government's fight against terrorism promises to be a long-term commitment, demanding vast resources and steady funding. With the lessons of a failed drug control policy in clear view, it is crucial that the government curb its tendency of blaming ethnic and religious minorities for problems associated with terrorism (Marable 2003; Robin 2003). Moreover, citizens ought not accept the false paradigm that diminished civil liberties is the price to pay for public safety (Ratner 2003). Indeed, rather than weakening national security, protection of civil liberties is symbolic of a strong democratic government. As Supreme Court Justice Louis D. Brandeis wrote in 1927, the framers of the U.S. Constitution knew that "fear breeds repression; that repression breeds hate; [and] that hate menaces stable government" (*Whitney v. California* 1927; see Human Rights Watch 2003, 2002b; Lawyers Committee for Human Rights 2003).

Conclusion

The war on terror continues to be politicized not only for election purposes but also to serve as a form of public relations hyping the government's claim that it is protecting Americans against terrorism. This chapter offers abundant evidence that the Bush administration has issued false claims of effectiveness. There has yet to emerge any compelling proof that the government has captured, prosecuted, and convicted large numbers of so-called terrorist king pins, contrary to multiple press conferences and speeches by Bush, Ashcroft, and Homeland Security Director Tom Ridge. In lieu of such success the government is left with a sad litany of bungled operations and cases that simply fell apart or backfired altogether, hardly the kind of law enforcement record worth bragging about (Cole, 2004; Krugman, 2004b; *New York Times* 2004d). Nevertheless, there are many dedicated investigators and counterterrorism experts within government who remain committed to their duty of public safety and national security, especially since the risk of terrorism is very real. Regrettably, however, when those employees complain publicly about egregious errors and mismanagement, they face the wrath of their superiors. Consider the case of Sibel Edmonds, a contract linguist who was dismissed by the FBI in 2002. Edmonds accused the Bureau of ineptitude by producing slipshod and incomplete translations of intelligence and that it did not aggressively investigate her claims of espionage against a co-worker (Lichtblau 2004c).

Issues surrounding the Edmonds' case are particularly troubling in three fundamental areas: vulnerabilities for the FBI; its ability to translate precisely sensitive counterterrorism evidence; and its treatment of internal whistle-blowers. In response to the Edmonds' case, the Justice Department predictably adhered to the Bush administration's well-established tactic of stonewalling, declaring details of her case to be a matter of "state secrets" (Lichtblau 2004c, A1). The Department of Justice has blocked Edmonds from testifying in a lawsuit brought by families of 9/11 victims. Furthermore, the Department has retroactively classified Congressional briefings given in 2002, and it has classified the Inspector General's entire report on its investigation into the case (also see Files 2005; Lichtblau 2004a; *New York Times* 2005a).

The problem with accurately translating materials containing information on terrorism persists. Three years after 9/11, more than 120,000 hours of potentially valuable terrorism-related recordings have not yet been translated by linguists at the FBI. Compounding matters, computer malfunctions have led to the erasing of some Al Qaeda audio recordings. Glenn A. Fine, inspector general for the Department of Justice, reported that the FBI still lacked the capacity to interpret all the terrorism-related evidence contained in wiretaps and other sources; moreover, the influx of new material continues to outpace the bureau's resources. Al Qaeda messages stating "Tomorrow is about to begin" and "The match is about to begin" were intercepted by the National Security Agency on September 10, 2001, but not translated until days after the attacks (Lichtblau 2004d, A1). The inspector general also learned that linguists for the FBI are supposed to undergo proficiency examinations but that requirement has been ignored, raising obvious concerns over the accuracy of translations. Congress has been vocal in criticizing the FBI for its ineptitude. "What good is taping thousands of hours of conversations of intelligence targets in foreign languages if we cannot translate promptly, securely, accurately, and efficiently?" asked Vermont Democratic Senator Patrick Leahy (Lichtblau 2004d, A22). Senator Charles Grassley, a Republican from Iowa, also weighed into the controversy: "Since terrorists attacked the United States on 9/11, the FBI has been trying to assure the Congress and the public that its translation program is on the right track. Unfortunately, this report shows that the FBI is still drowning in information about terrorism activities with hundreds of thousands of audio yet to be translated" (Lichtblau 2004d, A22; also see Scheuer 2004; Janofsky 2005; Weiser 2004).

Of course, the problems facing the war on terror discussed in this chapter are limited to those that have been brought to light by way of investigative journalism and audits conducted by inspectors general. It is difficult to know with any certainty just how bad the situation really is, especially since the government goes to great lengths to conceal errors, mismanagement, and poor decision-making in the realm of law enforcement and prosecution. As the next chapter demonstrates, there are a host of other problems in the way the government fights its war on terror, most notably policies and tactics that undermine civil liberties.

CHAPTER NINE

Assaulting Civil Liberties

The world has become a very dangerous place to live. We are winning the
war against terrorism . . . [and] respecting civil rights at the highest level
possible.

> —Attorney General John Ashcroft, quoted in A. Cowell, "Ashcroft,
> upbeat on Iraq, aims at corruption," *New York Times,* 2004

It appears that we are being transformed from an information society to
an informant society. Do the math. One tip per day per person and within
a year the whole country will be turned in, and we can put up a big fence
around the country and we'll be safe.

> —U.S. Congressman Dennis Kucinich, quoted in B. Berkowitz,
> "AmeriSnitch," *The Progressive,* 2002

Numerous legal scholars and civil liberties advocates remind us
that in an atmosphere of fear, the government embarked on
legislation that has dramatically altered the legal landscape
of post-9/11 America (Cole and Dempsey 2002; Gross 2003; Hentoff
2003c). So much so that many constitutionally protected rights hang in

the balance of decision making over how to enforce newly enacted provisions in the war on terror. As pointed out in previous chapters, the Justice Department—backed by the Patriot Act—has recklessly resorted to the round-ups, detentions, and deportations of Middle Eastern men who have no ties to terrorism. Consequently, those actions do not contribute to public safety or national security since no one is better off by arresting and detaining innocent people. Few in Congress openly questioned the dangers of the Patriot Act. The 342-page bill was complex and hastily written. There was virtually no public hearing or debate over the sweeping nature of the bill and it was accompanied by neither a conference report nor committee report. The House of Representatives passed it by a vote of 356 to 66. In the Senate, Russell Feingold of Wisconsin was the only senator to vote against the Patriot Act. In his memorable dissent, Feingold warned:

> Of course, there is no doubt that if we lived in a police state, it would be easier to catch terrorists. If we lived in a country that allowed the police to search your home at any time for any reason; if we lived in a country that allowed the government to open your mail, eavesdrop on your phone conversations; if we lived in a country that allowed the government to jail indefinitely based on what they write or think, or based on mere suspicion that they are up to no good, then the government would no doubt discover and arrest more terrorists. But that probably would not be a country in which we would want to live. And that would not a country for which we could, in good conscience, ask our young people to fight and die. In short, that would not be America. Preserving our freedom is one of the main reasons that we are now engaged in this war on terror. We will lose that war without firing a shot if we sacrifice the liberties of the American people. (2001; see Brill 2003)

As this chapter reveals, the Patriot Act—along with a host of counterterrorism tactics—poses grave threats to civil liberties since its broad ambit also has the potential to criminalize protest activities and stifle dissent. Examined here are several recent developments that warrant careful consideration as to where the war on terror is leading, and the deep impact it is having on a free society. The discussion begins with a critical survey of the USA Patriot Act, including concerns pertaining to fundamental civil liberties and freedoms guaranteed under the Constitution and its Bill of Rights.

Controversies over the USA Patriot Act

In her sharp and concise critique of the war on terror, Nancy Chang (2002) of the Center for Constitutional Rights focuses on three controversial aspects of the Patriot Act. First, that law jeopardizes First Amendment rights to speech and political associations by producing a broad new crime of "domestic terrorism" and denies entries of foreign nationals on the basis of ideology. Second, the act further undermines privacy, granting the government enhanced powers of surveillance. Finally, the Patriot Act erodes due process rights of noncitizens by permitting the government to use mandatory detention and removal on the basis of their political activities that have been recently recast as terrorist activities (see American Civil Liberties Union 2005, 2003a).

In the first area of concern, Section 802 of the Patriot Act creates a federal crime of "domestic terrorism" that widely extends to "acts dangerous to human life that are a violation of the criminal laws" if they "appear to be intended . . . to influence the policy of a government by intimidation or coercion," and if they "occur primarily within the territorial jurisdiction of the United States" (Section 802). Like many features of the Patriot Act, that section is vague and sweeping in scope; hence, it enables federal law enforcement agencies to place under surveillance and investigate political activists and organizations that protest government policies. In effect, the act allows the government to criminalize legitimate political dissent. Chang (2002) points out that confrontational protests are by their very nature acts that "appear to be intended . . . to influence the policy of a government by intimidation or coercion." Even instances of civil disobedience—including those that do not result in injuries or are entirely nonviolent—could be interpreted as "dangerous to human life" and "in violation of the criminal laws." Protestors that engage in direct action, such as environmentalists, anti-abortionists, and anti-globalization activists risk being arrested as "domestic terrorists," should prosecutors find their dissent particularly disruptive (see Welch 2000a, 1999b; Welch and Bryan 1998, 1997).

Similar clampdowns on unpopular politics are found in Section 411 of the Act that produce an ideological test for entry into the United States. According to that section, representatives of a political or social group "whose public endorsements of acts of terrorist activity the Secretary of State has determined undermines United States efforts to reduce or eliminate terrorist activities" can be denied entry to the country. The section echoes the McCarran-Walter Act (1952), which, dating back to the Cold

War, allowed the State Department to bar entry to foreign speakers based on their political beliefs. It was repealed in 1990 on the grounds that it abridged the First Amendment rights of U.S. citizens to hear controversial speakers. In a turnabout, Section 411 also bars noncitizens who have used their "position of prominence within any country to endorse or espouse terrorist activity," a determination made solely by the Secretary of State with virtually unchecked authority (Brown 2003; Chang 2002). The Patriot Act also unleashes a three-pronged attack on privacy, a freedom that many Americans take for granted.

> First, the act grants the executive branch unprecedented, and largely unchecked, surveillance powers, including the enhanced ability to track e-mail and Internet usage, conduct sneak-and-peek searches, obtain sensitive personal records from third parties, monitor financial transactions, and conduct nationwide roving wiretaps.
>
> Second, the act permits law enforcement agencies to circumvent the Fourth Amendment's requirement of probable cause when conducting wiretaps and searches for a criminal investigation as long as the investigation can be described as having a "significant purpose," the gathering of foreign intelligence.
>
> Third, the act allows for the sharing of information between criminal and intelligence agencies, including grand jury information, and thereby opens the door to a resurgence of domestic spying by the CIA. (Chang 2002, 47; see American Civil Liberties Union 2003b)

Several lawmakers acknowledged that the enhanced surveillance procedures contained in the Patriot Act present significant dangers to the privacy of U.S. citizens. As a partial safeguard, Congress included "sunset" clauses that would force some of the enhanced surveillance procedures to expire on December 31, 2005. Nevertheless, many of the provisions may be implemented beyond the expiration date, especially in cases involving foreign intelligence investigations. The Bush administration, which opposed the inclusion of "sunset" clauses, has stepped up its pressure on Congress to install permanently the enhanced surveillance procedures. While campaigning for re-election, President Bush pronounced: "Those who criticize the Patriot Act must listen to those folks on the front line defending America. The Patriot Act defends our liberty, is what it does, under the Constitution of the United States" (Nagourney 2004a, A18).

Upon passage of the Patriot Act, the Justice Department flooded the telecommunications industry with relentless requests for subscriber information. Moreover, rather than completing the required legal work to obtain such information (e.g., subpoena, court order), law enforcement agencies are exerting pressure on telecommunication companies to turn over records voluntarily in the name of national security and patriotism. Jeffrey Eisenach, president of the Progress and Freedom Foundation noted, "Consumers should know that information they give to America Online or Microsoft may very well wind up at the IRS or FBI" and that new technologies "will indeed soon give government the ability to monitor the whereabouts of virtually everyone" (Bensor 2002, 28; Parenti 2003).

The government's obsession with optimizing its capacity to gather information on its citizens has led them to libraries, a trend that Emily Sheketoff, executive director of the American Library Association (ALA) calls "scary" (Blumner 2002, 13A). But fending off accusations that the FBI is using the Patriot Act's Section 215 as a shield to investigate library records, Attorney General Ashcroft called the ALA's concern over protecting the privacy of its patrons "baseless hysteria." Sheketoff fired back: "If he's coming after us so specifically, we must be having an impact" (Lichtblau 2003g, A23). The press looked into the controversy, finding: "It is not known how many times federal agents have actually used the law to gain access to library records because that information is classified . . . and such records are bound by a gag order" (Lichtblau 2003g, A23). Days later, the Justice Department tried to put the matter to rest by publicly announcing that there was not a single case in which Section 215 was implemented to demand library records. Suspicion, however, did not subside as the question lingered: If the government has not used Section 215 to seize library records in pursuit of terrorists then why does it need the authority at all? Professor David Cole responded that the Patriot Act and its various sections are being used to produce a "substantial chilling effect" (Lichtblau 2003h, A20; Hentoff 2003d). In doing so, the government can create public fears of Big Brother while simultaneously assuaging those anxieties by denying any intrusions into personal space, becoming a perfect form of social control (see Parenti 2003; Staples 1997).[1]

Tools in the Patriot Act

Tactics that contribute to the Patriot Act's enhanced surveillance are found in its toolbox, including "sneak-and-peek searches," access to records in international investigations, and tracking Internet usage (Chang 2002; *New York Times* 2004k). Section 213 of the Patriot Act authorizes federal agents to perform covert— "sneak-and-peek"—searches of a person's home or office without notice of the execution of the search warrant until the completion of the search. Critics oppose such "sneak-and-peek" searches on the basis that they violate the common-law principle that law enforcement agents must "knock and announce" their arrival prior to conducting a search, as stipulated by the Fourth Amendment's reasonable requirement (*Wilson v. Arkansas* 1995). Furthermore, it contravenes Rule 41(d) of the Federal Rules of Criminal Procedure that requires the officer removing property to furnish (or leave) a copy of the warrant and a receipt for the property taken. What makes Section 213 even more remarkable is that it is not limited to terrorism investigations but applies to all criminal investigations; the section also is not subject to expiration (see *New York Times* 2004l).

The Patriot Act's surveillance powers are enhanced by Section 215 that lowers the requirements and extends the reach of the Foreign Intelligence Surveillance Act of 1978 (FISA: 50 U.S.C. 1978). Under that section, the FBI director (or a designee as low in rank as an assistant special agent) may apply for a court order demanding the production of "any tangible things (including books, records, papers, documents, and other items)" to accompany an investigation "to protect against international terrorism or clandestine intelligence activities." Civil liberties attorneys complain that Section 215 removes a key FISA restriction that obligates the government to specify in its application for a court order that "there are specific and articulable facts giving reason to believe that the person to whom the records pertain is a foreign power or an agent of a foreign power." The FBI need not suspect of any wrongdoing the person whose records are being sought. Section 215 applies not only to foreign powers and their agents but also to U.S. citizens and lawful permanent residents. Congressional oversight requires the Attorney General's Office to report twice annually its activities under Section 215. The section was renewed in March 2006.

The third controversial utensil in the Patriot Act's toolkit is the use of tracking devices on the Internet. When a U.S. attorney has certified that information to be obtained is "relevant to an ongoing criminal investigation," the courts in accordance to Section 216 are required to order the installation of a pen register (records phone numbers of outgoing calls) and a trap-and-trace device (records phone numbers from which incoming calls originate). Those devices track both telephone and Internet usage, including dialing, routing, addressing, and signaling information. Section 216 does not authorize the tracking of the contents; however, the act does not clarify exactly the boundary separating dialing (and routing, addressing, and signaling information) and content. Whereas dialing information is separate from content in telephone communications, that demarcation does not exist in email messages that move address and content information together. Section 216 also does not precisely state whether records of visiting websites and web pages constitute dialing, routing, addressing, and signaling information or content. Because the act fails to demonstrate any guidance on those concerns, the Patriot Act gives the government considerable leeway to determine what constitutes content.

Compounding matters, Section 216 allows the government to install its Carnivore (or DCS1000) system, a powerful tracking device that can intercept a wide variety of Internet activity: email messages, web page browsing, and Internet telephone communications. Moreover, the Carnivore consumes every bit of information traveling through an Internet service provider's network, not only information and content belonging to the target under surveillance but also that of all users in the network. The FBI claims that through its use of filters, the Carnivore isolates only messages strictly noted by court order. "However, neither the accuracy of Carnivore's filtering system nor the infallibility of its human programmers has been demonstrated" (Chang 2002, 55; Parenti 2003). Of great concern to civil liberties organizations, Section 216 is not set to expire.

Further unnerving civil liberties groups, as well as some lawmakers, is the Bush administration's brazen effort to step aside from its legal obligation to the Fourth Amendment, requiring judicial oversight and review of its surveillance activities. Assistant Attorney General Daniel J. Bryant of the Department of Justice's Office of Legislative Affairs sent a letter to key members of the Senate advocating for a suspension of the Fourth Amendment's warrant requirement for situations involving the investigation of a foreign national security threat. In that letter, Bryant offers the following reasoning: "Here, for Fourth Amendment purposes, the right to self-defense is not that of an individual, but that of the nation and its citizens. . . . If the government's heightened interest in self-defense justifies the use of deadly force, then it certainly would also justify warrantless searches"[2] (see Chang 2002, 56).

In a significant way, Section 218 of the Patriot Act advances the Bush team's agenda to erode the separation of powers doctrine. Specifically, the section permits warrantless searches by amending the FISA's wiretap and physical search provisions. "Under FISA, court orders permitting the executive to conduct surreptitious foreign intelligence wiretaps and physical searches may be obtained without the showing of probable cause of criminal conduct demanded by the Fourth Amendment in the case of criminal investigations" (Chang 2002, 56–54). Political and governmental responses to the attacks of 9/11 contributed enormously to the creation of Section 218 but there remain major obstacles. The government is bound by *United States v. United States District Court for the Eastern District of Michigan (Keith)* in which the U.S. Supreme Court rejected President Nixon's attempt to conduct warrantless wiretaps when investigating national security threats from domestic groups with no foreign ties. In its ruling, the Court reemphasized the importance of maintaining judicial oversight in applications for warrants, thereby upholding separation of powers and division of functions among different branches and levels of government. In light of the *Keith* Court, there remains doubt over the constitutionality of Section 218, creating potential problems for the government in its quest to prosecute criminal defendants based on evidence that does not satisfy the probable cause requirement of the Fourth Amendment. It is possible that the courts, citing the exclusionary rule, would reject such evidence as illegally gathered. Section 218 was renewed in March 2006 (Chang 2002; Lichtblau and Liptak 2003).[3]

Finally, the third controversial tool of the Patriot Act involves the stripping of constitutional protections for noncitizens. As Chapter 6 on profiling and detention clearly illustrates, the government has behaved recklessly with its many sweeps and round-ups of innocent Middle Eastern and South Asian men following the events of 9/11. Making matters worse, the Patriot Act deprives noncitizens of their due process and First Amendment rights, according to Sections 411 and 412. In the former, the Patriot Act widens the class of noncitizens that are subject to deportation on the grounds of terrorism by broadening the definition of the terms "terrorist activity," "engage in terrorist activity," and "terrorist organization." The latter grants greater authority to the government, allowing it to detain noncitizens while their deportation proceedings are pending (Cole 2003, 2002; Cole and Dempsey 2002).[4]

Setbacks for Counterterrorism Laws

Years after the enactment of the Patriot Act, the judiciary is considering the constitutionality of several controversial sections of the law. In a series of setbacks for the legislators and chief members of the executive branch who designed the Patriot Act, the courts have invalidated or called into questions key aspects of the act. In September 2004, a federal district judge, Victor Marrero in Manhattan, struck down a major surveillance provision, ruling that it broadly violated the Constitution by granting the government unchecked powers to obtain private information. The judge determined that Section 505 of the law violated both free speech guarantees and protection against unreasonable searches, and it is likely that other court challenges will emerge. The suit was brought by the American Civil Liberties Union against a kind of subpoena known as the National Security Letter (NSL) that the government has used to force Internet service providers to release personal information about subscribers, including customers' names, addresses, credit card data, and details of their online activity (*John Doe, American Civil Liberties Union v. John Ashcroft and FBI Director Robert Mueller* 2004).

The section also bars the Internet service provider from disclosing to anyone that it received such a subpoena, including an attorney. According to the section, the subpoena is issued without court order. Judge Marrero said that provision was unique in its "all-inclusive sweep" and had "no place in our open society" (Preston 2004a, A26). Specifically, the judge ruled that the subpoena violates the Fourth Amendment because it does not permit a court review. Commenting on the court ruling, Andrew Napolitano, a judge and media legal analyst, said: "This stops the FBI from writing their own warrants" (Hentoff 2004a, 26; see Preston 2004a).

In another setback, in 2003, the United States Court of Appeals for the Ninth Circuit in San Francisco threw into doubt parts of the 1996 Antiterrorism and Effective Death Penalty Act that make it a crime to provide support to groups designated terrorist. In a case involving two organizations that deliver humanitarian services and advocacy assistance to Kurds in Turkey and Tamils in Sri Lanka, the panel ruled that the law failed to require clearly that a suspect knowingly provided support to a terrorist group, posing as a dangerous zone for mortal innocents (*Humanitarian Law Project v. Ashcroft* 2003). According to the government's interpretation of the law, the court found that an individual who sends a financial contribution to an orphanage in Sri Lanka operated by a banned group or an individual who buys cookies at a bake sale that supports displaced Kurdish refugees could face a lengthy prison sentence for supporting terrorists. The court also affirmed a preliminary ruling that found unconstitutionally vague the ban on providing training and personnel for terrorist groups; moreover, it posed a danger to protected free speech. David Cole, the attorney who represented the humanitarian groups in the lawsuit, said: "The government's reading of this statute is extremely broad and it has had an extreme chilling effect on anyone who is interested in providing humanitarian aid where there might be a designated terrorist organization involved" (Lichtblau 2003i, A37).

In Michigan, the ACLU is challenging Section 215 of the Patriot Act that allows the FBI to obtain a court order to require any organization to turn over tangible evidence that the government believes is related to terrorist activity. Prior to the passage of the Patriot Act, investigators seeking to obtain concrete evidence had to convince the court that the organization or people were spies or terrorists for a foreign government. The ACLU declares that the section violates citizens' privacy, due process, and free speech, giving federal agents virtually unchecked authority to spy on Americans. The suit was filed on behalf of six Muslim groups, including a members of a mosque in Ann Arbor who maintain that they had been unfairly questioned and singled out by the FBI; some of its associates have been imprisoned and deported. Ann Beeson, the chief lawyer in the case, stated: "We think the Constitution is really on our side" (Lichtblau 2003j, A17; see Preston 2004a).

Stifling the First Amendment and Political Dissent

In the face national security threats, First Amendment freedoms, especially free speech and assembly, ought not be contracted since public participation in crucial decision making is the hallmark of a democratic society (Stone 2004; see Hitchens 2004; Kakutani 2004). As attorney Nancy Chang points out: "Crises force us to make decision on the weightiest of matters—whether to declare war, whether to take military action and compel military service, whether to curtail our political and personal freedoms, whom to call a friend and whom foe. The specter of casualties—both military and civilian, American and foreign—looms in the balance. Once made, these decisions are certain to carry long lasting repercussions extending far beyond the geographical confines of the United States" (2002, 92).

Yet, it is in times like these involving the war on terror—and by exten-sion the war in Iraq—that First Amendment values are vulnerable to au-thoritarian rule. Eerily, Justice Antonin Scalia, speaking at John Carroll University, proclaimed: "Most of the rights you enjoy go way beyond what the Constitution requires" because "the Constitution just sets mini-mums;" accordingly, in wartime "the protections will be ratcheted down to the Constitutional minimum" (Hentoff 2003b; see Lawyers Commit-tee for Human Rights 2003). As discussed in previous chapters, govern-ment secrecy undercuts public awareness and participation in crucial matters involving national security and war. Moreover, there are other recent developments in post-9/11 America that worry civil libertarians, including government efforts to impose guilt by association and tactics aimed at silencing political activists.

The First Amendment guarantees the freedom of expression along-side the right to associate freely with others for the purpose of collective political action (*Bates v. City of Little Rock* 1960; *NAACP v. Alabama ex rel Patterson* 1958). Equally important, the U.S. Supreme Court has ruled that membership of an organization having lawful as well as unlawful ac-tivities cannot serve as grounds for guilt (*NAACP v. Claiborne Hardware Co.* 1982; *Scales v. United States* 1961; *United States v. Robel* 1967). Controversies during the 1950s McCarthy era, remind us of dark periods of American history when loyalty-obsessed political leaders embarked on Communist witch-hunts, creating an atmosphere of suspicion that undermined free association (Goldstein 1978; Murphy 1972; Welch 2000a). Similarly, the Bush administration since 9/11 has taken ominous steps in pursuit of ter-rorists, vowing to hunt down not only those engaged in terrorist activities but also "anyone who espouses a philosophy that's terrorist" (Sanger 2002, A1). Whereas one might dismiss Bush's remarks as part and parcel of his "tough talk," his words resonate in tactics that impose guilt by as-sociation. In the name of the war on terror, the government is targeting citizens and noncitizens for participating in expressive activities on be-half of groups that the secretary of state deems terrorist (Chang 2002; *International Herald Tribune* 2003b).

In line with the Patriot Act and the Antiterrorism and Effective Death Penalty Act (1996), the executive branch possesses unprecedented au-thority to penalize those who associate with organizations the govern-ment considers terrorist. Criminal punishments are available to anyone who provides material support to any of the approximately 33 organiza-tions that the secretary of state has catalogued as a "foreign terrorist or-ganization" (FTO). Critics complain that the FTO list is based on loose standards of definition that can apply to virtually any revolutionary movement, even those that have never threatened directly or indirectly violence against the United States (Chang 2002; see *Imperial Hubris* 2004). Given that America's war on terror is swiftly becoming international in scope, the list of FTOs is likely to grow; furthermore, that form of net widening is then likely to snare increasingly more suspects, including those who do not pose a threat to American national security (Dreyfuss 2002a).

With similar fervor, the Bush administration has cracked down on political dissent, including nonviolent civil disobedience. In particular, the Justice Department and the FBI continue to funnel increasingly more funds and technical support to local police departments to monitor and infiltrate, and disrupt left-wing political groups (Dreyfuss 2002b; Hentoff 2004b, 2003a). Those so-called "red squads" have emerged in such cities as Denver where police maintained massive "Spy Files" on the peaceful political activities of more than 3,200 individuals and 208 organizations. Denver police placed under surveillance the American Friends Service Committee (AFSC) and Amnesty International, along with a host of groups involved in campaigns to improve police accountability, Native American rights, the indigenous rights in Chiapas, Mexico (Cart 2002; *New York Times* 2002). In 2002, the American Civil Liberties Union issued a class action suit on behalf of the AFSC and other "Spy File" targets, seeking an injunction ordering the Denver Police Department to halt its surveillance activities. The suit alleges that Denver police deployed undercover operatives to videotape and photograph persons who participated in peaceful demonstrations in the absence of any legitimate law enforcement purpose.

Additionally, the complaint accuses the Denver Police Department of sharing its "Spy Files" with other law enforcement agencies without ensuring that the information would not be disclosed further. The suit, citing First and Fourth Amendment violations, asserts that the Denver Police Department falsely designated as "criminal extremist" the AFSC, a pacifist Quaker group and recipient of the Nobel Peace Prize. In doing so, the Denver Police Department produced a chill effect that would force prospective activists to think twice about joining the organization for fear of being monitored, especially since the AFSC was labeled— albeit falsely—"criminal extremist" (*American Friends Service Committee, et al., v. City and Counter of Denver, Civil Action* 2002; Chang 2002).

Detailing the excesses of the government in curbing political expression and protest, the American Civil Liberties Union released a key report,

Freedom Under Fire: Dissent in Post-9/11 America (2003b). Three principle forms of dissent have been subject to increasingly punitive control, mass protests and rallies, messages on signs or clothing, and other acts of defiance by communities and individuals. "Police have beaten and maced protestors in Missouri, charged on horseback into crowds of demonstrators in New York, fired on demonstrators in California, helped FBI agents to spy on professors and students at the University of Massachusetts in Amherst" (*Civil Liberties Reporter* 2003, 1; see Sisario 2004).

In 2004, a law enforcement official in cooperation with the Joint Terrorism Task Force in Des Moines, Iowa, issued a subpoena to Drake University, ordering the disclosure of records on its student chapter of the National Lawyers Guild, including names of officers of the chapter, meeting agendas, and annual reports. Additionally, the government wanted to learn the identities of the attendees at the Guild-sponsored anti-war conference: "Stop the Occupation! Bring the Iowa Guard Home!" Prosecutors also subpoenaed several conference participants to testify before a grand jury and secured a court order barring Drake University from publicly commenting on the subpoena. When news of the government's actions hit the national press, however, the Justice Department withdrew quickly and cancelled the subpoenas, announcing that it had ended its investigation at Drake University. As noted previously, Attorney General Ashcroft in June 2002 issued guidelines allowing the FBI to attend public meetings of political and religious groups, even without a hint of criminal activity (see Solomon 2003b).

The war on terror and the war against anti-war activists were formally cemented in October 2003 when the FBI released a "terrorism" bulletin outlining the tactics of peace demonstrators, among them: using the Internet to raise funds and organize meetings. Anthony Romero, executive director of the ACLU commented: "The FBI is dangerously targeting Americans who are engaged in nothing more than lawful protest and dissent. The line between terrorism and legitimate civil disobedience is blurred" (Lichtblau 2003k, A1). As the Patriot Act was gaining support in Congress after 9/11, critics complained that the government's new definition of "domestic terrorism" could conceivably be applied to political demonstrations. Backers of the Patriot Act cried foul, characterizing civil libertarians as hysterical. Law professor David Cole shot back: "But the proof is in the pudding. The Feds maintain the Drake case had nothing to do with the Patriot Act, but when the government institutes federal grand jury proceedings about a student antiwar conference and rally and seeks records on the meeting and its attendees, it suggests that it doesn't have enough to do or that it sees monitoring of political dissent as an integral part of the 'war on terror'" (2004b, 5).

Before the Democratic and Republican national conventions unfolded in 2004, federal law enforcement agents stepped up their interest in so-called political troublemakers. The FBI urged agents to scour communities in search of information about planned disruption aimed at the political conventions. Agents questioned and in some cases subpoenaed persons involved in political protests but said that their investigations were in pursuit of possible crimes and not part of an overall plan to crack down on dissent. However, many of those who were visited by the FBI were mystified by the questions and felt that they were being hassled as well as intimidated from participating in political demonstrations. Sarah Bardwell, a 21-year-old intern at an anti-war group in Denver, said after being questioned by six investigators: "The message I took from it was that they were trying to intimidate us into not going to any protests and to let us know that, 'hey, were watching you'" (Lichtblau 2004e, A1). Armed with greater authority to monitor even lawful and peaceful political activity since the passage of the Patriot Act, the FBI has blurred the line between protecting national security in the age of terrorism and suppression free speech. In the end, a chilling effect takes hold. "People are going to be afraid to go to a demonstration or even sign a petition if they justifiably believe that will result in having an FBI file opened on you" (Lichtblau 2004e, A11; see Lichtblau 2004f; *New York Times* 2004m).

In the months leading up to the Republican National Convention in New York City, where President Bush was expected to remind Americans of the lasting significance of September 11 alongside his commitment to the war on terror, other government officials activated similar counter-terrorism rhetoric. At issue was the request by the group United for Peace and Justice to stage a huge anti-war demonstration on the Great Lawn in the City's Central Park. In rejecting the request, NYC Police Commissioner Raymond Kelly returned to concerns over possible terrorism while adding that citizens better get used to restrictions on the First Amendment so that government can improve public safety. Kelly explained that any congregation of significant numbers of people constitutes a terrorist target because of the potential for mass casualties. Then shifting into the language of a risk society in a post-9/11 world, Kelly announced: "I think demonstrators have to recognize that everybody's lives have changed, and they need some accommodation and some acceptance of the fact that it's a different environment that we're all living in now" (Cardwell 2004, B1; see Chang 2004).

With those anxieties in the backdrop, the Republican convention was fraught with fears of a terrorist strike along with concerns of a police clampdown on protestors, especially those who traveled long distances to New York City to criticize Bush for his politicization of 9/11. Stoking anger among demonstrators who felt they were being pushed to the margins of political expression, the City announced plans that police would implement the controversial use of closed four-sided pens to contain protestors. Additionally, police would be permitted to embark on a general search of protestors' personal bags. Civil liberties organizations challenged those measures in court. In his ruling, federal judge Robert W. Sweet barred the City's plans to allow police lax procedures in searching bags unless there was information of a specific threat. The judge also did not bar entirely the use of the containment pens but emphasized that protestors must be able to move freely in and out of them. The City as well as civil liberties groups claimed victory as Judge Sweet stated that he intended to strike "a delicate balance" that would "encourage free expression in a secure society" (Preston 2004b, B4; see Lee 2004).

No Fly Lists

In another sphere of civil liberties that has drawn tremendous controversy is the government's use of No Fly lists, barring certain individuals from boarding commercial aircrafts. In 2004, while traveling to the United States from London, the plane carrying Yusuf Islam, popularly known in the music world as Cat Stevens, was rerouted to Bangor, Maine, where the aircraft remained for four and a half hours. During the layover, Mr. Islam was removed from the plane because agents who detained and interrogated the famous singer said that he appeared on a No Fly list. The government claimed that it had evidence that Mr. Islam donated money to groups suspected of terrorism and chastised United Airlines for allowing him to board the aircraft (Wald 2004a). Reaction to the obvious blunder was swift and sharp. Britain's foreign minister, Jack Straw, formally criticized the Bush administration for deporting Mr. Islam, who has frequently toured the United States. In fact, earlier that year, Mr. Islam visited the White House Office of Faith-Based and Community initiatives to speak about philanthropy (*New York Times* 2004n, WK2). In addition to being renowned for his music, Mr. Islam is admired for his commitment to charity, generating funds for children victimized in Bosnia, for example. Upon his return to England, Mr. Islam announced: "Sadly, the latest horror to hit the U.S. looks to have been caused by people of Middle Eastern origin, bearing Muslim names. Again shame. This fuels more hatred for a religion and a people that have nothing to do with these events" (Tyler 2004b, A6).

While the targeting of Mr. Islam appears to embody ethnic and religious profiling, the reliability of No Fly lists sheds light on deeper problems that shake the faith of some who question whether the government is actually competent to safeguard its citizens. The degree of mismanagement is at times astonishing (see National Commission on Terrorist Attacks Upon the United States, 2004). Senator Edward M. (Ted) Kennedy, Democratic stalwart and one of the most recognizable faces in Washington, also had his name appearing on No Fly lists. Between March 1 and April 6 (2004), agents tried to block the senator from boarding airplanes on five occasions because his name resembles an alias used by a suspected terrorist. In one of those incidents, Kennedy was told that he could not purchase a ticket to fly to Boston. He asked: "Well, why not?" and was told: "We can't tell you" (Swarns 2004b, A18). Eventually, airline supervisors intervened and allowed Kennedy to travel but it took several weeks for Homeland Security to correct the problem.

Due in part to the celebrity status of Mr. Islam and Senator Kennedy, greater public awareness is being raised about the No Fly lists and their breach of civil liberties involving persons clearly not involved in terrorism. In 2004, a federal judge in San Francisco accused the government of relying on "frivolous claims" to avoid publicly disclosing who is banned from boarding airplanes on the basis of terrorism risks. The case stems from a lawsuit brought by the American Civil Liberties Union and others in pursuit of information explaining how hundreds of people have had their names entered on the No Fly list since 9/11. In his ruling, Judge Charles R. Breyer determined that the government lawyers had not met their burden of proving that the material was exempt from the Freedom of Information Act. The ACLU estimates that more than 500 people in San Francisco alone have been kept from boarding aircraft due to what the government cites as terrorist concerns. However, many of those barred from flying believe that they were targeted for their strong liberal politics and criticisms of the Bush administration. In one particular incident in 2002, two-dozen members of a group called Peace of Action of Wisconsin, including a nun and high school students who were traveling to a teach-in on the war in Iraq were detained in Milwaukee, missing their flight (Lichtblau 2004g).

Thomas Burke of the ACLU said the ruling is a significant victory in stripping away the secrecy shrouding the No Fly lists. It also might help people who have been mistakenly registered to get their names removed from the lists: "The end goal here is to determine how these names were even developed in the first place" (Lichtblau 2004h, A19). Indeed, the development of the No Fly lists is a tightly controlled secret but some government officials acknowledge that the standards for banning certain passengers due to terrorism concerns were "necessarily subjective" with no hard and fast rules" (Lichtblau 2004i, A9). The original No Fly list grew from 16 names on September 11, 2001, to more than a few thousand by year 2004, including about 10,000 names that appear on a secondary list that require that those passengers get closer scrutiny. The lists developed amid signs of internal confusion and dissension over how the list would be implemented. Civil liberties organizations complain that the use of No Fly lists violates airline passengers' constitutional protection against unreasonable searches and seizures and then denies their right to due process necessary to correct any mistakes. Moreover, the government has been criticized for its failure to put two of the 9/11 hijackers on the watch list even after their ties to terrorism became known.

Conclusion

It is true that terrorism threatens democracy, especially its commitment to civil liberties. However, in responding to terrorism, democracy itself is tested. As John Dean, former counsel to President Nixon, points out: "Thus, the great danger posed by terrorism for our democracy is not that terrorists can defeat us with physical or military force but rather that terrorism presents its real threat in provoking democratic regimes to embrace and employ authoritarian measures" (2004, 194). Similarly, University of Minnesota law professor, Oren Gross, weighs into the issue, drawing attention to authoritarian rule in a post-9/11 America. Given the direction of the war on terror, embodied in the Patriot Act along with the post-9/11 round-ups and travesties of justice at Guantanamo Bay—all shrouded in secrecy—there is evidence that the U.S. government has adopted tactics that: "(1) weaken the fabric of democracy; (2) discredit the government domestically as well as internationally; (3) alienate segments of the population from their government, thereby pushing more people to support (passively, if not outright actively) the terrorist organizations and their causes; and (4) undermine the government's claim to the moral high ground in the battle against terrorists, while gaining legitimacy for the latter" (Gross 2003, 1030). Succinctly stated, Gross believes that terrorists win when the United States becomes less democratic. Dean concurs, reminding us that the United States is less democratic today than before 9/11 (see Rosen 2004a, 2003).

Recent political and legislative activities advance the perception that indeed America is less democratic—and more authoritarian—than before September 11. On the eve of the second anniversary of 9/11, President Bush called for a significant broadening of law enforcement powers under the Patriot Act. Bush claimed that his administration was winning the war on terror but that "unreasonable obstacles" in the Patriot Act undermined its effectiveness. To a cheering crowd of federal investigators and troops, Bush went on to say that the Patriot Act did not go far enough, promising: "We will never forget the servants of evil who plotted the attacks, and we will never forget those who rejoiced at our grief" (Sanger 2002, A1). Specifically, Bush proposed letting federal law enforcement agencies deliver "administrative subpoenas" in terrorism cases without the approval of judges or grand juries. He also pushed to expand the federal death penalty to include more terrorism-related offenses and making it more difficult for those suspected of terrorism-related crimes to be released on bail. Incidentally, the provision for "administrative subpoenas" was in the original Patriot Act bill but was removed in the Congressional conference.

The Bush team seemed to have been thinking that the emotional second year anniversary of the terror attacks on New York City and Washington, D.C., would serve to strengthen his plea for greater law enforcement powers. However, many in Congress—from both parties—remained skeptical that federal agents would not abuse their expanding power. John Conyers, Jr., ranking Democrat on the House Judiciary Committee, sharply noted: "Removing judges from providing any check or balance on John Ashcroft's subpoena does not make us safer, it only makes us less free. Of course, terrorists should not be released on bail, but this administration has a shameful record of deeming law-abiding citizens as terrorists and taking away their rights" (Lichtblau 2004l, A19). In 2004, Bush pressed forward with his campaign to renew many of the provisions of the Patriot Act scheduled to expired at the end of 2005, including the controversial sneak-and-peek searches and the section that allows the government to demand records from libraries and bookstores (Lichtblau 2004j, A18: Stevenson and Lichtblau 2004). Adding to concerns that the executive branch of the federal government is becoming too powerful while undercutting the doctrine of separation of powers is the Republicans' response to recommendations by the 9/11 Commission.

Civil liberties groups along with some Democrats criticize a proposal—
what some call Patriot Act 2—that goes well beyond the Commission's sug-
gestions to include new authority to conduct electronic surveillance in terrorism cases. Congressman Conyers promptly railed the legislative draft,
saying: "It's as if the commission's recommendations have been supersized
with irrelevant fat and lard, representing a wish list of past reactionary proposals that would diminish our civil liberties" (Shenon 2004d, A18; see
Lee 2003).[5]

In his penetrating book, *The Soft Cage: Surveillance in America, from Slave
Passes to the War on Terror*, Christian Parenti surveys the contributions of
Michel Foucault (1979) who asserted that routine surveillance is bound
up with political repression. Still, such surveillance also lends itself to a
generative function, constructing politically useful forms of knowledge
and behavior. "In short, surveillance instills discipline by forcing self-
regulation. Constant surveillance brings forth loyal citizens, trained soldiers, obedient patients, productive workers, and docile, useful bodies"
(Parenti 2003, 9). As government (and corporations) expands and inten-
sifies its external observation, citizens over time internalize that gaze: not
only becoming increasingly willing to accept such intrusion but also adjusting their conduct accordingly (see Lyon 1994; Staples 1997). With particular significance to the war on terror, greater surveillance also serves
another generative purpose insofar as it defines who is an insider and
who is an outsider. That generative function resonates profoundly within
scapegoating in a post-9/11 America, particularly the displacement of
aggression—and blame—onto those considered religious, ethnic, and
political outsiders. As we shall discuss in the next, and final, chapter, those
developments have strong implications to a changing American culture,
characterized by denial.

CHAPTER TEN

Culture of Denial

For individuals, denial promotes a false narrative about self. For societies, it promotes a discourse of hatred, fear, and distortion.

—Joshua Miller and Gerald Schamess,
"The discourse of denigration and the creation of the other,"
Journal of Sociology and Social Welfare, 2000

The Bush administration's strategy has been to promote a culture of denial in which American abuses are first covered up, then acknowledged with shock and horror, then absorbed and neutralized ("excesses" by a few "rotten apples") and finally forgotten—so that when new scandals surface, a new cycle can begin.

—*Nation,* 2005

Given that American counterterrorism policies and practices continue to blend the metaphors and realities of war, it is important to consider cultural and social psychological products of the war on terror. In his deeply insightful book, *War is a Force That Gives Us Meaning,* Chris Hedges chronicles his experiences as a war correspondent in nations engulfed by conflict. Among his revelations are cultural transformations that fuel the myth of war. Offering a potent rationalization for aggression, the myth of war consumes people, altering their social world in ways that allow them to crystallize their identity as well as the identities of their enemies (see LaShan 1992). The myth of war is sustained by the popular view characterizing some forms of violence—including serious human rights violations—as noble, serving to defend the eternal good (Katz 1988). Hedges writes: "The myth of war is essential to justify the horrible sacrifices required in war, the destruction and death of innocents. It can be formed only by denying the reality of war, by the turning lies, the manipulation, the inhumanness of war into the heroic ideal" (2002, 26).

Similarly, the American war on terrorism is driven by the myth of war while adhering to an "othering" process in which Middle Eastern men are demonized, profiled, and suspected of terrorist activities. The accused are cast as menacing outsiders who threaten not only national security but the entire social order as well. That way of thinking about terrorism draws on popular fears in ways that lend support to government's clampdown on civil liberties and human rights. As described in previous passages of the book, those developments stem from the *criminology of the other* which is an anti-modern paradigm, rejecting modern concepts of crime and terrorism as well as enlightened ways of dealing with each of them (Garland 2001). From that perspective crime and terrorism are re-dramatized, and doing so reinforce a disaster mentality, retreating into intolerance and authoritarianism (see Young 1999). Such manifestations of collective anxiety in post-9/11 America have clear implications to multiple forms of scapegoating that possess "the ability to dehumanize and demonize relatively powerless populations defined as 'other'" (Miller and Schamess 2000, 47).

As an enduring theme, this chapter attends to the significance of culture and the role that key forms of collective denial play in undermining civil liberties and human rights in the war on terror. Amid the fallout of 9/11, it is important to consider both polarities of societal reaction: over-reaction, especially in the form of moral panic, as well as under-reaction, manifesting in denial (Cohen 2002, 2001; Welch 2003a). Because the war on terror is predicated on well-publicized criminal justice and militaristic imperatives aimed at those perceived as aggressors, it tends to deflect attention from collateral damage, innocent victims caught in the machinery of Bush-styled counterterrorism. Consequently, civil liberties and human rights violations are perpetuated by under-reaction whereby the plight of scapegoats quietly eludes public awareness. The discussion begins with an introduction into the sociology of denial then explores the significance of fighting back against government—and popular—repression. Finally, and fittingly, recommendations to improve counter-terrorist policies are offered, most notably in the realm of human rights and international relations.

Sociology of Denial

The violation of civil liberties and human rights in the wake of September 11 offer enormous implications to a sociology of denial. In *States of Denial: Knowing About Atrocities and Suffering,* Stanley Cohen examines critically the role of denial in perpetuating long-term social problems, especially those that produce and reproduce human rights violations (also see Kleinman 1997; Hamm 2002). More to the point of this analysis, Cohen's framework concentrates on the content of denial manifesting in three forms: literal, interpretive, and implicatory. Literal denial is as blunt as it is blatant (e.g., officials insist "that the atrocity did not occur"), serving as a blanket defense against acknowledging the undisputed facts. Under interpretive denial, however, the facts are not refuted but are given a different spin, thus altering the meaning (e.g., officials argue "what happened is not what you think it is"). By its very nature, reinterpretation is distinctly more intricate than literal denial typically because it relies on euphemism and legalism. According to Cohen: "The function of euphemism labels and jargon is to mask, sanitize, and confer respectability. Palliative terms deny or misrepresent cruelty or harm, giving them neutral or respectable status" (2001, 107). Political and military rhetoric is steeped in euphemisms, providing speakers and their audience insulation from the full meaning of harm, injury, and death. Consider the following examples: "collateral damage" rather than the killing of civilians; "transfer of population" rather than forced expulsion; "moderate physical pressure" rather than torture. Legalism also facilitates interpretive denial by employing an infinite array of logical (or illogical) maneuvers. "The legal discourse depicts a wholly non-pictorial world. This is a board game with a limited repertoire of fixed moves. One side claims that event X does not fit the appropriate category (right, law, article, or convention). Yes, this demonstrator was arrested and detained, but this was not a violation of freedom of expression. Yes, it was, comes the counter-move. Event Y may have been a violation of the Fourth Geneva Convention, but the Convention does not apply. Yes, it does" (Cohen 2001, 108).

In the third form of content denial, implicatory denial does not refute either the facts or their conventional meaning; rather, the psychological, political, or moral consequences are denied, minimized, or muted. By diminishing the significance of the harm of human rights violations and other atrocities, officials evade their responsibility to intervene. Whereas critical criminology is predicated on revealing truths about crime, especially in the social context of inequality and repression, Cohen's paradigm offers additional concepts in analyzing the content of official rhetoric. Applying the sociology of denial to the war on terror, it is clear that literal, interpretive, and implicatory denial contribute to persistent civil liberties and human rights abuses.

Literal Denial

Along with secrecy, stonewalling, and the knack for making outrageous claims proven to be false, most notably its mantra over Iraq's weapons of mass destruction and Saddam Hussein's links to Al Qaeda, literal denial has become a hallmark of the Bush administration (Weiser 2005). Consider the administration's perpetual denial of U.S. involvement in torture. Amid the controversy over "extraordinary rendition," in which the U.S. government stands accused of transporting terrorist suspects to other countries (e.g., Egypt, Morocco, Syria, and Jordan) for purposes of torture, statements of literal denial were emphatic. President Bush, on January 27, 2005, assured the world that "torture is never acceptable, nor do we hand people to countries that do torture" (Mayer 2005, EV1). Bush's denial is unacceptable to many who know that indeed the United States has rendered—a euphemism for kidnapping—suspects to other nations with the understanding that they will be abused and tortured (Beinart 2004; Priest and Gellman 2002). Moreover, those renditions are a matter of policy carried out by "the CIA under broad authority that has allowed it to act without case-by-case approval from the White House or the State or Justice Departments," according to current and former government officials (Jehl and Johnston 2005, A14).

A case in point is Maher Arar, a Canadian citizen born in Syria. On September 26, 2002, Arar was arrested at John F. Kennedy airport while changing planes; he had been on vacation with his family in Tunisia and was returning to his home in Canada. American officials said that Arar's name appeared on a watch list of suspected terrorists and detained and questioned him for 13 days but never formally charged him of any violation. Then, bound in handcuffs and leg irons, he was loaded onto an

executive jet to Syria where he was placed in the custody of Syrian interrogators. For a year, Arar was beaten and tortured. It was not until the Canadian government eventually took up his cause that he was released,
without charges (Herbert 2005b; Mayer 2005; see Greenberg and Dratel
2005). Former government officials say that "the CIA has flown 100 to
150 suspected terrorists from one foreign country to another, including
Egypt, Syria, Saudi Arabia, Jordan, and Pakistan" (Jehl and Johnston
2005, A14). Also it is not publicly known how many terrorist suspects are
being held secretly by the U.S. government. The CIA is reported to have
prisons—so called interrogation centers—in Afghanistan, Diego Gar-
cia, Qatar, and Thailand (Scheuer 2004; Hersh 2004; Priest and Gellman
2002). Incidentally, the Bush team's practice of extraordinary rendition
was so secretive that members of the 9/11 Commission were barred from
asking questions about it during its investigation (Hentoff 2005).

As mass detentions mounted in the weeks and months following September 11, civil liberties groups called attention to the mistreatment of detainees, including well-documented incidents in which young men were
kept from their attorneys, confined in jails without proper food, and in
some cases assaulted by guards and other prisoners (Human Rights Watch
2002b; Lawyers Committee for Human Rights 2003). Still, even in the face
of growing evidence, Attorney General Ashcroft resorted to literal denial
by failing to admit that there had been any "wholesale" abuse of those being held (see U.S. Department of Justice 2003a, 2003b; Chapter 6). Taking
a more nuanced view of the domestic war on terror in general, government secrecy—concealing the truth—represents a form of literal denial
since government officials refuse to acknowledge publicly the extent of
civil liberties and human rights violations. Ashcroft repeatedly denied access to basic information concerning those in detention, including their
names and where they were being held. Such secrecy has been denounced
by human rights and civil liberties advocates as well as by news organizations. Even some political leaders have complained that the attorney general had failed to explain adequately the need for those drastic measures.
Laura W. Murphy of the ACLU sharply criticized the government's approach to the domestic war on terror, stating: "We should not as a society
tolerate a law enforcement apparatus that operates in virtual secrecy"
(Goldstein and Eggen 2001, EV2; *New York Times* 2001).

Hiding the truth also leads to hiding other things, including prisoners. Although the Geneva Conventions of 1949 require the prompt registration of detainees so that their treatment can be monitored, Secretary
of Defense Donald Rumsfeld, at the request of the CIA, personally

ordered that certain prisoners in Iraq be hidden from the International Red Cross, in effect becoming "ghost detainees" for several months (Hersh 2004). Almost paradoxically, the issue of secrecy in the war on terror has been open to public discussion. Vice President Cheney spoke straightforwardly about the role of secrecy in the war on terror in an interview with "Meet the Press" five days after 9/11, saying that the government would have to "work through, sort of, the dark side." Cheney continued: "A lot of what needs to be done here will have to done quietly, without any discussion" (Mayer 2005, EV2).

Another extension of literal denial is covering up and looking the other way, for instance, when human rights abuses occur. In February 2005, John D. Negroponte was selected to become the nation's first director of national intelligence, a key post in the war on terror. While Negroponte is hailed for his distinguished government career, human rights advocates fumed. During his tenure as U.S. ambassador to Honduras in the 1980s, Negroponte was criticized for covering up and turning a blind eye to grave human rights violations, including kidnappings, torture, and killings (Harbury 2005). Oscar Reyes, whom the Honduran military seized in 1982 and tortured—along with his wife—was angered by Negroponte's nomination, expecting him to deny having knowledge of the human rights abuses in Honduran: "He'll say, I didn't know. But the U.S. embassy knew everything that was going on" (Shane 2005, A13). Reed Brody, counsel to Human Rights Watch, echoed a similar charge against Negroponte: "Unfortunately, today the United States is involved in serious human rights crimes committed in the process of collecting intelligence. Is he going to look the other way again?" (Shane 2005, A13). The controversy over outsourcing torture to other nations raises similar concerns. In interviews with the *New York Times,* several current and former government officials said "they believe that, in practice, the administration's approach may have involved in turning a blind eye to torture" (Jehl and Johnston 2005, A14). Even in his testimony to Congress, Porter J. Goss, the new CIA director, acknowledged that the United States can only provide so many safeguards against torture: "of course once they're out of our control, there's only so much we can do" (Jehl and Johnston 2005, A14).

Interpretive Denial

In defending controversial tactics in the war on terror, government officials also engage in interpretive denial, spinning euphemism and legalism. One such example of relying on soft language or euphemism to dampen criticism over harsh measures, is the Justice Department's use of the term "interview" rather than "interrogation" in reference to the government's plan to question foreign nationals (holding valid visas) in the months following 9/11. Journalists and political commentators not only detected the euphemism embodied in the term "interview," but ridiculed Ashcroft when he announced "We're being as kind and fair and gentle as we can" (Downes 2001, WK2). Lawrence Downes, in his op-ed piece published in the *New York Times,* parodied the Justice Department. Satirically, Downes writes:

> Dear Middle Eastern Man,
> A bunch of us federal agents were thinking about getting together sometime soon. Would you like to join us? How about next Wednesday, between 3:30 and 4:45? Nothing formal, just come as you are!
> We'll supply the coffee and cookies. But if you could answer the following questions (in black pen, please) and bring this sheet with you, that would be great.
> (1) Are you a terrorist?
> (2) Seriously, are you? (If so, please call us right away!)
> (3) Do you know any terrorists?
> (4) Do you know where Osama bin Laden is?
> (5) If not, do you know how we could get a package to him?
> (6) If we arrested you and held you for a while, would you have a problem with that?
> (7) What are all of you so mad about? (Downes 2001, WK2)

Despite the apparent humor, many civil liberties groups were not amused by the Justice Department's campaign to "interview" 82,000 Middle Eastern men, especially considering that hundreds were unjustly detained and deported. In response to the government heavy-handed tactics, the American Civil Liberties promptly prepared and distributed a pamphlet, *Know Your Rights: What to Do If You're Stopped by The Police, The FBI, The INS, or The Customs Service* (American Civil Liberties Union 2001, 2004; Tracy 2002).

Shortly after the attacks of September 11, Attorney General Ashcroft also participated in legalism, thereby deepening the government's commitment to interpretive denial in its domestic war on terror. Ashcroft proposed limiting judicial appeals of detentions and deportation and setting up a new legal standard for detention that requires only a "reason to believe" that someone is associated with terrorism (Povich 2001). Under the newly enacted USA Patriot Act, the Justice Department forged ahead with its broad powers, including the government's new rule to listen in on conversations between inmates and their lawyers—in effect suspending the Sixth Amendment right to effective counsel. In both instances, the government's legalistic tactics lend themselves to Cohen's observation on reinterpretation. "Powerful forms of interpretive denial come from the language of legality itself. Countries with democratic credentials sensitive to their international image now offer legalistic defences, drawn from the accredited human rights discourse" (Cohen 2001, 107). The Bush team's invention of the unlawful criminal combatant directive, allowing the U.S. government to detain indefinitely terrorist suspects, demonstrates a high degree of legalism intended to skirt U.S. Constitutional law, international law, and the Geneva Conventions.

Adding to evidence that the government routinely relies on interpretive denial in the war on terror, the FBI ordered supervisors in its 56 field bureaus to develop "demographic" profiles by counting the number of mosques and Muslims in their areas. As *Newsweek,* reported: "Those profiles are then being used, along with other factors to set up specific numerical goals for counterterrorism investigations and secret national-security wiretaps in each region" (Isikoff 2003, 6). FBI officials said the tactic is justified on the basis that there exist undetected "sleeper cells" and troublesome evidence that some mosques may be serving as cover for terrorist activity. A top FBI supervisor said: "This is not politically correct, no question about it. But it would be stupid not to look at this given the number of criminal mosques that may be out there" (Isikoff 2003, 6). When the news story broke, civil rights advocates and Arab-American leaders denounced the directive, accusing the government of furthering its campaign of ethnic profiling.

In a sharp turnaround, FBI officials countered with their own form of interpretive denial saying the agency was focusing "primarily on vulnerabilities, and mosques in the past that have been target for violence," according to Cassandra Chandler, an assistant director of the FBI (Lichtblau 2003c, EV1). Chandler's remarks, however, do not square with those of Wilson Lowery, Jr., executive director of the FBI who told Congressional officials "that the information would be used to help establish a yardstick for the number of terrorism investigations and intelligence warrants that a field office could reasonably be expected to produce" (Lichtblau 2003c, EV1). Still, one Congressional aide, responded: "On its face, it certainly sounds like the FBI is pressuring agents to use a profile.

It's beyond eyebrow-raising. It seems like a bloody waste of law enforcement resources, and it's pure profiling in its worst form" (Lichtblau 2003c, EV1). The ACLU said the tactic was "tailor-made for a witch hunt" and compared it to the ethnic census information collected during World War II as a precursor to the internment of Japanese-Americans" (Lichtblau 2003c, EV1; see American Civil Liberties Union 2003). The controversy over monitoring mosques is compounded further by the crackdown on Islamic charities, especially amid charges that the FBI falsified evidence against certain groups (Goodstein 2003b).

Implicatory Denial

Implicatory denial also abounds in the war on terror, particularly given the tendencies for government officials and intelligence operatives to deny the psychological, political, and moral implications of such tactics as ethnic profiling, abusive detention, and even torture. Several of the national security officials interviewed by reporters of the *Washington Post* defended the use of violence against captives as just and necessary. Moreover, they expressed confidence that the American public would back them, especially in light of a new climate encouraging abuse in the wake of 9/11. As noted an FBI agent told reporters: "It could get to that spot where we could go to pressure" (Priest and Gellman 2002, A1). While arguing that torture ought not be "authorized," Robert Litt, a former Justice Department official, suggested it could be used in an "emergency" (Williams 2001, 11). Again, a government operative who has supervised the capture and transfer of accused terrorists: "If you don't violate someone's human rights some of the time, you probably aren't doing your job. I don't think we want to be promoting a view of zero tolerance on this. That was the whole problem for a long time with the CIA" (Priest and Gellman 2002, A1).

Due in large part to graphic photos documenting abuse, the Abu Ghraib prison scandal became a worldwide embarrassment for the United States. Promptly, the Bush team set out to control the blaming process, unleashing the standard "bad apples" explanation to counter suspicion that the use of torture was systemic, and a matter of counterterroism policy in a post-9/11 world (Harbury 2005, Hersh 2004). Strangely, however, some members of Congress swam against the tide of international condemnation by suggesting that their ill treatment was somehow deserved. Senator James Inhofe, a Republican from Oklahoma and member of the Senate Armed Services Committee insisted: "These prisoners . . . you know they're not there for traffic violations. If they're in Cellblock 1-A or 1-B, these prisoners, they're murderers, they're terrorists, they're insurgents. Many of them probably have American blood on their hands, and here we're so concerned about the treatment of those individuals" (Sontag 2004, 42; see Rich 2004a).

In a parallel vein, former Senate majority leader Trent Lott defended the interrogation techniques, commenting: "Most people in Mississippi came up to me and said: 'Thank Goodness. America comes first.' Interrogation is not a Sunday-school class. You don't get information that will save American lives by withholding pancakes" (Solomon, 2004, 15). Journalist Deborah Solomon confronted Lott, pointing out that unleashing killer dogs on naked prisoners is not the same as withholding pancakes. Lott responded: "I was amazed that people reacted like that. Did the dogs bite them? Did the dogs assault them? How are you going to get people to give information that will lead to the saving of lives?" (Solomon 2004, 15). Contributing to the wave of implicatory denial, Secretary of Defense Rumsfeld, who insisted that Iraqi prisoners, as unlawful combatants, do not have any rights under the Geneva Convention, mocked restrictions on stress and duress positions (like standing) for a maximum of four hours: "I stand for 8–10 hours a day. Why is standing limited to 4 hours?" (Jehl 2004b, A10).

Considering ethnic profiling, detention, and reliance on secrecy, Ashcroft and other government officials engaged further in implicatory denial by arguing that such measures are necessary to ensure national security even though such repressive tactics have failed to identify clear links to terrorism (Marable 2003; Ratner 2003). With such spin, government officials diminish the universal values of immigrants' rights, civil liberties, and human rights. As noted previously, Glenn A. Fine, inspector general at the Department of Justice, confirmed suspicions that the government's approach to the war on terror was plagued with serious problems. The report concluded that the government's round-up of hundreds of illegal immigrants in the aftermath of 9/11 was a mistake since it forced many people with no connection to terrorism to languish behind bars in unduly harsh conditions. The inspector general found that even some of the lawyers in the Justice Department expressed concerns about the legality of its tactics only to be overridden by senior administrators. Despite strong evidence of civil rights violations contained in the report, Justice Department officials defended themselves saying that they believed they had acted within the law in pursuing terrorist suspects. Barbara Comstock, a spokeswoman for the department announced: "We make no apologies for

finding every legal way possible to protect the American public from further terrorist attacks" (Lichtblau 2003b, A1). The implication then is that
such abuses were not that serious and even so they were justified in the
name of national security.

Each of these forms of denial—literal, interpretive, and implicatory—
all serve the government's wider interest in averting blame and refusing
to take responsibility for its policies and actions. Taken together, they
contribute to the dynamic of passing the hot potato that would otherwise
force government officials to be held accountable for their trampling of
civil liberties and human rights, activities that have become a defining
emblem on the war on terror. As we turn to the next segment, those
manifestations of denial are becoming increasingly apparent at the cultural level, especially since September 11.

Cultural Denial

Denial becomes official when it is public, collective, and highly organized. Unlike totalitarian regimes that go to great lengths to rewrite history and block out the present, denial in democratic societies is subtle,
often taking the form of spin-doctoring and public agenda setting. But
similar to totalitarianism, democratic nations also build denial into the
ideological facade of the state, turning to fraud rather than force (Cohen
2001; Willis 1999). Eventually, entire societies are subject to slipping into
collective modes of denial and when that occurs, citizens adopt potent
defense mechanisms against acknowledging atrocities within their own
nation. In the war on terror, cultural denial and official denial operate in
tandem, developments that pose grave threats to civil liberties and human rights (see Neier 2003; Schulz 2004).

As the government rounded up and detained more than 1,200 immigrants of Middle Eastern descent shortly after 9/11, some concerned citizens took notice, most notably those who had previously suffered similar forms of detention (i.e., Japanese-Americans). However, polls showed
that Americans supported such racial/ethnic profiling (Nieves, 2001).
Even more distressing is the degree of public support for torture. A CNN
poll revealed that 45 percent of those surveyed would not object to having someone tortured if it would provide information about terrorism
(Williams, 2001). To repeat, Dana Priest, one of the reporters who exposed the use of torture by the CIA long before the Abu Ghraib scandal,
was asked why there's been so little follow-up in the rest of the media. "It's

hard," Priest explained, "to keep a story going when there's no outrage, as in Congress—where there have been no calls for hearings" (Hentoff 2003e, 33).

A further look into the media since September 11 offers a valuable opportunity to understand how denial persists as the war on terror continues. As a pillar in the culture industry, the media possesses the ability to influence public opinion; as a result, it remains on the "front lines in the state's battle to formulate a sense of cohesive purpose and national identity, particularly during wartime" (Robin 2003, 54). Political and corporate elites often go to great lengths to ensure that their agendas are supported by the mainline media. The case of Bill Maher, a political humorist and host of ABC's show *Politically Incorrect*, exhibits the thrust of such influence. In the wake of 9/11, Maher shocked the political and military establishment by saying: "We have the cowards, lobbing cruise missiles from two thousand miles away. . . . Staying in the airplane, when it hits the building—say what you want about that, it's not cowardly" (Silverglate 2002, A21). The White House was infuriated by Maher's remarks and Press Secretary Ari Fleischer warned that Americans "need to watch what they say" (Huff 2001, 112).

In a classic ritual of shaming, Maher was forced to make a public apology. Eventually, the network cancelled *Politically Incorrect,* an irony that is not lost given that the show was living up to its name. Looking back on those events, Maher quipped: "I was the first one to be Dixie Chicked," referring to the country band that openly criticized Bush for the invasion of Iraq only to be blackballed by the music industry (Goldstein 2003, 51). A similar form of shaming—and intimidation—emerged on college campuses and, in November 2001, the American Council of Trustees and Alumni (ACTA), a conservative think tank founded by Lynne Cheney (wife of the vice president) released a report titled *Defending Civilization: How Our Universities Are Failing America and What Can Be Done About It.* The report accused professors by name for making statements "short on patriotism and long on self-flagellation" (American Council of Trustees and Alumni, 2001, EV8; see Mashberg 2001; Scigliano 2001).

Corporate media continues to follow the strictures of the state's war on terror. One month following the attacks, Condoleezza Rice, national security advisor for President Bush, met with network chiefs from ABC, CBS, NBC, Fox, and CNN, issuing them a protocol for airing videotaped statements of Osama bin Laden (FAIR 2001a). CNN went further by requiring its staff to pair any scene of civilian casualties in Afghanistan caused by U.S. military with reminders of the victims of September 11

(FAIR 2001b). Fairness and Accuracy in Reporting (FAIR) released an in-depth report documenting the pro-U.S. military bias in the nation's most prestigious newspapers (FAIR 2001c). Political scientist Corey Robin observed: "While some of this bias can be attributed to the media's horror over the attacks of 9/11 as well as heartfelt jingoism, some of it is a response from above which is then translated to staffers below" (2003, 56). Erik Sorenson, president of MSNBC, who generally identifies with conservative ideologies in the war on terror concedes that he and other executives are careful not to provoke public opinion: "Any misstep and you can get into trouble with these guys and have the Patriotism police hunt you down" (Stanley 2001, B4).

A critical analysis of post-9/11 America offers a glimpse into the nation's cultural psyche, including intensified conflicts over free expression and political dissent. Clearly, there is evidence of a growing authoritarianism that espouses a rigid respect for authority and its symbols of patriotism, nationalism, militarism, and civil religion. That form of authoritarianism, however, is not entirely a top to bottom phenomenon since it is shared by a wide segment of American society. Such values maintain a society that tends to shun anti-establishment expression, and in doing so upholds hierarchies that marginalize voices of dissent (Welch, Sassi, and McDonough 2002). As a relatively young democracy, the United States is still grappling with the complexities of liberty and free expression, and strong anti-dissent attitudes—especially during wartime—reflect "societal insecurities, especially deep fears that the nation is 'coming apart,' and demonstrates a widespread misunderstanding of the substance of political freedom" (Goldstein 1995, 253; Welch 2000a). In the fallout of the attacks on the World Trade Center and the Pentagon there is a renewed sense of patriotism, and support for American militarism has taken on a new resonance. Since those acts of terrorism, there has been considerable debate over how to balance national security with civil liberties, specifically in light of the government's use of racial profiling, mass detention, and secrecy. More to the point of this discussion, there is growing concern over the government's response to political dissent. Attorney General Ashcroft, defending his tactics for the war on terrorism, declared that any public criticism of the Bush administration and its policies would be aiding terrorists. Revealingly, that narrow view of civil liberties has considerable support among a large proportion of Americans, according to public opinion polls (Toner and Elder 2001).

As an example of how strongly some Americans feel about political dissent in post-9/11 America, Janis Besler Heaphy, publisher of the

Sacramento Bee and commencement speaker at California State University at Sacramento, was booed off the stage for calling for the protection of civil liberties in the government's response to terrorism. When Heaphy urged that citizens safeguard their rights to free speech, the crowd of 10,000 graduates and guests booed louder. When she wondered what would happen if racial profiling became routine, the audience cheered. Heaphy struggled to complete her speech and when she proposed that "the Constitution makes it our right to challenge government policies" a clapping chant and further heckling forced her off the stage (Egan 2001, B1). Observers of civil liberties and free speech quickly weighed in on the incident. A representative of the American Civil Liberties Union stated "if you took the Bill of Rights to the street and asked most people to sign it, you would be unable to get a majority of Americans to do so" (Egan 2001, B4).

This discussion lends itself to further elaboration, particularly in light of an emerging cultural criminology that affirms the assumption that "the criminalization process then is that cultural process whereby those in power come to define and shape dominant forms of social life and give them specific meanings" (Presdee 2000, 17; see Ferrell and Sanders 1995). Antagonism toward civil liberties and human rights in the aftermath of September 11 reveal a compelling degree of obedience among the masses to comply with the authorities. Ironically though, by engaging in informal control such as censoring, harassing, and ridiculing those who engage in insubordination, citizens strengthen an apparatus of formal social control that reproduces hierarchies and structural inequality, thus undermining a democratic society.

Fighting Back

As stressed throughout this discussion, the war on terror is fraught with multiple forms of denial, all of which contribute to a culture of denial that dismisses violations of civil liberties and human rights. In fighting back, however, groups such as the American Civil Liberties Union, Amnesty International, the Center for Constitutional Rights, Human Rights First, and Human Rights Watch set out to confront official lying, deception, and disinformation (literal denial) along with official renaming (interpretive denial).[1] Furthermore, advocates for human rights are challenging cultural denial by engaging in rigorous public consciousness-raising, making it difficult for citizens to overlook the serious nature of such violations (see Drinan 2001; Shattuck 2003). By doing so, human rights campaigns mobilize citizens to take action against such injustices by confronting government officials who rely on denial, euphemisms, and spin as political tactics.

There is evidence that citizens are beginning to fight back against the tide of government authoritarianism that has gained a thrust of momentum since September 11. Four states (Alaska, Hawaii, Maine, Vermont) and more than 310 cities, towns, and countries across the nation have passed Bill of Rights resolutions condemning key sections of the Patriot Act, including ethnic, religious, and political profiling, secret detentions, sneak-and-peek searches, and the snooping into library and bookstore records. In doing so, those communities have established civil liberties safe zones, a term coined by Nancy Talanian, director of the original Bill of Rights Defense Committee in Northhampton, Massachusetts, where the grassroots renewal of constitutional democracy started (Hentoff 2003c). Whereas many of those resolutions are symbolic, some may actually have some legal teeth (Chang 2004).

Many mainstream citizens who until recently did not pay much attention to the government's war on terror tactics have begun to take notice of some of the extreme responses by federal agents. In Maryland, a 12-year-old student at the Boys' Latin School got an unexpected visit from the FBI after he had using the Internet to research the Chesapeake Bay Bridge for a class project (Chang 2004). Moreover, the grassroots resistance against the Patriot Act has some backing by key political figures. Former Vice President Al Gore called for a complete repeal of the statute, saying: "I want to challenge the Bush administration's implicit assumption that we have to give up many of our traditional freedoms in order to be safe from terrorists. It is simply not true" (Doty 2003). Even more significant, conservative Republican James Sensenbrenner, chairman of the House Judiciary Committee, made it known to his colleagues that he would not consider reauthorization of the Patriot Act until the end of 2005, presenting a key obstacle for the Bush team in their efforts to renew sections of the Act before they expire (Hentoff 2004a). Other conservatives expressed their discontent for the Patriot Act, especially its surveillance measures and secret warrants. Republican Phil Kent, former aide to Senator Strom Thurmond, opined: "The fact is, we should not be making suspects out of 280 million Americans" (Lichtblau 20031, A19).

Perhaps feeling the pressure from an array of critics, Attorney General Ashcroft embarked on a massive campaign, touring the country in support of renewing the Patriot Act. Ashcroft pushed his message, "We are winning the war on terrorism" to invitation-only forums, often packed with uniformed police as his audience (Lichtblau 20031, A19). Outside, however, protestors continued to stalk the attorney general with signs denouncing him as a "fascist." Ashcroft's tour was so visibly robust that some Democrats accused him of violating federal ethics laws that ban lobbying and political activities by officials from the executive branch. Many newspapers panned the speeches by Ashcroft, observing that they had "an air of desperation" about them (Lichtblau 20031, A19). Ashcroft clearly selected his audience carefully so as not to be confronted or even forced to debate the wisdom of the Patriot Act.

Other forms of fighting back have also emerged, including Ashcroft's foes in the American Library Association who prepared some *technically* legal placards for libraries to post without violating the gag order imposed on librarians that prohibits them from notifying patrons that the FBI has targeted them:

> We're sorry! Because of national-security concerns, we are unable to tell you if your Internet surfing habits, passwords and e-mail content are being monitored by federal agents; please act appropriately.

> The FBI has not been here. [Watch very closely for the removal of this sign.]

> Q. How can you tell when the FBI has been in your library?
> A. You can't. The Patriot Act makes it illegal for us to tell you if your computers are monitored; be aware. (Talbot 2003, 19)

Interestingly, even groups at the front lines of the war on terror are fighting back by the very agency that employs them. In 2004, the Department of Homeland Security issued a directive requiring its employees to sign a nondisclosure agreement so restrictive that it might be unconstitutional. The provision barred department workers from giving the public "sensitive but unclassified" information and permits the government to "conduct inspections at any time or place" to ensure that the agreement is obeyed (Wingfield 2004, A20). Workers expressed anger that their civil liberties were under threat by the very agency that employed them, prompting their unions to challenge the agreement. The National Treasury Employees and the American Federation of Government Employees challenged the Department for its "unprecedented leeway to search homes and personal belongings in violation of the Fourth Amendment" (Wingfield 2004, A20). In the face of worker resistance, the Department backed off. In place of the nondisclosure agreement, the Department reported that it would institute procedures to ensure that employees have the proper training for handling sensitive information (Files 2005, A17; see also Pear 2005).

Social movements opposing the Patriot Act and related tactics go beyond the special interests of government workers and librarians, for example. Nowadays, resistance against authoritarianism also questions the prevailing rationale driving the war on terror: "There are people and governments in the world who believe that in the struggle against terrorism, ends always justify means. But that is also the logic of terrorism. Whatever the response to this outrage, it must not validate that logic. Rather, it must uphold the principles that came under attack yesterday, respecting innocent life and international law. That is the way to deny the perpetrators of this crime their ultimate victory" (Human Rights Watch 2001, 1). As the ethics troubling the war on terror continue to undergo scrutiny, it is important to bear in mind the role of international relations in devising and implementing counterterrorism policies and practices. As explored in the next, and final, segment of this book, these and other crucial developments in the legal arena affecting human rights loom large.

Policy and Legal Implications

By adopting the *criminology of the other* along with a host of mystical condemnations (e.g., evil, evildoers, wicked), a coherent understanding of political violence is obscured. Especially since September 11, the prevailing war on terror is fraught with self-defeating measures: the post-9/11 round-ups, a special registration program, and mass—and indefinite—detentions, are proven to be dysfunctional and ineffective in reducing the threat of terrorism in the United States. Additionally, those problems are compounded further by secrecy, casting doubt and suspicion on government officials who sidestep public scrutiny and accountability. Here key areas of policy are examined in an effort to improve counterterrorism strategies, in particular the importance of protecting civil liberties and human rights while cultivating international relations.

For counterterrorism policies to become effective both in the short- and long-term, issues surrounding civil liberties and human rights must be taken serious. Regrettably, governmental leaders—especially in the United States—have politicized efforts to deal with terrorism in ways that stoke and exploit public fear (Ratner 2003; Robin 2003). Indeed, the prevailing politics of fear has allowed the Bush administration to use national security and threats of terrorism as the "ultimate all-purpose trump card. The Bush crowd will play it anywhere" (Cole 2004c, 5). In the realm of civil liberties, the trump card of national security perpetuates the false paradigm that in order to fight effectively the war on terror, citizens must surrender some of their freedoms. Attacks on civil liberties not only undermine democratic institutions but they also fail to improve national security. Once again, no one can be made safe by arresting the wrong people since by doing so it not only violates their civil rights but also abandons public safety as well (Glasser 2003).

The Bush administration also has issued its trump card to shield itself from criticism over secret detentions (Dow 2004, 2001). Legal experts strongly urge the government to amend its tactics in the war on terror so that its actions may be subject to public scrutiny. To reiterate, three areas of accountability are recommended. First, the Justice Department must release information about those it detains, including their names and location. Secret detentions such as those used by the Justice Department in its anti-terrorism campaign violate the *Declaration on the Protection of All Persons from Enforced Disappearances,* a non-binding resolution by the United Nations General Assembly in 1992. Second, independent monitoring groups must be granted unrestricted access to detention facilities so as to ensure that detainees are treated in a fair and humane manner (Human Rights Watch 2003). Third, immigration proceedings must no longer be conducted in secrecy (Cole, 2003b; Cole and Dempsey, 2002).

Recently appealing a landmark human rights case to the U.S. Supreme Court, the Bush administration once again has played the trump card. Invoking national security, the U.S. government has argued that enforcing human rights protection could undermine public safety. The case *Sosa v. Alvarez-Machain* involves the Alien Tort Claims Act of 1789 that provides human rights victims a legal avenue to hold violators liable for crimes against humanity. Specifically, the Alien Tort Claims Act permits foreign citizens to use the U.S. federal courts to sue for damages committed overseas. *Sosa v. Alvarez-Machain* is a joint appeal by the U.S. government and a Mexican citizen, Jose Francisco Sosa, who was hired by American drug enforcement officials to kidnap a Mexican physician and bring him across the border. The physician, Humberto Alvarez-Machain, was indicted on charges of participating in the torture and murder of federal agent Enrique Camarena-Salazar in Guadalajara (Mexico) in 1990.

Dr. Alvarez-Machain, however, was acquitted of all charges and re-turned to Mexico. In 1993, he sued both the U.S. government and Sosa, claiming that he had been subject to false arrest in violation of interna-tional law. A federal district court dismissed the suit against the U.S. gov-ernment that was filed under the Federal Tort Claim Act but allowed the case against Sosa to proceed under the Alien Tort Claims Act. In that case, a jury awarded Alvarez-Machain $25,000 in damages. On appeal, the Ninth Circuit Court of Appeals not only upheld the judgment but also reinstated Alvarez-Machain's suit against the U.S. government. The Bush administration urged the Supreme Court to overturn the judg-ment, arguing that should federal courts enforce international human rights norms, such rulings could weaken the government's war on terror. To that Professor David Cole comments: "But of course, the whole point of international law is to limit the prerogatives of nations, at least when it comes to fundamental rights owed to all persons" (2004c, 5; Green-house, 2004c).

In 2004, the U.S. Supreme Court ruled in *Sosa v. Alvarez-Machain* (2004) to keep federal courts open to lawsuits by foreigners who allege that they were victims of brazen human rights violations occurring any-where in the world. The Court's interpretation of the Alien Tort statute is welcomed by human rights groups, especially since it rejects the Bush administration claim that the statute ought to be narrowed. Human rights lawyers are hopeful that the Court's decision will apply to univer-sally recognized violations, including genocide, slavery, and prolonged arbitrary detention (Greenhouse 2004c). The legal reasoning evident in *Sosa v. Alvarez-Machain* reflects growing interest in the internationaliza-tion of human rights. In a key development revealing international pres-sure on the U.S. criminal justice system, the International Court of Jus-tice, located in The Hague, issued a resounding ruling when it ordered American courts to undertake "an effective review" of the death sen-tences imposed on fifty-one Mexicans. The United Nation's highest court determined that the Mexican prisoners' rights were violated under in-ternational law. The Court found that the prisoners were repeatedly de-nied the right to speak with Mexican consular officials after their arrest. Similar cases recently have been filed in the Court against the United States involving prisoners from Germany and Paraguay.

The United States recognizes the jurisdiction of the Court to resolve disputes between nations arising under the 1963 Vienna Convention on Consular Relations, spanning 165 countries. Under the Convention, per-sons arrested abroad have the right to consult with representatives of their government and they must be advised of such a right. Still, elected leaders in the United States resist the application of international law in American cases. Governor Rick Perry, who succeeded President Bush stated: "the International Court of Justice does not have jurisdiction in Texas" (Simons and Weiner 2004, A8). U.S. State and Justice Department officials insist that international law is an intrusion into the American criminal justice system. Although the Court's decisions are binding, it has no power to enforce them (Liptak 2004b). In a bold step in 2005, Bush ordered the United States to exit from the International Court of Justice. Legal experts harshly criticized the withdrawal from the world judicial body: "It's a sore-loser kind of move. If we can't win, we're not going to play," said Peter J. Spiro, law professor at the University of Georgia (Liptak 2005, A16). Similarly, Harold Hongiu Koh, dean of the Yale Law School, characterized the move as counterproductive: "International adjudication is an important tool in a post-cold-war, post-9/11 world (Liptak 2005, A16).[2]

At the center of any criminal justice campaign is its perceived legitimacy. Crime control and counterterrorism tactics that appear out of step with civil liberties and human rights are bound to erode public support (see Welch 2005d, 2005e). This consideration is even more important as the war on terror becomes increasingly global. Hard-line anti-terrorism strategies that trample the rights of people do not contribute to national security; rather, they undermine it. Moreover, effective counterterrorism policies and practices are contingent upon good international relations. Such cooperation within the international community is especially important for the United States, given that anti-Americanism is at an all-time high around the world. Fueling such resentment is the widespread view of the U.S. government's reputation for ignoring principles of international law and human rights (e.g., the controversies over Guantanamo Bay and the Abu Ghraib prison scandal; see Knowlton, 2005).

Former national security advisor serving President Carter, Zbigniew Brzezinski contends in his book, *The Choice: Global Domination or Global Leadership* (2004), that America's safety is dependent on international security. As the link between national sovereignty and national security dissolves, America's domestic security is increasingly in the hands of others. With those developments fully recognized, Brzezinski takes issue with the Bush administration for adopting a demonization approach to terrorism in which the government must locate and take out of circulation those who are evil and pose a danger to the nation. Like the *criminology of the other,* a demonization perspective on terrorism is not only too abstract but also politically unsustainable, leading to scare mongering and scapegoating. Moreover, that response presents an inadequate diagnosis of terrorism, prompting other nations to refuse to cooperate. Brzezinski also insists that an effective counterterrorism platform requires that the problem be understood in its proper historical and political context. At the heart of every act of terrorism is a political conflict, and its sources must be addressed in order to present a strategy that is both informed and legitimate. In an effort to improve not only national security for the United States but for other countries as well, Brzezinski advocates the expansion of zones of global stability by recognizing that political violence is caused in large part by misery and injustice. The preservation of zones of global stability rests on human rights and a commitment to democracy, rather than the impulse of unilateral authority (see Barak 2001; Cohen 2001; Wallace and Kreisel 2003).

Final Thoughts

While elaborating on his views on the culture of control, sociologist David Garland notes that the conservative shift toward greater social control is not a generalized phenomenon but rather one targeting particular groups and their behaviors. The new conservatism sends "a message exhorting everyone to return to the values of family, work, abstinence, and self control, but in practice its real moral disciplines fastened onto the behaviour of unemployed workers, welfare mothers, immigrants, offenders, and drug users" (Garland 2001, 99–100). As the culture of control tightens the grip on those marginalized by economic conditions, it perpetuates fear across the social spectrum, enabling the *criminology of the other* to divert attention from progressive criminology. The popular notion of criminals—and terrorists—transcends both reality and humanity, with criminals becoming imaginary figures that political conservatives manipulate and exploit. Consequently, harsh criminal justice and counterterrorism tactics often are erroneously seen as practical and rational since they are aimed at taking so-called dangerous or evil persons "out of circulation" (Douglas 1992, 1982). The culture of control also resists attempts to reevaluate tough on crime strategies that would otherwise reveal the fallacies of labeling and the detrimental effects of mass imprisonment. The same holds true for ineffective and unjust counterterrorism tactics that rely on profiling and indefinite detention, creating an array of human rights violations (see Fekete 2002; Schmid 2003; Reitan 2003).

Worldwide concern over the threats of terrorism is indeed warranted. Still, it is important to remain critical of the politics of fear that empower governments to use threats to national security as an all-purpose trump card. Especially in the United States, many social issues are superficially linked to fighting terrorism, from the American invasion of Iraq to the detention of Haitians seeking safe haven in the United States (Welch 2004c; Welch and Schuster 2005a). Even the debate over gay marriages has been framed with national security in mind. "So argued a woman interviewed by NPR (National Public Radio) at the National Association of Evangelicals convention in Colorado Springs. Her reasoning: By breaking down the family, we're not having enough kids, while 'other countries' with an agenda to hurt America are having boatloads of babies. If we legalize gay marriage, the terrorists will eventually outnumber us" (Cole 2004c, 5). Ridiculous attempts to locate threats of terrorism—or evil—in other spheres of society, such as gay marriages, obscure an intelligent understanding of the nature of political violence as well as the formulation of coherent plans to prevent acts of terrorism (see Gearty 2004, 1997). Understandably, the tragic events of September 11 have had a tremendous impact on American society. If, however, the government's activities since 9/11 are any indication of where the war on terror is taking America, it is likely that civil liberties and human rights will remain in flux for the foreseeable future, producing an ever growing number of scapegoats.

NOTES

Chapter 1: Talking About Terror

1. The debate over definitions of terrorism continues to shape popular and political discourse over political violence. A French dictionary, in 1796, described terrorism as a positive activity until the 9th of Thermidor when the term was reversed to a negative connotation, linking it to criminal activity. Throughout history, the term terrorism has fluctuated between subjective viewpoints, commonly reinforcing the dictum that "one man's terrorist is another man's freedom fighter" (Onwudiwe 2002; see Gearty 1997). Since 1983, the U.S. government has defined terrorism as the "premeditated, politically motivated violence perpetrated against noncombatant targets by subnational groups or clandestine agents, usually intended to influence an audience" (United States Department of State 2002; see Garrison 2004; Nunberg 2004).

2. The following are the other "Biggest Lies Bush Told Us About Iraq." Lies #2 and #3—Imminent Threats: Iraq's Bio-Chem and Nuclear Weapons Program; Lie #4—It Will Be Easy: Iraq as a 'Cakewalk'"; Lie #5—The Moral Justification: Iraq as a Democratic Model (Scheer, Scheer, and Chaudhry 2003).

3. In 2005, the U.S. Comptroller General warned all federal agencies against producing newscasts promoting administration policies without clearly stating that the government itself is the source. The Comptroller's office has caught federal agencies distributing prepackaged televised television programs using paid spokesmen acting as newscasters, a violation of federal law (Kornblut 2005; also see Barstow and Stein 2005; Bumiller 2005).

Chapter 2: Seeking a Safer Society

1. Scrambling to correct the imbalance in funding formula, lawmakers have pushed for more spending for large metropolitan areas (Lipton 2004).

Chapter 5: Hate Crimes as Backlash Violence

1. There is considerable deliberation and debate over proposals and policies for dealing with hate crimes. Indeed, both sides of the debate offer compelling arguments for their respective positions (see Bakken 2000, 2002; Human Rights Watch 2002a; Jacobs and Potter 1998; Levin 2002; Perry 2003b). However, given the scope and thrust of this chapter, I reluctantly bypass that crucial area of the hate crime literature. Instead, the focus remains squarely on the descriptive and analytical components of backlash violence and their meaning in post-9/11 America.

Chapter 6: Profiling and Detention in Post-9/11 America

1. Another controversial law enforcement tactic in the war on terror with implications to profiling is the FBI monitoring of mosques. That practice has outraged Muslim religious leaders as well as civil liberties organizations (American Civil Liberties Union 2003c. Lichtblau 2003c; *Newsweek* 2003; see chapter 9).

Chapter 7: State Crimes in the War on Terror

1. "A recent poll indicated that nearly 70 percent of Americans believed that an Iraqi leadership probably was involved" in the attacks of 9/11 (Associated Press 2003a).
2. Constitution of the United States, Article II, Section 4: The President, Vice President and all civil officers of the United States, shall be removed from office on impeachment for, and conviction, of treason, bribery, or other high crimes and misdemeanors. Articles of impeachment have been drafted by former attorney general, Ramsey Clark (www.votetoimpeach.org and www.impeachbush.org).
3. The following websites attempt to document the human death toll in the war in Iraq: Iraq Body Count: (Iraqbodycount.net) and Iraq Coalition Casualty Count: (Icasualties.org/oif).
4. In another area of controversy, the U.S. military stands accused of deliberately targeting journalists in Iraq. On April 3, 2003, "a US warplane swooped in and fired a rocket at Al Jazeera's office," killing correspondent Tareq Ayyoub. And on April 8, 2003: "a US Abrams tank fired at the Palestine Hotel, home and office to more than 100 unembedded international journalists. . . . The shell smashed into the fifteenth floor of the Reuters office, killing two cameramen" (*Nation* 2005c, 4–5.).

Chapter 8: Claiming Effectiveness

1. As an example of how counterterrorism aimed at preserving public safety is undermined by gaps in gun control legislation, the Government Accounting Office discovered that dozens of terror suspects on federal watch lists were allowed to

buy firearms legally in the United States. "People suspected of being members of a terrorist group are not automatically barred from legally buying a gun [including assault rifles], and the Government Accounting Office indicated that people with clear links to terrorist groups had regularly taken advantage of this gap" (Lichtblau 2005, A1; *New York Times* 2005b).

Chapter 9 Assaulting Civil Liberties

1. In July 2004, an amendment to the Patriot Act that would have prevented the government from obtaining records from libraries and bookstores in some terrorism investigations failed by one vote in a highly partisan and bitter battle in the House of Representatives (Lichtblau 2004k, A16).
2. Page 9 of an undated letter of Assistant Attorney General Daniel Bryant sent to Senators Bob Graham, Orrin Hatch, Patrick Leahy, and Richard Shelby while the USA Patriot Act was under consideration by Congress. A copy of the letter is on file with Nancy Chang at the Center for Constitutional Rights (see Chang 2002, 56).
3. Civil liberties organizations also are concerned over other provisions of the Patriot Act, including Section 203 that allows the sharing of sensitive criminal and foreign intelligence information. At issue is the disclosure of grand jury proceedings that are subject to strict rules of secrecy so as to ensure that witnesses may testify freely and openly. Section 203 threatens to undermine the integrity of grand juries should confidential disclosures be shared with other federal agencies, including the CIA (American Civil Liberties Union 2003a, 2003b; Chang 2002).
4. Civil liberties groups and defense attorneys express enormous concern that the government is strategically trying to create a chill effect that would discourage lawyers from representing terrorist suspects. The fall-out involving the case of Lynne F. Stewart is being carefully watched (Glaberson 2005d). Stewart represents Sheik Omar Abdel Rohman who in 1995 was convicted of conspiracy to attack New York City landmarks and is serving a life sentence in federal prison. In 2005, Stewart was convicted on five counts of providing material aid to terrorism and lying to the government when she pledged to obey federal rules that barred her client from communicating with his followers (Preston 2005). Critics complain that the new rules allowing the government to listen and record conversations between attorneys and their clients violate the Sixth Amendment right to effective counsel (Napolitano 2005).
5. In February 2003, the Justice Department was grilled for a draft that it prepared for further expansion of law enforcement powers. The 80-page document marked "Confidential—Not for Distribution Draft Jan. 9, 2003" was delivered to House Speaker Dennis Hastert and to Vice President Dick Cheney in his capacity as president of the Senate. Eventually, it was leaked and posted on the website of the Center for Public Integrity (www.publicintegrity.org/dtaweb/home.asp). The proposal included several controversial measures, including the following:

> Invalidate state legal consent decrees that seek to curb police spying. The authors argued that such orders could hinder terrorism investigations.
> Eliminate the requirement that the attorney general personally has to authorize using certain intelligence evidence in a criminal case, permitting him to designate an assistant attorney general to make such authorization.

Allow the collection of DNA samples by "such means as are reasonably necessary" from suspected terrorists being held by federal authorities. Failing to cooperate would be crime.

Flatly bar Freedom of Information Act efforts to gain information about detainees, because litigation over such issues costs the Justice Department resources.

Allow citizenship to be stripped from people who support groups that the United States considers terrorist organizations. (Clymer 2003a, A10)

Chapter 10: Culture of Control

1. Some moral panic research tends to overlook the ironic and symbiotic relationship between moral crusaders and those they demonize. Correcting that deficiency, McRobbie and Thornton (1995) recognize that social worlds have become increasingly multimediated. Therefore, targets of moral panic and campaigns of criminalization often are able to fight back using the media to challenge authority and legitimacy of moral guardians (see Ferrell 1996; Welch, Sassi, and McDonough 2002).

2. One of the 51 Mexican cases is that of Roberto Moreno Ramos who was sentenced to death after being convicted of murdering his wife in 1992. In addition to being denied his right to consult the Mexican consulate, his lawyer contends that he has evidence that Ramos is mentally retarded, a finding not raised by previous defense attorneys. The Mexican government sponsors a legal assistance program because diplomats realize that many Mexicans who are arrested in the United States are bewildered by American legal procedures and many speak poor English. Mexican officials informed the court that in cases when consular protection was permitted, life sentences were more likely than death sentences (Liptak 2004b). The court's ruling would apply to more than 120 foreign prisoners from 29 nations currently on death row. Reed Brody of Human Rights Watch commented: "The right to see your consul is not just a technicality, it is a way to avoid all kinds of errors and miscarriages of justice. Of course, this right is just as important for Americans abroad" (Simons and Weiner 2004, A8). The hypocrisy is clear since the United States rarely recognizes the International Court of Justice unless the Court rules in its favor.

CASES

American Friends Service Committee, et al., v. City and Counter of Denver, Civil Action
    No. 02-N-0740 (D. Colo.) (2002)
Bates v. City of Little Rock, 361 U.S. 516 (1960)
John Doe, American Civil Liberties Union v. John Ashcroft and FBI Director Robert Mueller,
    317 F. Supp. 2d 488; 2004 U.S. (New York)
Hamdi v. Rumsfeld, 542 U.S. 507 (2044)
Humanitarian Law Project v. Ashcroft, 309 F. Supp. 2d 1185, (2004)
NAACP v. Alabama ex rel Patterson, 357 U.S. 449 (1958)
NAACP v. Claiborne Hardware Co., 458 U.S., 886, 932 (1982)
Rasul v. Bush, 542 U. S. 466 (2004)
Rumsfeld v. Padilla, 542 U.S. 426 (2004)
Scales v. United States, 367 U.S. 203, 229 (1961), reh'g denied, 367 U.S. 978 (1961)
Sosa v. Alvarez-Machain, 124 S. Ct. 2739; 159 L. Ed. 2d 718; 2004 U.S.
United States v. Koubriti, 305 F. Supp. 2d 723 (2003)
United States v. Koubriti, 336 F. Supp. 2d 676, (2004)
United States v. Robel, 389 U.S., 258, 262, (1967)
United States v. United States District Court for the Eastern District of Michigan (Keith),
    407 U.S. 297 (1972)
Whitney v. California, 274 U.S. 357 (1927)
Wilson v. Arkansas, 514 U.S. 927, 929 (1995)
Zadvydas v. Underdown, 185 F.3d 279 (5th Cir. 1999), 121 S. Ct. 876 (2001)

REFERENCES

Note: EV refers to electronic version of the publication

Abraham, N. 1994. Anti-Arab racism and violence in the United States. In *The develop-ment of Arab-American identity,* 155–214, edited by Ernest McCarus. Ann Arbor: University of Michigan Press.

Adams, K. 1996. The bull market in corrections. *Prison Journal* 76: 461–467.

Adorno, T. W., E. Frenkel-Brunswik, D. J. Levinson, and R. Nevitt Sanford. 1969. *The authoritarian personality.* New York: W.W. Norton.

Allen, J. L., Jr. 2004. The campaign comes to Rome. *New York Times,* June 3, A27

Allison, G. 2004. *Nuclear terrorism: The ultimate preventable catastrophe.* New York: Henry Holt and Company.

Allport, G. 1954. *The nature of prejudice.* Boston: Beacon Press.

Altheide, D. J. 2002. *Creating fear: News and the construction of crisis.* New York: Aldine de Gruyter.

American-Arab Antidiscrimination Committee 2001a. *ADC fact sheet: The condition of Arab Americans post 9/11.* Washington, DC: ADC.

———. 2001b. *Statement by ADC President Ziad Asali.* Press Release, September 14, EV1–3.

American Civil Liberties Union. 2001. *Know your rights: What to do if you're stopped by the police, the FBI, the INS, or the customs service.* www.aclu.org.

———. 2003a. What the USA PATRIOT Act means to you. *Civil Liberties* (fall): 7.

———. 2003b. *Freedom under fire: Dissent in post-9/11 America.* New York: American Civil Liberties Union.

———. 2003. *ACLU calls FBI Mosque-counting scheme blatant ethnic and religious profiling.* Press Release, February 6, E1–2.

————. 2004. *Worlds apart: How deporting immigrants after September 11 tore families apart and shattered communities.* New York: American Civil Liberties Union.

————. 2005. *2005 Workplan.* New York: American Civil Liberties Union.

American Council of Trustees & Alumni. 2001. Defending civilization: How our universities are failing America and what can be done about it. November 3, www.goacta.org/Reports/def-civ.pdf.

Amnesty International. 2001. *US government may be considering use of torture for detainees.* Press Release, October 26.

————. 2003a. *Annual report.* New York: Amnesty International.

————. 2003b. *Amnesty International condemns Ashcroft's ruling to indefinitely detain non-U.S. citizens, including asylum-seekers.* Press Release, April 28.

Anderson, C. 2003. Ashcroft rules on immigrants' detention. Associated Press, April 4, EV1–2.

Anderson, M., and P. H. Collins.1995. Preface to Part 4. In *Race, class and gender: An anthology,* 350–362, edited by Margaret Anderson and Patricia Hill Collins. Belmont, CA: Wadsworth.

Aronson, E. 1980. *The social animal.* 3rd ed. San Francisco: Freeman & Company.

Ashcroft, J. 2003.*Testimony of attorney general John Ashcroft before a hearing of the senate judiciary committee on DOJ oversight: Preserving our freedoms while defending against terrorism,* December 6. Washington, DC: U.S. Government Printing.

Associated Press. 2000. Cheney: Swift retaliation needed. October 13.

————. 2003a. Bush Saddam not involved in 9/11. September 18.

————. 2003b. 'Terrorism' cases in New Jersey relate mostly to test cheating. March 3, 1.

Asylum Protection News 21. 2003. Court TV film, inspired by Lawyers Committee case, shines a light on U.S. detention of asylum seekers. EV1–6.

Asylum Protection News 22. 2004. Tibetan nun detained in Virginia jail denied parole again. EV1–4.

Bakken, T. 2000. Liberty and equality through freedom of expression: The human rights questions behind 'hate crime' laws. *International Journal of Human Rights* 4 (2): 1–12.

Bakken, T. 2002. The effects of hate crime legislation: Unproven benefits and unintended consequences. *International Journal of Discrimination and the Law* 5: 231–246.

Bamford, J. 2004. *A pretext for war: 9/11, Iraq, and the abuse of America's intelligence agencies.* New York: Doubleday.

————. 2004. This spy for rent. *New York Times,* June 13, WK13.

Banerjee, N. 2004. Christian conservatives press issues in statehouses. *New York Times,* December 13, A1, A12.

Barak, G. 2001. Crime and crime control in an age of globalization: A theoretical dissection. *Critical Criminology: An International Journal* 10 (1): 57–72.

————. 2003. *Violence and nonviolence: Pathways to understanding.* Thousand Oaks, CA: Sage.

————. 2005. A reciprocal approach to peacemaking criminology: Between adversarialism and mutualism. *Theoretical Criminology* 9 (2): 131–152.

Barlow, M., D. E. Barlow, and T. G. Chiricos. 1995a. Economic conditions and ideologies of crime in the media: A content analysis of crime news. *Crime & Delinquency* 41 (1): 3–19.

————. 1995b. Mobilizing support for social control in a declining economy: Exploring ideologies of crime within crime news. *Crime & Delinquency* 41 (2): 191–204.

Barstow, D. and R. Stein. 2005. Under Bush, a new age of prepackaged news. *New York Times,* March 13, A1, 34–35.

Beck, U. 1992. *Risk society: Towards a new modernity.* London: Sage.

Beck, U., A. Giddens, and S. Lash. 1994. *Reflexive modernity: Politics, tradition, and aesthetics in the modern social order.* Cambridge, UK: Polity Press.

Bellah, R.1975. *The broken covenant.* New York: Seabury.

———. 1988. Civil religion in America. *Daedalus* 117 (3): 97–118.

Benson, J. 2004. Homeland security reduces aid for Jersey City and Newark areas in 2005. *New York Times,* December 4, B5.

Bensor, M. 2002. Tech firms feel the heat as U.S. snoops on citizens. *Times Picayune,* April 1, 28.

Berger, P. L. 1967. *The sacred canopy: Elements of a sociological theory of religion.* Garden City, NJ: Doubleday.

Berkowitz, B. 2002. AmeriSnitch. *The Progressive* (May): 27–28.

Best, J. 1994. *Troubling children: Studies of children and social problems.* New York: Aldine de Gruyter.

———. 1999. *Random violence: How we talk about new crimes and new victims.* Berkeley: University of California Press.

"Bismillah" retrieved on September 11, 2001, from http://groups.yahoo.com/group/-ymaonline. Accessed by subscribing to Young Muslim Association Yahoogroup and viewing archives.

Blumner, R. 2002. Book police thwarted by Colorado ruling. *Milwaukee Journal Sentinel,* April 16, 13A.

Bok, S. 1979. *Secrets: On the ethics of concealment and revelation.* New York: Vintage.

Bonner, R. 2004. Marine defends Guantanamo detainee, and surprises Australians. *New York Times,* March 28, 13.

Bottoms, A. 1995. The philosophy and politics of punishment and sentencing. In *The Politics of Sentencing Reform,* 28–41, edited by C. Clarkson and R. Morgan. Oxford: Clarendon Press.

Bravin, J., G. Fields, C. Adams, and R. Wartzman. 2001. Justice Department quickly moves to use new broad authority in detaining aliens. *Wall Street Journal,* September 26, EV1–3.

Brill, S. 2003. *After: How America confronted the September 12 era.* New York: Simon and Schuster.

Bronowski, J. 1972. The scapegoat king. In *The scapegoat: Ritual and literature,* 67–82, edited by J. Vickery and J. Sellery. Boston: Houghton Mifflin.

Brooks, R. 2003a. The character myth: To counter Bush, the Democrats must present a different vision of a safe world. *Nation* (December 29): 25–28.

———. 2003b. A nation of victims: Bush uses well-known linguistic techniques to make citizens feel dependent. *Nation* (June 30): 20–22.

Brown, C. 2003. *Lost liberties: Ashcroft and the assault on personal freedom.* New York: New Press.

Brown, L. E., and R. Stivers. 1998. The legend of 'nigger' lake: Place as scapegoat. *Journal of Black Studies* 28 (6): 704–723.

Brzezinski, Z. 2004. *The choice: Global domination or global leadership.* New York: Basic Books.

Bumiller, E. 2003. Bush orders a 3-year delay in opening secret documents. *New York Times,* March 26, A15.

———. 2005. Bush advisor to repair tarnished U.S. image abroad. *New York Times,* March 12, A2.

Burns, R., and C. Crawford. 1999. School shootings: The media and public fear, in-gredients for a moral panic. *Crime, Law, and Social Change* 32 (2): 147–68.

Burson, P. 2001. Terrorist attacks; driver arrested in hate crime at mall. *Newsday*, September 13, 12.

Calhoun, C. 2002. *Understanding September 11*. New York: New Press.

———. 2004. Gerhard Lenski: Some false oppositions, and *The Religious Factor*. *Sociological Theory* 22 (2): 194–204.

Campbell, E. 2004. Police narrativity in the risk society. *British Journal of Criminology* 44: 695–714.

Campbell, J. 1973. *Myths to live by*. London: Souvenir Press.

Cardwell, D. 2003. Muslims face deportation, but say U.S. is their home. *The New York Times*, June 13, A22.

———. 2004. The contest of liberties and security: Protestors and officials see the City differently. *New York Times*, July 26, B1, B7.

Carey, B., and A. O'Connor. 2004. As public adjusts to threat, alerts cause less unease. *New York Times*, August 3, A11.

Carroll, J. 2004a. *Crusade: Chronicles of an unjust war*. New York: Metropolitan Books/Henry Holt.

Chomsky, N. 1996. *The culture of terrorism*. Boston, MA: South End Press.

Chomsky, Noam, and Edward S. Herman. 1988. *Manufacturing consent: The political economy of the mass media*. New York: Pantheon Books.

———. 2004b. The Busch crusade: Sacred violence, again unleashed in 2001, could prove as destructive as in 1096. *Nation* (September 20): 14–22.

———. 2004c. The 'E' word: What does the age-old concept of evil mean in a post-9/11 world? *New Times Book Review*, January 11, 7.

Cart, J. 2002. Denver police spied on activists, ACLU says. *Los Angeles Times*, March 22, A1.

Chambliss, W. 1999. *Power, politics, and crime*. Boulder, CO: Westview.

Chang, N. 2002. *Silencing political dissent: How post-September 11 anti-terrorism measures threaten our civil liberties*. New York: Seven Stories Press

———. 2004. The war on dissent. *Nation* (September 13), 8.

Charleston Gazette (West Virginia). 2004. Holey moley!: Who concocts this gibberish? September 22, 16.

Chermak, S., F. Bailey, and M. Brown. 2004. *Media representations of September 11*. New York: Praeger.

Chicago Police Department. 2002. *Hate crimes in Chicago: 2001*. Chicago: Chicago Police Department.

Chicago Tribune. 2001. Concerns rise of civil rights being ignored. October 17, EV1–3.

Chomsky, N. 1996. *The culture of terrorism*. Boston: South End Press.

———. 2003. *Hegemony or survival: America's quest for global dominance*. New York: Henry Holt and Company.

Civil Liberties Reporter. 2003. Report released: Dissent post 9/11. 37 (2): 1.

Clarke, R. 2004. *Against all enemies: Inside America's war on terror*. New York: Simon and Schuster.

Clymer, A. 2003a. Justice Dept. draft on wider powers draws quick criticism. *New York Times*, February 8, A10.

———. 2003b. Ashcroft calls on news media to help explain antiterrorism laws. *New York Times*, June 20, 12.

———. 2003c. Government openness at issue as Bush holds on to records. *New York Times*, January 3, A1, A18.

Cohen, L. P. 2001. Denied access to attorneys some INS detainees are jailed without charges. *Wall Street Journal,* November 1, EV1–3.

Cohen, R. 2004. The war on terror: An obsession the world doesn't share. *New York Times,* December 5, WK4, 6.

Cohen, S. 1985. *Visions of social control.* Cambridge, MA: Polity Press.

———. 2001. *States of denial: Knowing about atrocities and suffering.* Cambridge, UK: Polity.

———. 2002. *Folk devils and moral panics: The creation of the mods and rockers.* 3rd ed. London: Routledge.

Cole, D. 2002. Enemy aliens. *Stanford Law Review* 54 (May): 953–1004.

———. 2003a. *Enemy aliens: Double standards and constitutional freedoms in the war on terror.* New York: New Press.

———. 2003b. Blind sweeps return. *Nation* (January 13/20): 5.

———. 2004a. Ashcroft: 0 for 5,000. *Nation* (October 4): 6–7.

———. 2004b. Spying on the guild. *Nation* (March 1): 5–6.

———. 2004c. Playing the security card. *Nation* (April 12): 5–6.

———. 2005. Accounting for torture. *Nation* (March 21): 4–5.

Cole, D., and James X. Dempsey. 2002. *Terrorism and the constitution: Sacrificing civil liberties in the name of national security.* New York: Free Press.

Connell, R. 1987. *Gender and power.* Stanford, CA: Stanford University Press.

Convention against torture and other cruel, inhuman or degrading treatment or punishment. 1984. Adopted by the General National Assembly Resolution 39/46, 10 December.

Cooperman, A. 2002. Sept.11 backlash murders and the state of 'hate': Between families and police, a gulf on victim count. *Washington Post,* January 20, 1.

Coulter, A. 2001. This is war. *Ann Coulter archive,* September 14, EV3.

Council on American-Islamic Relations. 1995. *A special report on anti-Muslim stereotyping, harassment, and hate crimes: Following the bombing of Oklahoma City's Murrah federal building.* Washington, DC: CAIR.

———. 2002a. Anti-Muslim incidents. Retrieved on September 8, 2002, from http://cair-net.org.

———. 2002b. Number of reported incidents by category. Council on American-Islamic Relations, retrieved on August 30, from http://cair-net.org/html/bycategory.htm.

———. 2002c. Poll: Majority of U.S. Muslims suffered post September 11 bias. August 21, retrieved on August 28, 2002, from http://cair-net.org/asp/article.asp?articleid=895&articletype=3.

Cowell, A. 2004. Ashcroft, upbeat on Iraq, aims at corruption. *New York Times,* January 23, A10.

———. 2004. Five Britons released from Guantanamo Bay arrive home. *New York Times,* March 10, A8.

———. 2005. Blair, on defensive, releases a secret memo on Iraq war. *New York Times,* April 29, A9.

Danner, M. 2004. *Torture and truth: America, Abu Ghraib, and the war on terror.* London: Granta Books.

———. 2005. Taking stock in the forever war. *New York Times Magazine,* September 11, 44–53, 68–87.

Davey, M. 2005. An Iraqi police officer's death, a soldier's varying accounts. *New York Times,* May 23: A1, A14.

Davies, N. 1981. *Human sacrifice: In history and today.* New York: William Morrow.

Dean, J. 2004. *Worse than Watergate: The secret presidency of George W. Bush.* New York: Little, Brown and Company.

DeSantis, J. 2005a. Officer urges murder case be dropped against Marine. *New York Times,* May 14, A10.

———. 2005b. Marine cleared in deaths of 2 insurgents in Iraq. *New York Times,* May 27, A18.

De Tocqueville, A. 1835. *Democracy in America.* London: Saunders and Otley.

Didion, J. 2003. *Fixed ideas: America since 9/11.* New York: New York Review Books.

Donohue, B. 2001. Rights groups prodding feds for information on detainees. *Star-Ledger* (Newark, NJ), October 30, EV1–2.

Doty, C. 2003. Gore criticizes expanded terrorism law. *New York Times,* November 10, A19.

Douglas, M. 1966. *Purity and danger: An analysis of concepts of pollution and taboo.* New York: Praeger.

———. 1982. *Natural symbols: Explorations in cosmology.* 2nd ed. New York: Pantheon.

———. 1986. *Risk acceptability according to the social sciences.* London: Routledge.

———. 1992. *Risk and blame: Essays in cultural theory.* London: Routledge.

Douglas, T. 1995. *Scapegoats: Transferring blame.* London: Routledge.

Dow, M. 2001. We know what INS is hiding. *Miami Herald,* November 11, EV1–3.

———. 2004. *American gulag: Inside U.S. immigration prisons.* Berkeley: University of California Press.

Dowd, M. 2003. A tale of two Fridays. *New York Times,* April 20, WK9.

Downes, L. 2001. Hope you can come! *New York Times,* December 2, WK2.

Dreyfuss, R. 2002a. Colin Powell's list. *Nation* (March 25): 21.

———. 2002b. The cops are watching you. *Nation* (June 3): 12.

Drinan, R. F. 2001. *The mobilization of shame: A world view of human rights.* New Haven, CT: Yale University Press.

Durkheim, E. 1995. *Elementary forms of religious life.* New York: Free Press.

Eckholm, E. 2005. U.S. mishandled $96.6 million in rebuilding Iraq, report finds. *New York Times,* May 5, A16.

Eckstrom, K. 2001. Graham heir keeps stance on Islam talk. *The Times Union* (Albany, NY), November 24, 1.

Edison/Mitofsky. 2004. Surveys conducted by Edison Media Research of Somerville, N.J. and Mitofsky International of New York City for the National Election Pool, a consortium of ABC News, Associated Press, CBS News, CNN, Fox News, and NBC News.

Egan, T. 2001. In Sacramento, A publisher's questions draw the wrath of the crowd. *New York Times,* December 21, B1, B4.

Egan, T. 2004. Computer student on trial over Muslim web site work: Case hinges on use of antiterrorism law. *New York Times,* April 27, A16.

Elias, N. 1994. *The civilizing process.* Oxford: Basil Blackwell.

Elliott, A. 2003. In Brooklyn, 9/11 damage continues. *New York Times,* June 7, A9.

Equal Employment Opportunity Commission. 2002. EEOC provides answers about the workplace rights of Muslims, Arabs, South Asians and Sikhs. Press Release, Equal Employment Opportunity Commission, May 15, 2002; retrieved on September 23, 2002, from http://eeoc.gov/press/5–15–02.html.

Erikson, E. 1964. *Insight and responsibility.* New York: W.W. Norton.

Erikson, K. 1966. *Wayward Puritans: A study in the sociology of deviance.* New York: John Wiley & Sons.

Esposito, J. (1992) *The Islamic threat: Myth or reality.* Oxford: Oxford University Press.

FAIR. 2001a. *Networks accept government guidance.* New York: Fair Media Advisory. October 12.

———. 2001b. *CNN says focus on civilian casualties would be 'perverse.'* New York: Fair Media Advisory. November 1.

———. 2001c. *Op-Ed echo chamber: Little space for dissent to the military line.* New York: Fair Media Advisory. November 2.

Farragher, T., and K. Cullen. 2001. Plan to question 5000 raises issue of profiling. *Boston Globe,* November 11, EV1–4.

Federal Bureau of Investigation. 2002. *Crime in the United States.* October 30. Washington, DC: U.S. Government Printing.

Feeley, M., and J. Simon. 1992. The new penology: Notes on the emerging strategy of corrections and their implications. *Criminology* 30 (2): 449–474.

Feingold, R. 2001. On the anti-terrorism bill. October 25. (www.senate.gov/'feingold/releases/01/10/102501at.html).

Fekete, L. 2002. *Racism: The hidden cost of September 11th.* London: Institute of Race Relations.

Fellman, G. 1998. *Rambo and the Dalai Lama: The compulsion to win and its threat to human survival.* Albany: State University of New York.

Ferrell, J. 1996. *Crimes of style: Urban graffiti and the politics of criminality.* Boston: Northeastern University Press.

Ferrell, J., and C. R. Sanders. 1995. *Cultural criminology.* Boston: Northeastern University Press.

Files, J. 2005. Justice Dept. opposes bid to revive case against FBI *New York Times,* February 26, A9.

Fine, M., L. Weis, and J. Addelston. 1997. (In) Secure times: Constructing white working class masculinities in the late twentieth century. *Gender and Society* 11 (1): 52–68.

Fineman, H. 2003. Bush and God. *Newsweek,* March 10, 23–30.

Foderaro, Lisa W. 2004. Study weighs terror threat to Kensico dam. *New York Times,* August 20, B7.

Foucault, M. 1979. *Discipline and punish: The birth of the prison.* New York: Vintage.

Fox, B. 2001. Attacks probed in closed courts. Associated Press, October 4, EV1–3.

Freud, S. 1989. *Civilization and its discontents.* New York: W.W. Norton.

Freudenburg, W. 1997. Contamination, corrosion, and the social order. An overview. *Current Sociology* 45 (3): 19–40.

Friedrichs, D. 1998. *State crime: Volumes I and II.* Aldershot, UK: Aldershot/Dartmouth.

Frontline. 2004. The Jesus factor. Raney Aronson, producer, writer, and director. Produced by WGBH, Boston, and a Little Rain Productions. Aired April 29.

Frum, D., and R. Perle. 2003. *An end to evil: How to win the war on terror.* New York: Random House.

Gall, C. 2004. 3 Afghan youths question U.S. captivity. *New York Times,* March 12, A10.

Gamson, W., and A. Modigliani. 1989. Media discourse and public opinion on nuclear power: A constructionist approach. *American Journal of Sociology* 95: 1–37.

Garland, D. 2001. *The culture of control: Crime and social order in contemporary society.* Chicago: University of Chicago Press.

———. 2002. *Mass imprisonment: Social causes and consequences.* London: Sage.

Garrison, A. 2004. Defining terrorism: Philosophy of the bomb, propaganda by deed and change through fear and violence. *Criminal Justice Studies* 17 (3): 259–279.

Gates, A. 2004. Seeing a mushroom cloud in New York. *New York Times,* September 9, E10.

Gearty, C. 1997. *The future of terrorism.* London: Phoenix.

————. 2004. *Principles of human rights adjudication.* Oxford: Oxford University.

————. 2005. With a little help from our friends. *Index on Censorship* 34 (1): 46–51.

George, J., and M. Santora. 2004. After beheading, rising anger in New Jersey. *New York Times,* June 20, 16.

General Accounting Office. 2003. *Better management oversight and internal controls needed to ensure accuracy of terrorism-related statistics.* Washington, DC: General Accounting Office.

Gerth, J. 2003. C.I.A. chief won't name officials who failed to add hijackers to watch list. *New York Times,* May 15, A25.

Girard, R. 1977. *Violence and the sacred.* Translated by P.Gregory. Baltimore, MD: Johns Hopkins University Press.

————. 1986. *The Scapegoat.* Translated by Y. Freccero. Baltimore, MD: Johns Hopkins University Press.

————. 1987a. Generative scapegoating. In *Violent origins,* 7–105, edited by R. Hamerton-Kelly. Stanford, CA: Stanford University Press.

————. 1987b. *Things hidden since the foundation of the world.* Translated by S. Bann and M. Metteer. Stanford, CA: Stanford University Press.

Glaberson, W. 2001. Detainees accounts of investigation are at odds with official reports. *New York Times,* September 29, EV1–3.

————. 2005a. Defense for Sheik and aide is suspicious of tape gaps. *New York Times,* January 5, B3.

————. 2005b. Focus shifting in terror case against Sheik. *New York Times,* January 20, A1, B8.

————. 2005c. Federal court jury finds Sheik guilty of conspiracy and financing terrorism. *New York Times,* March 11, B1, B6.

————. 2005d. Lawyers take uneasy look at the future. *New York Times,* February 11, B8.

Glaberson, W., Ian Urbin, and Andy Newman. 2004. Terror case hinges on a wobbly key player. *New York Times,* November 27, A1, B4.

Glanz, J., and E. Wong. 2004. Cameraman details Marine's role in mosque shooting. *New York Times,* November 22, A13.

Glasser, I. 2003. Arrests after 9/11: Are we safer? *New York Times,* June 8, WK12.

Glassner, B. 1999. *The culture of fear: Why Americans are afraid of the wrong things.* New York: Basic Books.

Golden, T., and D. Van Natta, Jr. 2004. U.S. said to overstate value of Guantanamo Bay detainees. *New York Times,* June 21, A1, A12.

————. 2005a. In U.S. Report, brutal details of 2 Afghan inmates' deaths. *New York Times,* May 20a: A1, A12.

————. 2005b. Army faltered in investigating detainee abuse. *New York Times,* May 20b: A1, A18.

Goldstein, R. J. 1978. *Political repression in modern America: From 1870 to the present.* Cambridge, MA: Schenkman.

————. 1995. *Saving "Old Glory": The history of the American flag desecration controversy.* Boulder, CO: Westview.

————. 2003. Neo-macho man: Pop culture and post-911 politics. *Nation* (March 24): 16–18.

Goldstein, A., and D. Eggen. 2001. U.S. to stop issuing detention tallies. *Washington Post,* November 9, EV1–2.

Gonzales, A. R. 2002. Memorandum to the president. Re: Standards for conduct for interrogation under 18 U.S.C. Sections 2340–2340A. August 1.

Goode, E., and N. Ben-Yehuda. 1994. *Moral panics: The social construction of deviance.* Cambridge, MA: Blackwell.

Goodstein, L. 2001. American Sikhs contend they have become a focus of profiling at airports. *New York Times,* November 10, B6.

———. 2003. Seeing Islam as 'evil' faith, Evangelicals seek converts. *New York Times,* May 27, A1, A23.

———. 2004. Politicians talk more about religion, and people expect them to. *New York Times,* July 4, sec. 4, 2.

Goodstein, L., and W. Yardley. 2004. President benefits from efforts to build a coalition of religious voters. *New York Times,* November 5, A22.

Gore, A. 2003. This administration is using fear as a political tool. *New York Times,* November 25, A9.

Gould, S. J. 1981. *The mismeasure of man.* New York: W.W. Norton.

Gourevitch, A. 2003. Detention disorder: Ashcroft's clumsy round-up of foreigners lurches forward. *American Prospect* (January): EV1–7.

Gramsci, A. 1971. *Selections from the prison notebooks.* New York: International.

Greenberg, D. 2002. Striking out in democracy. *Punishment & Society* 4 (2): 237–252.

Greenberg, K. J. and J. L. Dratel. 2005. *The torture papers: The road to Abu Ghraib.* Cambridge: Cambridge University Press.

Greenhouse, L. 2004a. Administration says a 'zone of autonomy' justifies its secrecy on energy task force. *New York Times,* April 25, 16.

———. 2004b. Justices affirm legal rights of 'enemy combatants.' *New York Times,* June 29, A1, A14.

———. 2004c. Justices hear case about foreigner's use of federal courts. *New York Times,* March 3, A16.

Greider, W. 2004. Under the banner of the 'war' on terror. *Nation* (June 21): 11–16.

Gross, O. 2003. Chaos and rules: Should responses to violent crisis always be constitutional? *Yale Law Review* 112: 1011–1030.

Gross, S., and D. Livingston. 2002. Racial profiling under attack. *Columbia Law Review* 102 (5): 1413–1438.

Haddad, Y. 1998. The dynamics of Islamic identity in North America. In *Muslims on the Americanization path?,* 21–56, edited by Yvonne Yazbeck Haddad and John Esposito. Atlanta, GA: Scholars Press.

Hakim, D. 2004a. Inquiries begun into handling of Detroit terror cases. *New York Times,* January 29, A23.

———. 2004b. Defendant is released in Detroit terror case. *New York Times,* October 13, A16.

Hakim, D., and E. Lichtblau. 2004. After convictions, the undoing of a U.S. terror prosecution. *New York Times,* October 7, A1, A32.

Hamerton-Kelly, R. 1987. *Violent origins: Ritual killing and cultural formation.* Stanford, CA: Stanford University Press.

Hamm, M. S. 1994a. *American skinheads: The criminology and control of hate.* Westport, CT: Praeger.

———. 1994b. *Hate crime: International perspectives on causes and control.* Cincinnati, OH: Anderson.

———. 2002. *In bad company: America's terrorist underground.* Boston: Northeastern University Press.

———. 2005. After September 11th: Terrorism research and the crisis in criminology. *Theoretical Criminology* 9 (2): 237–230.

Hannaford, A. 2004. What's not to love about Bush? *The Guardian Weekly,* August 27–September 2, 20.

Harbury, J. 2005. *Truth, torture, and the American way: The history and consequences of U.S. involvement in torture.* Boston: Beacon Press.

202 REFERENCES

Hartung, W. D. 2004. Making money on terrorism. The Bush administration's apparent motto: Leave no defense contractor behind. *Nation* (February 23): 19–21.

Hedges, C. 2002. *War is a force that gives us meaning.* New York: Anchor Books.

Heir, S. 2003. Risk and panic in late-modernity: Implications of the converging sites of social anxiety. *British Journal of Sociology* 54 (1): 3–20.

Henriques, D. B. 2003. The catch-22 of Iraq contracts: Law requires public disclosure but U.S. demands secrecy. *New York Times,* April 12, C1, C3.

Hentoff, N. 2003a. Conservatives rise for the Bill of Rights: Everyone in this room is a suspect. *Village Voice,* April 30-May 6, 33.

———. 2003b. Vanishing liberties: Where's the press. *Village Voice,* April 16–22, 31.

———. 2003c. *The war on bill of rights and the gathering resistance.* New York. Seven Stories Press.

———. 2003d. Criminalizing librarians. *Village Voice,* December 24–30, 18.

———. 2003e. Our designated killers: Where is the outrage? *Village Voice,* February 19–25, 33.

———. 2004a. Cuffing Bush and the FBI: A serious setback to the Patriot Act, despite the victorious Bush's unstinting support. *Village Voice,* November 17–23, 26.

———. 2004b. Declarations of independence. *Village Voice,* June 16–22, 32.

———. 2004c. John Ashcroft's achievements: The fearsome attorney general is leaving, but his legacy, and the resistance, remain. *Village Voice,* November 24–30, 20.

Herbert, B. 2004, A war without reason. *New York Times,* October 18, A17.

———. 2005a. Torture, American style. *New York Times,* February 11, A25.

———. 2005b. On Abu Ghraib, the big shots walk. *New York Times,* April 28, A25.

Herman, Edward S., and N. Chomsky. 1988. *Manufacturing consent.* New York: Pantheon.

Hersh, S. M. 2004. *Chain of command: The road from 9/11 to Abu Ghraib.* New York: HarperCollins Publishers.

Hill, A. 2002. Acid house and Thatcherism: Noise, the mob and the English countryside. *British Journal of Sociology* 53 (1): 89–105.

Hinds, L. 2005. The US election: Looking backward and looking forward. *Socialist Lawyer* (April): 16–20.

Hitchens, C. 2004. War of words: During military conflicts, the government has struggled with the right to free speech. *New York Times Book Review,* November 7, 8–9.

Holl, J. 2004. Jersey City police chief says terror duties strain budget. *New York Times,* August 16, B4.

Hollway, W., and T. Jefferson. 1997. The risk society in an age of anxiety: Situating fear of crime. *British Journal of Sociology* 48 (2): 255–265.

Howard, M. 2005. Civilians bear the brunt of Iraqi insurgency. *Guardian,* July 15, 15.

Hsu, H. 2003. The control model in a mega prison: Governing prisons in Taiwan. *International Criminal Justice Review* 13: 149–167.

Hu, W. 2004. Mayor scolds security chief on U.S. funds to protect city. *New York Times,* June 5, B2.

Huff, R. 2001. White House sees red over Maher's remarks. *Daily News* (New York), September 27, 112.

Human Rights Watch. 2002a. *We are not the enemy: Hate crimes against Arabs, Muslims, and those perceived to be Arab or Muslim after September 11.* New York: Human Rights Watch.

———. 2002b. *Presumption of guilt: Human rights abuses of post-September 11th detainees.* New York: Human Rights Watch.

———. 2002c. Interview with Joshua Salaam of the Council on American-Islamic Relations. February 21.

————. 2003. *World report 2003: Events of 2002.* New York: Human Rights Watch.

————. 2004a. *Afghanistan: Abuses by U.S. forces, beatings in detention; no legal process.* New York: Human Rights Watch.

————. 2004b. *Material witness law is being abused.* (www.hrw.org) May 27.

————. 2004. *Afghanistan: Abuses by U.S. forces, beatings in detention; no legal process.* New York: Human Rights Watch.

————. 2005. *New Accounts of torture by U.S. troops: Soldiers say failures by command led to abuse.* (www.hrw.org) September 25.

Humphries, D.1999. *Crack mothers: Pregnancy, drugs, and the media.* Columbus: Ohio State University.

Husak, D. 2002. *Legalize this! The case for decriminalizing drugs.* New York: Verso.

International Committee of the Red Cross. 2001. *Discover the ICRC.* Geneva: International Committee of the Red Cross.

International convention on the elimination of all forms of racial discrimination (CERD), article 2 (1).

International Covenant on Civil and Political Rights (ICCPR), article 26.

International Herald Tribune. 2003a. An unpatriotic act. August 26, 6.

————. 2003b. Bush won't commit White House on Sept. 11 documents. October 28, 2.

————. 2005. Iraq's WMD: Case closed. January 14, 6.

Isikoff, M. 2003. The FBI says, count the mosques. *Newsweek,* February 3: 6.

Jacobs, J., and K. Potter. 1998. *Hate crimes: Criminal law & identity politics.* New York: Oxford University Press.

Jacoby, S. 2004. In praise of secularism: To arms, freethinkers! Religious zealots have hijacked your government. *Nation* (April 19): 14–18.

Janofsky, M. 2003. War brings new surge of anxiety for followers of Islam. *New York Times,* March 29, B15.

————. 2004. Rights experts see possibility of a war crime. *New York Times,* November 13, A8.

————. 2005. FBI director faults himself for delays on software. *New York Times,* February 4, A15.

Jealous, B. 2004. Profiles of the profiled. *Amnesty International: The Magazine of Amnesty International USA* (winter): 16–18.

Jeffrey, V. 1992. The search for scapegoat deviant. *Humanist* 52 (5): 10–14.

Jehl, D. 2003. U.S. general apologizes for remarks about Islam. *New York Times,* October 18, A6.

————. 2004a. C.I.A. classifies much of a report on its failings. *New York Times,* June 16, A13.

————. 2004b. Files show Rumsfeld rejected some efforts to toughen prison rules. *New York Times,* July 23, A10.

————. 2005a. British memo on U.S. plans for Iraq war fuels critics. *New York Times,* May 20, A10.

————. 2005b. Questions left by C.I.A. chief on torture use: Goss vouches only for current practices. *New York Times,* March 18, A1, A11.

————. 2005c. Terrorism will not stop, report says: Intelligence agencies say Iraq could be training ground. *International Herald Tribune,* January 15–16, 4.

Jehl, D., and D. Johnston. 2004. Reports that led to terror alert were years old, officials say. *New York Times,* August 3, A1, A10.

Jenkins, P. 1998. *Moral panic: Changing concepts of the child molester in modern America.* New Haven, CT: Yale University Press.

————. 2003. *The mythology of modern terrorism: Why we don't understand terrorists and their motives.* New York: Aldine de Gruyter.

Jilani, H. 2002. Antiterrorism strategies and protecting human rights. *Amnesty Now* (a publication of Amnesty International) 27 (2): 1, 16–17.

Johnston, D. 2004. Somali is accused of planning a terror attack at a shopping center in Ohio. *New York Times,* June 15, A16.

Johnston, D., and D. Jehl. 2003. Bush refuses to declassify Saudi section of report. *New York Times,* July 30, A1, A10.

———. 2004a. Report cites lapses across government and 2 presidents. *New York Times,* July 23, A1, A13.

———. 2004b. C.I.A. sends terror experts to tell small towns of risk: FBI coordinates intelligence briefings. *New York Times,* July 18, 18.

Johnston, D., and R. W. Stevenson. 2004. Ashcroft, deft at taking political heat, hits a rocky patch. *New York Times,* July 1, A14.

Jones, B. 2003. Asylum seeker feels sting of post-9/11 immigration laws: A 'culture of no' casualty. *New York Newsday* November 3, EV1–4.

Jung, C. 1953–1979. *The collected works* (Bollingen Series XX). 20 vols. Translated and edited by R. Hull. Princeton, NJ: Princeton University Press.

Kakutani, M. 2004. Protecting the freedom to dissent during war. *New York Times,* November 5, 35–47.

Kaminer, W. 1995. *It's all the rage: Crime and culture.* New York: Addison-Wesley.

Kaplan, E. 2004a. Follow the money: Bush has revived the Christian right through direct federal largesse. *Nation* (November 1): 20–23.

———. 2004b. *With God on their side: How Christian fundamentalists trampled science, policy, and democracy in George W. Bush's White House.* New York: New Press.

Karabell, Z. 1995. The wrong threat: The United States and Islamic fundamentalism. *World Policy Journal* (summer): 37–48.

Katz, J. 1988. *Seductions of crime: Moral and sensual attraction in doing evil.* New York: Basic Books.

Kauzlarich, D., R. Matthews, and W. J. Miller. 2001. Toward a victimology of state crime. *Critical Criminology* 10: 173–194.

Kearney, R.1999. Aliens and others: Between Girard and Derrida. *Cultural Values* 3 (3): 251–262.

Kelman, H. C., and L. Hamilton. 1989. *Crimes of obedience: Toward a social psychology of authority and responsibility.* New Haven, CT: Yale University Press.

Kershaw, S., and E. Lichtblau. 2004a. Spain had doubts before U.S. held lawyer in blast: Fingerprint copy at issue, Court records show that FBI was confident of '100 percent' match. *New York Times,* May 26, A1, A20.

———. 2004b. Questions about evidence in U.S. arrest in bombing. *New York Times,* May 22, A14.

Killingbeck, D.1999. The role of television news in the construction of school violence as a 'moral panic.' *Journal of Criminal Justice and Popular Culture* 8 (3): 186–202.

Kimmage, M. 2004. Scared stiff: In the view of one political scientist, fear has tainted liberalism for centuries. *New York Times Book Review,* November 28, 31.

Kinzer, S., and T. S. Purdum. 2004. An American debate: How severe the threat? *New York Times,* August 5, A13.

Kirchgaessner, S. 2001. Some immigration lawyers wary of INS powers. *Financial Times,* September 30, EV1–3.

Kirkpatrick, D. D. 2004a. Wrath and mercy: The return of the warrior Jesus. *New York Times,* April 4, sec. 4, p. 1.

———. 2004b. Republicans admit mailing campaign literature saying liberals will ban the Bible. *New York Times,* September 24, A22.

———. 2005a. House approves election in event of deadly attack: What to do if more than 100 are killed. *New York Times,* March 4, A18.

———. 2005b. Evangelical leader threatens to use his political muscle against some Democrats. *New York Times,* January 1, A10.

———. 2005c. House and Senate reach accord on $82 billion for costs of wars. *New York Times,* May 4, A5.

Kleinman, A. 1997. *Social suffering.* Berkeley: University of California Press.

Knowlton, B. 2004. State Department doubles estimate of '03 terror toll. *International Herald Tribune,* June 23, 1, 8.

———. 2005. Poll shows modest changes in levels of anti-U.S. Mood. *International Herald Tribune,* June 24, EV1–3.

Kornblut, A. E. 2005. Administration is warned about its publicity videos. *New York Times,* February 19, A11.

Kramer, R. C., and R. J. Michalowski. 2005. War, aggression and state crime: A criminological analysis of the invasion and occupation of Iraq. *British Journal of Criminology* 45: 446–469.

Krassner, P. 2003. Is image everything? Ask the propaganda experts. *New York Press,* December 17–23, 28.

Kristof, N. D. 2004a. Apocalypse (almost) now. *New York Times,* November 24, A23.

———. 2004b. Travesty of justice. *New York Times,* June 15, A23.

Krugman, P. 2004. Ignorance isn't strength. *New York Times,* October 8, A27.

Kundera, M. 1984. *The unbearable lightness of being.* New York: Harper & Row.

LaHaye, T., and J. B. Jenkins. 2003. *Glorious appearing.* New York: Tyndale House Publishers.

Landler, M. 2004. Retrial of suspect in 9/11 attacks begins in Germany. *New York Times,* August 11, A12.

Langer, G. 2004. A question of values. *New York Times,* November 6, A19.

Lasch, C. 1979. *The culture of narcissism.* New York: W.W. Norton.

LaShan, L. 1992. *The psychology of war.* New York: Helios.

Lawyers Committee for Human Rights. 2003. *Imbalance of powers: How changes to U.S. law & policy since 9/11 erode human rights and civil liberties.* New York: Lawyers Committee for Human Rights.

———. 2004. *In liberty's shadow: U.S. detention of asylum seekers in the era of homeland security.* New York: Lawyers Committee for Human Rights.

Lea, J. 2002. *Crime and modernity: Continuities in left realist criminology.* London: Sage.

Lee, C. 2003. Devil in the details: Patriot Act II, and means to weigh it, emerge in bits. *Village Voice,* June 18–24, 38.

———. 2004. Security or suppression: Examining NYPD crackdowns on activists. *Village Voice,* April 30-May 6, 29–30.

Legum, J., and D. Sirota 2004. Vote for Bush or die: The Republicans politicize terror. *Nation* (September 27): 13–15.

Lenski, G. 1961. *The religious factor.* New York: Doubleday Anchor.

Lerner, J., R. M. Gonzalez, D. A. Small, B. Finchoff. 2003. Effects of fear and anger on perceived risks of terrorism. *Psychological Science* 14 (2) (March): 144–150.

Levin, J. 2002. *The violence of hate: Confronting racism, anti-Semitism, and other forms of bigotry.* Boston: Allyn and Bacon.

Levi-Strauss, 1968. *Structural anthropology.* New York: Penguin.

Lewin, T., and A. L. Cowan. 2001. Dozens of Israeli Jews are being kept in federal detention. *New York Times,* November 21, B7.

Lewis, A. 2005. Guantanamo's long shadow. *New York Times,* June 21, EV1.

Lewis, N. A. 2003. Court blocks efforts to protect secret Cheney files. *New York Times,* July 9, A16.

——. 2004a. US military describes findings at Guantanamo. *New York Times,* March 21, 8.

——. 2004b. Suit contests military trials of detainees at Cuba base. *New York Times,* April 8, A25.

——. 2004c. Relatives of prisoners at Guantanamo Bay tell of anger and sadness at detentions. *New York Times,* March 8, A13.

——. 2004d. Fate of Guantanamo Bay detainees is debated in federal court. *New York Times,* December 2, A36.

——. 2005b. Judge extends legal rights for Guantanamo Bay detainees: Approves examinations by U.S. courts. *New York Times,* February 2, A12.

——. 2005c. Judge says U.S. terror suspect can't be held as an enemy combatant. *New York Times,* March 1, A14.

Lewis, N. A., and E. Schmitt. 2005. Inquiry finds abuses at Guantanamo Bay: Pentagon's report follows FBI complaints about practices. *New York Times,* May 1, 35.

Lichtblau, E. 2003a. Bush issues racial profiling ban but exempts security inquiries: Use of race and ethnicity in 'narrow' instances. *New York Times,* June 19, A1, A16.

——. 2003b. U.S. report faults the roundup of illegal immigrants after 9/11: Many with no ties to terror languished in jail. *New York Times,* June 3, A1, A18.

——. 2003c. FBI tells offices to count local Muslim mosques. *New York Times,* February 6, EV1–3.

——. 2003d. FBI admits secret seizure of documents from Associated Press and opens inquiry. *New York Times,* April 24, A20.

——. 2003e. Terror cases rise, but most are small-scale, study says. *New York Times,* February 14, A16.

——. 2003f. U.S. uses terror law to pursue crimes from drugs to swindling: Broad steps anger critics of expanded powers. *New York Times,* June 3, A1, A32.

——. 2003g. Ashcroft mocks librarians and other who oppose parts of counterterrorism law. *New York Times,* September 16, A23.

——. 2003h. U.S. says it has not used new library records law. *New York Times,* September 19, A20.

——. 2003i. Appeals court casts doubt on parts of key antiterrorism law. *New York Times,* December 4, A37.

——. 2003j. Suit challenges constitutionality of powers in antiterrorism law. *New York Times,* July 31, A17.

——. 2003k. FBI scrutinizes antiwar rallies: Officials say effort aims at extremist elements. *New York Times,* November 23, A1, A29.

——. 2003l. Counterterror proposals are a hard sell. *New York Times,* September 11, A19.

——. 2004a. Another FBI employee blows whistle on agency: Says a terror investigation was thwarted. *New York Times,* August 2, A15.

——. 2004b. For voters, Osama replaces the common criminal. *New York Times,* July 18, 4WK.

——. 2004c. Whistle-blower said to be a factor in an FBI firing: Classified investigation, translator alleged bureau had poorly translated terror documents. *New York Times,* July 29, A1, A14.

——. E. 2004d. FBI said to lag on translations of terror tapes: A Justice Dept. inquiry, computer problems and shortage of linguists are cited in report. *New York Times,* September 28, A1, A22.

————. 2004e. FBI goes knocking for political troublemakers. *New York Times,* August 16, A1, A11.

————. 2004f. Inquiry into FBI questioning is sought. *New York Times,* August 18, A20.

————. E. 2004g. Government's 'no fly' list is challenged in a lawsuit. *New York Times,* April 23, A17.

————. 2004h. Judge scolds U.S. officials over barring jet travelers. *New York Times,* June 16, A19.

————. 2004i. Papers show confusion as watch list grew quickly. *New York Times,* October 9, A9.

————. 2004j. Bush aide calls criticism of Patriot Act uninformed. *New York Times,* October 27, A18.

————. 2004k. Effort to curb scope of antiterrorism law falls short. *New York Times,* July 9, A16.

————. 2005. Terror suspects buying firearms, U.S. report finds: Gaps exist in gun laws, FBI says that concerns about personal privacy constrain actions. *New York Times,* March 8, A1, A10.

Lichtblau, E., with A, Liptak. 2003. On terror, spying and guns, Ashcroft expands reach. *New York Times,* March 15, A1, A8.

Lifton, R. J. 2003a. *Superpower syndrome: America's apocalyptic confrontation with the world.* New York: Nation Books.

————. 2003b. American apocalypse. *Nation* (December 22): 11–17.

Lilly, J. R., and M. Deflem.1996. Profit and penality: An analysis of the corrections-commercial complex. *Crime & Delinquency* 42 (1): 3–20.

Lilly, J. R., and P. Knepper.1993. The corrections-commercial complex. *Crime & Delinquency* 39 (2): 150–166.

Lind, M. 2004. A tragedy of errors: The neoconservatives' war has proved a disaster. No wonder they're running for cover. *Nation* (February 23): 23–32.

Lindorff, D. 2005. Chertoff and torture. *Nation* (February 14): 6–8.

Lippman, W. 1929. *Public opinion.* New Brunswick, NJ: Transaction Publishers.

Liptak, A. 2003. For jailed immigrants a presumption of guilt. *New York Times,* June 3, A18.

————. 2004a. For post-9/11 material witness, it is a terror of a different kind. *New York Times,* August 19, A1, A20.

————. 2004b. A court decision is one thing; enforcing it is another. *New York Times,* April 1, A8.

————. 2005. U.S. says it has withdrawn from world judicial body. *New York Times,* March 10, A16.

Lipton, E. 2004. Big cities will get more in antiterrorism grants: New York City has the largest increase. *New York Times,* December 22, A20.

————. 2005a. U.S. lists possible terror attacks and likely toll. *New York Times,* March 16, A1, A16.

————. 2005b. Nominee says U.S. agents abused power after 9/11. *New York Times,* February 3, A19.

————. 2005c. Terror suspects buying firearms, U.S. report finds: Gaps exist in gun laws, FBI says that concerns about personal privacy constrain action. *New York Times,* March 8, A1, A18.

Los Angeles County Commission on Human Relations. 2002. *Compounding tragedy*: The other victims of September 11. Los Angeles: Los Angeles County Commission on Human Relations.

Lott, T., and R. Wyden. 2004. Let's end the abuse in government secrecy. *International Herald Tribune,* August 30, 8.

Lueck, T. J. 2004a. 3 assailants sought in beating of Sikh man. *New York Times,* July 12, B5.

———. 2004b. Nadar calls for impeachment of Bush over the war in Iraq. *New York Times,* May 25, A21.

Lustick, S. 1996. Fundamentalism, politicized religion and pietism. *MESA Bulletin* 30: 26.

Lyon, D. 1994. *The electronic eye: The rise of surveillance society.* Minneapolis: University of Minnesota Press.

Mamdani, M. 2004. *Good Muslim, bad Muslim: America, the Cold War, and the roots of terror.* New York: Pantheon.

Marable, M. 2003. 9/11: Racism in a time of terror. In *Implicating empire: Globalization & resistance in the 21st century world order,* 3–14, edited by S. Aronowitz and H. Gautney. New York: Basic Books.

Marquis, C. 2003. Muslims object to Graham. *New York Times,* April 18, B10.

Marty, M. E. 2003. The sin of pride. *Newsweek,* March 10, 32–33.

Mashberg, T. 2001. Pro or con, war talk's risky campus. *Boston Herald,* December 16, 23.

Mayer, J. 2005. Outsourcing torture. *New Yorker,* February 21, EV1–14.

McCarus, E. 1994. *The development of Arab-American identity.* Ann Arbor: University of Michigan Press.

McKinney, J. 2001. Cooksey: Expect racial profiling. *Advocate* (Baton Rouge, LA), September 19, 1.

McLuhan, M.1964. *Understanding media: The extension of man.* New York: McGraw-Hill.

McRobbie, A. 1994. *Post-modernism and popular culture.* London: Routledge.

McRobbie, A., and S. Thornton. 1995. Rethinking moral panics for multi-mediated social worlds. *British Journal of Sociology* 46 (4): 559–574.

Mead, G. H. 1964. The psychology of punitive justice. In *Selected writings,* 212–239, edited by A. J. Reck. Chicago: University of Chicago Press.

Mellema, G. 2000. Scapegoats. *Criminal Justice Ethics* (winter/spring): 3–9.

Merkin, D. 2004. Terror-filled: Preparing for the worst by never ceasing to think about it. *New York Times Magazine,* August 15, 13–14.

Michalowski, R.1985. *Law, order and power.* New York: Random House.

———.1996. Critical criminology and the critique of domination: The story of an intellectual movement. *Critical Criminology* 7 (1): 9–16.

Miller, J., and G. Schamess 2000. The discourse of denigration and the creation of the other. *Journal of Sociology and Social Welfare* 27 (3): 39–62.

Miller, J. 1996. *God has ninety-nine names: A reporter's journey through a militant Middle East.* New York: Simon and Schuster.

Millett, K. 1994. *The politics of imprisonment: An essay on the literature of political imprisonment.* New York: W.W. Norton.

Molenaar, B., and R. Neufeld. 2003. The use of privatized detention centers for asylum seekers in Australia and the UK. In *Capitalist punishment: Prison privatization & human rights,* 127–139, edited by A. Coyle, A. Campbell, and R. Neufeld. Atlanta: Clarity Press.

Moore, Kathleen. 1995. *Al-Mughtaribun: American law and the transformation of Muslim life in the United States.* Albany, NY: SUNY Press.

Moore, K. 1998. The *Hijab* and religious liberty: Anti-discrimination law and Muslim women in the United States. In *Muslims on the Americanization path?,* 129–148, edited by Y. Yazbeck Haddad and J. Esposito. Atlanta, GA: Scholars Press.

Morrow, L. 2003. *Evil: An investigation.* New York: Basic Books.

Murphy, D. E. 2004. Security grants still streaming to rural states. *New York Times,* October 12, A1, A18.

Murphy, P. 1972. *The Constitution in crisis times, 1918–1969.* New York: Harper & Row.

Nagourney, A. 2004a. Kerry sees hope of gaining edge on terror issue: Promises a safer nation. *New York Times,* July 25, 1, 16.

———. 2004b. Bush draws terrorism law into campaign: Stumps for its renewal, an issue he will make central to his run. *New York Times,* April 21, A18.

Napolitano, A. P. 2005. No defense. *New York Times,* February 17.

Nation. 2004a. The GOP hijacks 9/11. September 20, 3.

———. 2004b. The haunted archives. May 3, 3–4.

———. 2005a. Blair's illegal war. April 18, 8.

———. 2005b. Anti-war, pro-democracy. May 30, 3–4.

———. 2005c. Shooting the messenger. March 7, 4–5.

———. 2005d. Command of truth. October 4, 3.

National Commission on Terrorist Attacks Upon the United States. 2004. *The 9/11 commission report.* New York: W.W. Norton and Company.

Naureckas, J. 1995. The jihad that wasn't. *Extra,* July, 6–10, 20.

Neier, A. 2003. *Taking liberties: Four decades in the struggle for rights.* New York: Public-Affairs.

Newburn, T. 2005. Privatized security—Developments, dilemmas, and prospects. Plenary presentation. *British Society of Criminology,* Leeds, England, July 12.

Newsweek. 2003. The FBI says, count the Mosques. February 3, EV1.

New York Times. 2001. Disappearing in America. November 10, A22.

———. 2002. Denver police files raise rights concern. March 14, A12.

———. 2003a. Report finds U.S. misstated terror verdicts. February 22, A10.

———. 2003b. Secrecy: The Bush byword. March 28, A16.

———. 2003c. Stonewalling the 9/11 commission. November 23, 10WK.

———. 2004a. Repeated vandalism of mosque is to be investigated as bias crime. April 24, B6.

———. 2004b. What the Bush administration said. June 10, 4.

———. 2004c. Abu Ghraib, whitewashed. July 24, A12.

———. 2004d. A very bad deal. October 8, A26.

———. 2004e. The FBI messes up. May 26, A22.

———. 2004f. 2 ex-terror suspects face fraud charges. December 16, A37.

———. 2004g. No conviction for student in terror case: Saudi was accused of aiding Hamas. June 11, A14.

———. 2004h. U.S. drops charges for Saudi student. July 1, A12.

———. 2004i. Despite fears of terror tie, suspect goes back to Syria. June 3, A20.

———. 2004j. The mystery deepens. April 3, A14.

———. 2004k. Politics and the Patriot Act. April 21, A22.

———. 2004l. In defense of civil liberties. September 24, A24.

———. 2004m. Interrogating the protestors. August 17, A20.

———. 2004n. Singer non grata. September 26, WK2.

———. 2005a. FBI agent who wrote critical memo retires at age 50. January 1, 16.

———. 2005b. Terror suspects' right to bear arms. March 9.

———. 2005c. Army officer convicted in Iraqi's death is freed. April 2, A5.

———. 2005d. Soldier charged in Iraqi killing is acquitted. May 27, A18.

———. 2005e. Abu Ghraib, whitewashed again. March 11, A22.

———. 2005f. Patterns of abuse. May 23, A18.

———. 2005g. 2 officers punished in 2003 for mistreatment of detainees. May 18, A10.

———. 2005h. Detainee's suit gains support from jet's log. March 30, A1, A9.

Nieves, E. 2001. Recalling internment and saying 'never again. *New York Times,* September 28, EV1–2.

Nunberg, G. 2004. The –ism schism: How much wallop can a simple word pack?: TERRORISM. *New York Times,* July 11, WK7.

O'Brien, T. L. 2003. Treasury dept. to refuse Senate a list of Saudis investigated for terror links. *New York Times,* August 5, A8.

Office of the Attorney General of Florida. 2002. *Hate crimes in Florida.* Tallahassee, Florida: Office of the Attorney General.

Onwudiwe, I. D. 2002. Terrorism. In *Encyclopedia of crime and punishment,* 1614–1624, edited by D. Levinson. Thousand Oaks, CA: Sage.

Orwell, G. 1950. *1984.* London: Penguin.

Ostling, R. N. 2002. Falwell labels Muhammad 'terrorist' in TV interview. *ChicagoTribune,* October 4, 7.

Parenti, C. 2003. *The soft cage: Surveillance in America, from slave passes to the war on terror.* New York: The New Press.

———. 2004. The freedom: Shadows and hallucinations in occupied Iraq. New York: The New Press.

Pear, R. 2004. U.S. health chief, stepping down, issues warning: flu and terror worries. *New York Times,* December 4, A1.

———. 2005. 4 unions sue over new rules for Homeland Security workers. *New York Times,* January 28, A20.

Pepinsky, H. 1991. *The geometry of violence and democracy.* Bloomington: Indiana University Press.

Perera, S. B. 1986. *The scapegoat complex: Toward a mythology of shadow and guilt.* Toronto, Canada: Inner City Books.

Perry, B. 2002. Backlash violence: Anti-Muslim/Anti-Arab crime in the aftermath of 9/11. American Society of Criminology annual meeting, Chicago, Illinois.

Perry, B. 2003a. Anti-Muslim retaliatory violence following the 9/11 terrorist attacks. In *Hate and bias crime: A Reader,* 184–201, edited by B. Perry. New York: Routledge.

———. 2003b. *Hate and bias crime: A Reader.* New York: Routledge.

Phillips, K. 2004. *American dynasty: Aristocracy, fortune, and the politics of deceit in the house of Bush.* New York: Viking.

Pok, A. 1999. Atonement and sacrifice: Scapegoats in modern Eastern and Central Europe. *East European Quarterly* 32 (4): 531–548.

Presdee, M. 2001. *Cultural criminology and the carnival of crime.* New York: Routledge.

Press, E. 2003. In torture we trust. *Nation* (March 31): 1–6.

Preston, J. 2004a. Judge strikes down section of Patriot Act allowing secret subpoenas of Internet data. *New York Times,* September 30, A26.

———. 2004b. Searches of convention protestors limited. *New York Times,* July 20, B4.

———. 2005. Lawyer is guilty of aiding terror: Stewart carried messages while defending Sheik. *New York Times,* February 11, A1, B8.

Priest, D., and B. Gellman. 2002. U.S. decries abuse but defends interrogations 'stress and duress' tactics used on terrorism suspects held in secret overseas facilities. *Washington Post,* December 26, A1.

Quinney, R. 2000. Socialist humanism and the problem of crime: Thinking about Erich Fromm in the development of critical/peacemaking criminology. In *Erich Fromm and critical criminology: Beyond the punitive society,* 21–30, edited by K. Anderson and R. Quinney. Chicago: University of Illinois.

Rampton, S., and J. Stauber. 2003. *Weapons of mass deception: The uses of propaganda in the Bush's war in Iraq.* New York: Jeremy P. Tarcher/Penguin.

Ratner, M. 2003. Making us less free: War on terrorism or war on liberty? In *Implicating empire: Globalization & resistance in the 21st century world order,* 31–46, edited by S. Aronowitz and H. Gautney. New York: Basic Books.

Reinarman, C., and H. Levine. 1997. *Crack in America: Demon drugs and social justice.* Berkeley: University of California Press.

Reitan, R. 2003. Human rights in U.S. policy: A casualty of the 'war on terror'? *International Journal of Human Rights* 7 (4): 51–62.

Reuters. 2001a. Bush signs new anti terrorism law. October 26, EV1.

———. 2001b. US to listen in on some inmate-lawyer talks. November 13, EV1–3.

———. 2003. Rumsfeld praises army general who ridicules Islam as 'Satan.' October 17.

Rich, F. 2004a. It was the porn that made them do it. *New York Times,* May 30, sec. 2, pp. 1, 16.

———. 2004b. Distraction. Propaganda. Roll'em! *International Herald Tribune,* June 26, 27, 7.

———. 2005. Message: I care about the black folks. *New York Times,* September 18, WK 12.

Ridgeway, J. 2004. Flying in the face of facts: Lots of people dialed 911 to the U.S. before 9–11. Who put them on hold? *Village Voice,* July 21–27, 26–27.

Risen, J. 2004. Evolving nature of Al Qaeda is misunderstood, critic says. *New York Times,* November 8, A18.

Riverkeeper. 2004. *Chernobyl on the Hudson?* Riverkeeper, Inc. (www.Riverkeeper.org), http://www.riverkeeper.org/document.php/317/Chernobyl_on_th.pdf., September 20.

Robin, C. 2003. Fear, American style: Civil liberty after 9/11. In *Implicating empire: Globalization & resistance in the 21st century world order,* 47–64, edited by S. Aronowitz and H. Gautney. New York: Basic Books.

———. 2004. *Fear: The history of a political idea.* New York: Oxford University Press.

Robbins, T. 2004. Short fuses on 9–11: Lights out for a Muslim electrician's job after he argues over Trade Center attack. *Village Voice,* July 28-August 3, 18.

Rohde, D. 2003. U.S.-deported Pakistanis: Outcasts in 2 lands. *New York Times,* January 20, A1, A9.

———. 2004. U.S. rebuked on Afghans in detention. *New York Times,* March 8, A6.

Rosen, J. 2004. *The naked crowd: Reclaiming security and freedom in an anxious age.* New York: Random House.

———. 2004b. How to protect America, and your rights. *New York Times,* February 6, A27.

Rosenbaum, D. E. 2004. Call it pork, or necessity, but Alaska comes out far above the rest in spending. *New York Times,* November 21, 28.

Rosenthall, E. 2004. Study puts Iraqi deaths of civilians at 100,000. *New York Times,* October 29, A8.

Ross, J. I. 2000a. *Controlling state crime: An introduction.* 2nd ed. New Brunswick, NJ: Transaction Publishers.

———. 2000b. *Varieties of state crime and its control.* Monsey, NY: Criminal Justice Press.

Roth, K. 2002. *United States: Reports of torture of Al-Qaeda suspects.* December 27. New York: Human Rights Watch.

Rothe, D., and S. L. Muzzatti. 2004. Enemies everywhere: Terrorism, moral panic, and US civil society. *Critical Criminology* 12: 327–350.

Rovella, D. E. 2001. Clock ticks on terrorism-related detentions. *National Law Journal* October 31, EV1–3.

Said, E. W. 1978. *Orientalism.* New York: Pantheon.

———. 1996. A devil theory of Islam. *Nation* (August 12): 28–32.

———. 1997. *Covering Islam: How the media and the experts determine how we see the rest of the world.* New York: Vintage Books.

San Antonio Express-News. 2002. News Roundup. February 14, 1.

Sanders, E. 2002. Understanding turbans: Don't link them to terrorism. *Seattle Times,* October 9, 10.

Sandman, P. 1994. Mass media and environmental risk: Seven principles. *Risk: Health, Safety and Environment* (summer): 251–260.

Sanger, D. E. 2002. President urging wider U.S. powers in terrorism law: He says 'unreasonable obstacles' hinder pursuit of suspects. *New York Times,* September 11, A1, A19.

———. 2004a. Key Bush aide to leave security job. *New York Times,* November 6: A9.

———. 2004b. Bush on offense, says he will fight to keep tax cuts. *New York Times,* January 6, A1.

———. 2005. Bush tells Iowa crowd what he learned from Sept. 11th. *New York Times,* July 21, A16.

Sanger, D. E., and D. M. Halbfinger. 2004. Cheney warns of terror risk if Kerry wins: Bush contends rival adopts antiwar talk. *New York Times,* September 8, A1, A18.

Sante, L. 2004. The Abu Ghraib photos: Here's-me-at-war.jpeg. *International Herald Tribune,* May 12, 6.

Santora, M. 2004. Key evidence cast in doubt on a claim of terrorism. *New York Times,* August 18, B1, B8.

Scheer, C., R. Scheer, and L. Chaudhry. 2003. *The five biggest lies Bush told us about Iraq.* New York: Seven Stories Press.

———. 2004. Bush's lies about Iraq. *Nation* (March 29): 13.

Scheuer, Michael. 2004. *Imperial hubris: Why the west is losing the war on terror.* Washington, DC: Brassey's, Inc.

———. 2005. A fine rendition. *New York Times,* March 11, A23.

Schmid, E. 2003. *A permanent state of terror?* London: Campaign Against Criminalising Communities in Association with Index on Censorship.

Schmitt, E. 2004. Marine set for questioning in death of wounded Iraqi. *New York Times,* November 17, A12.

———. 2005. 3 in 82nd Airborne say beating Iraqi prisoners was routine. New York Times, *September 24, A1, A6.*

Schultz, William. 2003. *Tainted legacy: 9/11 and the ruin of human rights.* New York: Nation Books.

Schuman, M. 2004. Falluja's health damage. *Nation* (December 13): 5–6

Scigliano, E. 2001. Naming-and un-naming names. *Nation* (December 31): 2.

Sciolino, E. 1996. The red menace is gone. But here is Islam. *New York Times,* January 21, sec. 4, p.1.

Seelye, K. Q. 2004a. Moral values cited as a defining issue of the election. *New York Times,* November 4, P4.

———. 2004b. Gore says Bush betrayed the U.S. by using 9/11 as a reason for war in Iraq. *New York Times,* February 9, A18.

Sengupta, S. 2001a. Arabs and Muslims steer through an unsettling scrutiny. *New York Times,* September 13, EV1–3.

———. 2001b. Ill fated path to America jail and death. *New York Times,* November 5, EV1–4.

———. 2001c. Refugees at America's door find it closed after attacks. *New York Times,* October 29, EV1–3.

Serrano, R. 2001a. Detainees face assaults other violations lawyers say. *Los Angeles Times,* October 15, EV1–3.

———. 2001b. Ashcroft denies wide detainee abuse. *Los Angeles Times* October 17, EV1–4.

Shaheen, J. 1984. *The TV Arab.* Bowling Green, OH: Bowling Green University.

———. 1999. Hollywood's reel Arabs and Muslims. In *Muslims and Islamization in North America: Problems and prospects,* 179–202, edited by A. Haque. Beltsville MD: Amana Publications.

Shaidle, K. 2001. Full pews and empty gestures. *Toronto Star,* December 2, 24.

Shane, S. 2005. '01 memo to Rice warned of Qaeda and offered plan. *New York Times,* February 12, A1, A10.

Shane, S., S. Grey, and M. Williams 2005. C.I.A. expanding terror battle under guise of charter flights. *New York Times,* May 31, EV1–4.

Shattuck, J. 2003. *Freedom on fire: Human rights wars and America's response.* Cambridge: Harvard University Press.

Shelden, R. G., and W. Brown. 2000. The crime control industry and the management of the surplus population. *Critical Criminology* 9 (1–2): 39–62.

Shenon, P. 2003a. New asylum policy comes under fire. *New York Times,* March 19, A22.

———. 2003b. Deal on 9/11 briefings let White House edit papers. *New York Times,* November 14, 24.

———. 2004a. Ridge asserts action halted terror attack. *New York Times,* April 5, A21.

———. 2004b. G.O.P. blames Clinton for intelligence failures. *New York Times,* July 2, A17.

———. 2004c. 9/11 Report calls for a sweeping overhaul of intelligence: WE ARE NOT SAFE, Commission warns of another catastrophe under status quo. *New York Times,* July 23, A1, A10.

———. 2004d. Opponents say Republicans plan sequel to Patriot Act. *New York Times,* September 23, A18.

Shenon, P., and R. Toner. 2001. US widens policy on detaining suspects. *New York Times,* September 19, EV1–4.

Silverglate, H. 2002. First casualty of war. *National Law Journal,* December 3, A21.

Simon, J. 2001. Fear and loathing in late modernity. *Punishment and Society* 3 (1): 21–33.

Simons, M., and T. Weiner. 2004. World court rules U.S. should review 51 death sentences. *New York Times,* April 1, A1, A8.

Singer, P. 2004. *The president of good and evil: The ethics of George W. Bush.* New York: Dutton.

Sisario, B. 2004. Activist asserts harassment. *New York Times,* October 1, A13.

Solomon, A. 2003a. From Baghdad to Brooklyn: Immigrants brace for backlash but fear alerting NYPD. *Village Voice,* April 2–8, 26.

———. 2003b. The big chill. *Nation* (June 2): 17–22

———. 2004. Questions for Trent Lott. *New York Times Magazine,* June 20, 15.

Sontag, S. 2004. The photographs *are* us. *New York Times Magazine,* May 23, 24–29, 42.

South Asian American Leaders of Tomorrow. 2002. *American backlash: Terrorists bring war home in more ways than one.* Retrieved on August 28, from http://saalt.org/biasreport.pdf.

Sparks, R. 2001. Degrees of estrangement: The cultural theory of risk and comparative penology. *Theoretical Criminology* 5 (2): 159–176.

Springhall, J. 1998. *Youth, popular culture, and moral panics: Penny gaffs to gangsta-rap, 1830–1996.* New York: St. Martin's Press.

Stam, J. 2003. Bush's religious language. *Nation* (December 22): 27.

Stanley, A. 2001. Opponents of war are scarce on television. *New York Times,* November 9, B4.

Stanley, A. 2004. Understanding the president and his god. *New York Times,* April 29, E1, E5.

Staples, W. G. 1997. *The culture of surveillance: Discipline and social control in the United States.* New York: St. Martin's Press.

Stenson, K., and R. Sullivan. 2000. *Crime, risk, and justice: The politics of crime control in liberal democracies.* Devon, England: Willan.

Stevenson, R. 2003. For Muslims, a mixture of White House signals. *New York Times,* April 28, A13.

Stevenson, R. W., and E. Lichtblau. 2004. Bush pushes for renewal of antiterrorism legislation. *New York Times,* April 18, 16.

Stivers, R. 1993. The festival of light of the theory of the three milieus: A critique of Girard's theory of ritual scapegoating. *Journal of the American Academy of Religion* 61 (3): 505–539.

Stockton, R. 1994. Ethnic archetypes and the Arab image. In *The development of Arab-American identity,* 119–153, edited by E. McCarus. Ann Arbor: University of Michigan Press.

Stolberg, S. G., and F. Lee 2004. Bush nominee for archivist is criticized for his secrecy. *New York Times,* April 20, A14.

Stone, G. 2004. *Perilous times: Free speech in wartime, from the sedition act of 1789 to the war on terrorism.* New York: W.W. Norton & Company.

Stout, D. 2005. Court backs bush on trials for Qaeda suspects at Guantánamo. *New York Times,* July 15, EV1–2.

Suleiman, M. 1999. Islam, Muslims and Arabs in America: The other of the other of the other . . . *Journal of Muslim Minority Affairs* 19 (1): 33–48.

Suskind, R. 2004. Faith, certainty and the presidency of George W. Bush. *New York Times Magazine,* October 17, 44–51, 64, 102, 106.

Suskind, R. 2004. *The price of loyalty: George W. Bush, the White House, and the education of Paul O'Neill.* New York: Simon and Schuster.

Swarns, R. L. 2003. More than 13,000 may face deportation. *New York Times,* June 7, A9.

———. 2004a. Program's value in dispute as a tool to fight terrorism: Many face deportation after registering. *New York Times,* December 21, A26.

———. 2004b. Senator? Terrorist? A watch list stops Kennedy at airport. *New York Times* August 20, A1, A18.

Sykes, G. M., and D. Matza. 1957. Techniques of neutralization: A theory of delinquency. *American Sociological Review* 22: 664–670.

Szasz, T. 1970. *The manufacture of madness.* New York: Harper and Row.

Talbot, M. 2003. Subversive reading: Is it possible that librarians could be the biggest threat to the Patriot Act? *New York Times Magazine,* September 28, 19.

Talvi, S. 2003a. Round up: INS 'Special Registration' ends in mass arrests. *In These Times,* February 17, 3.

———. 2003b. It takes a nation of detention facilities to hold us back: Moral panic and the disaster mentality of immigration policy. (www.lipmagazine.org) January 15, EV1–8.

Tate, M. 2001. Mesquite seeks clues in killing of gas-store owner. *Dallas Morning News,* October 5, 1.

Thomas, W. I. 1923. *The unadjusted girl.* Boston: Little, Brown.

Toner, R., and J. Elder. 2001. Public is wary but supportive on rights curbs. *New York Times,* December 12, A1, B9.

TRAC (Transactional Records Access Clearinghouse). 2003. *Criminal enforcement against terrorists and spies in the year after the 9/11 attacks.* Syracuse, NY: Syracuse University.

Tracy, J. 2002. *The civil disobedience handbook: A brief history and practical advice for the politically disenchanted.* San Francisco: Manic D Press.

Tulsky, F. 2000a. Asylum seekers face tougher U.S. laws, attitudes. *San Jose Mercury News,* December 10, EV1–9.

———. 2000b. Asylum seekers face lack of legal help. *San Jose Mercury News,* December 30, EV1–2.

Tyler, P. E. 2004a. Ex-Guantanamo detainee charges beating. *New York Times,* March 12, A10.

———. 2004b. U.N. chief ignites firestorm by calling Iraq war 'illegal.' *New York Times,* September 17, A11.

———. 2004c. British singer calls his deportation a mistake. *New York Times,* September 24, A6.

Uchitelle, L., and J. Markoff. 2004. Terrorbusters, Inc.: The rise of the Homeland Security-Industrial complex. *New York Times,* October 17, BU1, 8, 12.

Ungar, S. 1990. Moral panics, the military industrial complex and the arms race. *Sociological Quarterly* 31(2): 165–185.

———. 1992. *The rise and fall of nuclearism: Fear and faith as determinants of the arms race.* University Park, PA: Penn State Press.

———. 1998. Hot crises and media reassurance: A comparison of emerging diseases and Ebola Zaire. *British Journal of Sociology* 49 (1): 36–56.

———. 1999. Is strange weather in the air: A study of US national news coverage of extreme weather events. *Climatic Change* 41 (2): 133–150.

———. 2000. Knowledge, ignorance and the popular culture: Climate change versus the ozone hole. *Public Understanding of Science* 9 (3): 297–312.

———. 2001. Moral panic versus the risk society: The implications of the changing sites of social anxiety. *British Journal of Sociology* 52 (2): 271–291.

United Press International. 2002. Death sentence for revenge killing. April 4, 1.

United States Department of Justice. 2003a. *Supplemental report on September 11 detainees' allegations of abuse at the metropolitan detention center in Brooklyn,* New York. Office of the Inspector General. December. Washington, DC: U.S. Government Printing.

———. 2003b. *The September 11 detainees: A review of the treatment of aliens held on immigration charges in connection with the investigation of the September 11 attacks.* Office of the Inspector General. June. Washington, DC: U.S. Government Printing.

Van Natta, D., and L. Wayne. 2004. Al Qaeda seeks to disrupt U.S. economy, experts warn. *New York Times,* August 2, A12.

Vaughan, B. 2002. The punitive consequences of consumer culture. *Punishment & Society* 4 (2): 195–211.

Village Voice. 2004. Say what? December 15–21, 24.

Viorst, M. 1994. *Sandcastles: The Arabs in search of the modern world.* New York: Knopf.

Von Zielbauer, P. 2003a. Detainees' abuse is detailed. *New York Times,* December 19, A32.

Wald, M. L. 2004a. Group predicts catastrophe if Indian Point is attacked. *New York Times,* September 8, B5.

———. 2004b. Accusations on detention of ex-singer. *New York Times,* September 23, A18.

Waldman, A. 2004. Guantanamo and jailers: Mixed review by detainees. *New York Times,* March 17, A6.

Wallace, D. H., and B. Kreisel. 2003. Martial law as a counterterrorism response to terrorist attacks: Domestic and international legal dimensions. *International Criminal Justice Review* 13: 50–75.

Wan, W. 2002. Four airlines sued for alleged post-Sept.11 discrimination. *Cox News Service,* June 4, 1.

Washington Post. 2001a. Lawmaker tries to explain remark; Rep. Chambliss, a senate hopeful, commented on Muslims. November 21, 2.

———. 2001b. War on terrorism. October 22, 25.

———. 2002. Mr. Robertson's incitement. February 24, 22.

Watney, S. 1987. *Policing desire: Pornography, AIDS, and the media.* Minneapolis: University of Minnesota Press.

Weiser, B. 1997. In lawsuit, I.N.S. is accused of illegally detaining man. *New York Times,* September 16, B2.

———. 2004. U.S. videos of Qaeda informer offer glimpse into a secret life: But evidence now poses a problem for prosecutors. *New York Times,* May 1, A1, B2.

Weisman, S. R. 2005. Jail term for soldier in abuse case. *New York Times,* May 23, A10.

Weitzer, R., and C. E. Kubrin. 2004. Breaking news: How local TV news and real world conditions affect fear of crime. *Justice Quarterly* 21 (3): 497–520.

Welch, M. 1999a. *Punishment in America.* Thousand Oaks, CA & London: Sage Publications, Inc.

———. 1999b. Social movements and political protest: Exploring flag desecration in the 1960s, 1970s, 1980s. *Social Pathology* 5 (2): 167–186.

———. 2000a. *Flag burning: Moral panic and the criminalization of protest.* New York: de Gruyter.

———. 2000b. The role of the immigration and naturalization service in the prison industrial complex. *Social Justice: A Journal of Crime, Conflict & World Order* 27 (3): 73–88.

———. 2002a. *Detained: Immigration laws and the expanding I.N.S. jail complex.* Philadelphia: Temple University Press.

———. 2002b. Detention in I.N.S. jails: Bureaucracy, brutality, and a booming business. In *Turnstile justice: Issues in American corrections.* 2nd ed., 202–214, edited by R. Gido and T. Alleman. Englewood Cliffs, NJ: Prentice Hall.

———. 2003a. The trampling of human rights in the war on terror: Implications to the sociology of denial. *Critical Criminology: An International Journal* 12 (2): 1–20.

———. 2003b. Ironies of social control and the criminalization of immigrants. *Crime, Law & Social Change: An International Journal* 39: 319–337.

———. 2003c. Force and fraud: A radically coherent criticism of corrections as industry. *Contemporary Justice Review* 6 (3): 227–240.

———. 2004a. *Corrections: A critical approach.* 2nd ed. New York: McGraw-Hill.

———. 2004b. Profiling and detention in the war on terror: Human rights predicaments for the criminal justice apparatus. In *Visions for change: Crime and justice in the twenty-first century.* 3rd ed., 203–218, edited by R. Muraskin and A. Roberts. Englewood Cliffs, NJ: Prentice Hall.

———. 2004c. Quiet constructions in the war on terror: Subjecting asylum seekers to unnecessary detention. *Social Justice: A Journal of Crime, Conflict & World Order* 31 (1–2): 113–129.

———. 2004d. War on terror and the criminology of the other: Examining detention and the rise of a global culture of control. *Societies of Criminology 1st Key Issues Conference,* Paris, France. May 13–15.

———. 2005a. *Ironies of imprisonment.* Thousand Oaks, CA and London: Sage Publications, Inc.

———. 2005b. Immigration lockdown before and after 9/11: Ethnic constructions and their consequences. In *From slavery to globalization: How race and gender shape punishment in America,* edited by M. Bosworth and J. Flavin. New Brunswick, NJ: Rutgers University Press.

―――. 2005c. Moral panic. In *Encyclopedia of criminology,* edited by R. Wright and J. M. Miller. New York: Routledge.

―――. 2005d. Restoring prison systems in war torn nations: Correctional vision, monitoring, and human rights. For the panel Justice system in conflict torn nations: Establishing standards and making them work (sponsored by the Academy of Criminal Justice Sciences). Ancillary Meeting at the *Eleventh United Nations Congress on Crime Prevention and Criminal Justice,* Bangkok, Thailand, April 18–25.

―――. 2005e. Restoring prison systems in war torn nations: Correctional vision, monitoring, and human rights. *International Journal of Comparative Criminology.*

Welch, M., and J. L. Bryan. 1997. Flag desecration in American culture: Offenses against civil religion and a consecrated symbol of nationalism. *Crime, Law and Social Change: An International Journal* 26: 77–93.

―――. 1998. Reactions to flag desecration in American society: Exploring the contours of formal and informal social control. *American Journal of Criminal Justice* 22 (2): 151–168.

Welch, M., H. Bryan, and R. Wolff. 1999. Just war theory and drug control policy: Militarization, mortality, and the war on drugs. *Contemporary Justice Review* 2 (1): 49–76.

Welch, M., E. Price, and N. Yankey. 2002. Moral panic over youth violence: *Wilding* and the manufacture of menace in the media. *Youth & Society* 34 (1): 3–30.

―――. 2004. Youth violence and race in the media: The emergence of *Wilding* as an invention of the press. *Race, Gender & Class* 11 (2): 36–48.

Welch, M., M. Fenwick, and M. Roberts. 1997. Primary definitions of crime and moral panic: A content analysis of experts' quotes in feature newspaper articles on crime. *Journal of Research in Crime and Delinquency* 34 (4): 474–494.

―――. 1998. State managers, intellectuals, and the media: A content analysis of ideology in experts' quotes in featured newspaper articles on crime. *Justice Quarterly* 15 (2): 219–241.

Welch, M., J. Sassi, and A. McDonough. 2002. Advances in critical cultural criminology: An analysis of reactions to avant-garde flag art. *Critical Criminology: An International Journal,* 11 (1): 1–20.

Welch, M., and L. Schuster. 2005a. Detention of asylum seekers in the UK and US: Deciphering noisy and quiet constructions. *Punishment & Society: An International Journal of Penology* 7 (4): 397–417.

―――. 2005b. Detention of asylum seekers in the US, UK, France, Germany, and Italy: A critical view of the globalizing culture of control. *Criminal Justice: The International Journal of Policy and Practice* 5 (4): 331–355.

Welch, M., and F. Turner. 2004. Globalization in the sphere of penality: Tracking the expansion of private prisons around the world. *Prisons and Penal Policy: International Perspectives,* City University, Islington, London. June 25.

Welch, M., R. Wolff, and N. Bryan. 1998. Decontextualizing the war on drugs: A content analysis of NIJ publications and their neglect of race and class. *Justice Quarterly* 15 (4): 719–742.

West, C., and S. Fenstermaker. 1995. Doing difference. *Gender and Society* 9 (1): 8–37.

Wiener, J. 2004. The archives and Allen Weinstein. *Nation* (May 17): 17–19.

Williams, P. J. 2001. By any means necessary. *Nation* (November 26): 11.

Willis, E. 1999. *Don't think, smile! Notes on a decade of denial.* Boston: Beacon Press.

Wills, G. 2003. With God on his side. *New York Times Magazine,* March 30, 26–29.

Winant, H. 1997. Where culture meets structure. *Race, class and gender in a diverse society,* 27–38, edited by Diana Kendall. Boston: Allyn and Bacon.

Wingfield, B. 2004. Unions for border workers criticize rules on disclosure. *New York Times,* November 30, A20.

Wood, P. J. 2003. The rise of the prison industrial complex in the United States. In *Capitalist punishment: Prison privatization & human rights,* 16–29, edited by A. Coyle, A. Campbell, and R. Neufeld. Atlanta, GA: Clarity Press.

Woodward, B. 2002. *Bush at war.* New York: Simon and Schuster.

World Conference Against Racism, Racial Discrimination, and Related Intolerance, Programme of Action (WCAR) 2002.

Wright, E. 2004a. Dead-checking in Falluja. *Village Voice,* November 24–30, 22–24.

———. 2004b. *Generation kill: Devil dogs, Iceman, Captain America, and the new face of American war.* New York: G.P. Putnam's Sons.

Wuthnow, R. 2000. *Religion and politics survey.* Princeton, NJ: Princeton University.

———. 2004. *The religious factor:* Revisited. *Sociological Theory* 22 (2): 205–218.

Wuthnow, R., and J. H. Evans. 2001. *The quiet voice of God: Faith-based activism and mainline Protestantism.* Berkeley: University of California Press.

York, M. 2005. 3rd antiwar defendant is held in contempt. *New York Times,* September 23, B3.

Young, I. M. 1990. *Justice and the politics of difference.* Princeton, NJ: Princeton University Press.

Young, J. 1971. The role of the police as amplifiers of deviancy, negotiators of reality and translators of fantasy. In *Images of deviancy,* 27–61. Edited by S. Cohen. Harmondsworth: Penguin.

———. 1999. *The exclusive society.* London: Sage.

Yourish, K. 2003. Delivering the 'good news.' *Newsweek,* March 10, 28.

Zgoba, K. 2004. Spin doctors and moral crusaders: The moral panic behind child safety legislation. *Criminal Justice Studies* 17 (4): 385–404.

INDEX

Convention Against Torture. *See* United Nations Convention Against Torture

Convertino, Richard C., 129

corrections-industrial complex, 31

Coulter, Ann, 46

criminology of the other, 15, 36, 40–42, 44, 45, 165, 180, 183–185. *See also* Garland, David

cultural theory, 15, 39. *See also* Douglas, Mary

culture of control, 15, 40–41, 45, 77–76, 184. *See also* Garland, David

Davies, Nigel, 35

Dean, John, 141, 161

Dearlove, Sir Richard, 106–107

Declaration on the Protection of All Persons from Enforced Disappearances, 138, 181

Defending Civilization: How Our Universities Are Failing America and What Can Be Done About It, 175

Douglas, Mary, 15, 37, 39–40, 44, 184; thought styles, 39, 44, 45. *See also* cultural theory

Douglas, Tom, 35–37, 44

Durkheim, Emile, 37

Edmonds, Sibel, 143

Erikson, Erik, 38

extraordinary renditions, 16, 167–169

faces of oppression, 16, 63–64, 74–75,

Fairness and Accuracy in Reporting (FAIR), 176

federal hate crimes statute, 67–68

Fishback, Captain Ian, 113–114. *See also* Camp Mercury

Flynn, Edith, 82

Foreign Intelligence Surveillance Act (FISA). *See* Patriot Act

Foucault, Michel, 163

Freud, Sigmund, 37

Frustration/aggression theory, 42

Garland, David, 15, 40–42, 165, 184. *See also* criminology of the other; culture of control

Geneva Conventions, 16, 113, 115–116, 118–119, 120, 166; Article 3, 110;

"ghost detainees," 168–169; indefinite detention, 171; stress and duress positions, 173

Girard, Rene, 37, 39, 45

Goldsmith, Lord, 107

Gramsci, Antonio, 18

Green, Judge Joyce Hens, 118

Greider, William, 6

Guantanamo Bay, 15–16, 28, 104, 113, 116–120, 125, 161–162, 183; Combatant Status Review Tribunals, 118

Guttentag, Lucas, 83

Hamdi v. Rumsfeld, 117

Hedges, Chris, 103, 164–165; myth of war, 165

Humanitarian Law Project v. Ashcroft, 131, 153

Illegal Immigration Reform and Immigrant Responsibility Act, 100

Indian Point nuclear plant, 23

International Court of Justice, 183, 190n2

International Covenant on Civil and Political Rights, 93, 122

International Criminal Court, 107

International Red Cross, 169

Islam, Yusuf. *See* Stevens, Cat

Jenkins, Jerry B., 49. *See also* LaHaye, Tim

Jesus, as warrior. *See* LaHaye, Tim; Jenkins, Jerry B.

John Doe, American Civil Liberties Union v. John Ashcroft and FBI Director Robert Mueller, 153

Jungian psychology, 37–38

Kendura, Milan, 102

Kennedy, Ted, 17, 127, 160

knowledge-ignorance paradox, 24

LaHaye, Tim, 49. *See also* Jenkins, Jerry B.

Langer, Gary, 51. *See also* moral values

language: blaming, 8, 9–10, 13; domination, 8, 10–11, 13; fabrication, 8, 10–11, 13; mystified, 8, 13; rumors, 8, 11, 13; tough talk, 8–9, 13, 28, 43

Lenski, Gerhard, 48–49

ABOUT THE AUTHOR

MICHAEL WELCH is professor in the Criminal Justice program at Rutgers University, New Brunswick, New Jersey (USA). He received a Ph.D. in sociology from the University of North Texas and his research interests include punishment, social control, and human rights. He has published numerous articles for academic journals, edited volumes and other scholarly publications. His key writings have appeared in *Punishment & Society, Justice Quarterly, Journal of Research in Crime & Delinquency, The Prison Journal, International Journal of Comparative Criminology, Criminal Justice: The International Journal of Policy and Practice, Crime, Law & Social Change, Social Justice, Youth & Society, Race, Gender & Class,* and *Critical Criminology.* Also he is author of *Ironies of Imprisonment* (2005, Sage), *Detained: Immigration Laws and the Expanding I.N.S. Jail Complex* (2002, Temple University Press), *Flag Burning: Moral Panic and the Criminalization of Protest* (2000, de Gruyter), *Punishment in America* (1999, Sage), and *Corrections: A Critical Approach* (2nd ed., 2004, McGraw-Hill). In 2005, and 2006–2007, Welch is a visiting fellow at the Centre for the Study of Human Rights, London School of Economics. He invites you visit his website at www.professormichaelwelch.com.